# THE KIDS NEXT DOOR

# THE KIDS NEXT DOOR

## Sons and Daughters Who Kill Their Parents

### GREGGORY W. MORRIS

William Morrow and Company, Inc.
New York

Library of Congress Cataloging in Publication Data

Morris, Greggory W.
    The kids next door.

    Includes index.
    1. Parricide—United States—Case studies.
    2. Abused children—United States—Case studies.
    I. Title.
HV6542.M67  1985      364.1'523      85-3033
ISBN 0-688-02851-9

Printed in the United States of America


    2 3 4 5 6 7 8 9 10

BOOK DESIGN BY RICHARD ORIOLO

For my mother, father, sister, and brother.
And my editor.

# Foreword

"Children are the hope of a society's future." I remember reading such a statement when I was a graduate student of child psychology. Funny that I can't remember who said it now, almost twenty years later. Younger and more idealistic then, I believed we were a child-centered society. Reading Greggory Morris's descriptions of the families in this book will make you focus on the fact that we may not have a future, if we are judged by the way these children have been treated. Their families have brutally beaten, sexually abused, and psychologically damaged them. All the while, we—that is, you and me and all of us—looked on or turned away when it offended our sensibilities. And when the children got old enough to try to stop their own abuse, they killed their parents. A few demonstrated how well they had learned their abusers' lessons—they too had become abusive. Sadly, the killings may have been the only way they could have stopped being battered!

You will learn that as a society, we turn our backs on these children by not giving them an adequate defense or a chance to heal and become whole again. You will be shocked and perhaps offended by the stories you are about to read, and might like to put down this book so as to forget these children exist. *Don't do it!* Their lives concern you. Family violence eventually spills out into the streets and poisons us all. Child victims rarely talk as openly as they did to Gregg Morris. Force yourself to read and know that attorneys make deals that benefit themselves rather than their young clients, that

judges play at being mental health professionals, picking and choos-
ing whom to believe without the information needed to make informed judgments, and that doctors untrained in the dynamics of
family violence commit gross errors that might be considered mal-
practice if their clients were not so young and vulnerable and ren-
dered invisible.

Stories about family violence are ugly. Those of us who work in
the field and hear them daily must find ways to deal with our own
feelings of outrage that children continue to be harmed by those who
should protect and love them. For the past ten years I have been
immersed in the study and treatment of abuse victims and the appli-
cation of this knowledge to their legal issues. For me, I continuously
must ask the question *why?* Why does a judge allow a fifteen-year-old
girl, like Mary Jane, who has been sexually abused by the father she
has just shot and killed, to be placed in a virtually all-male psychiatric facility? Why does the doctor befriend her, get her to open up
and talk to him, and then tell Mary Jane that her talking about
incest makes him uncomfortable! How many other mental health
professionals provide incest victims with less than adequate treatment, betraying these children once again? Why does a judge like
Maryland's Vincent Femia temper justice with mercy for a son who
killed his abusive father, but not for a daughter who allegedly conspired with others? Why does one prosecutor demand a sentence of
life for a fourteen-year-old, while another is tried in the more treat-
ment-oriented juvenile court?

These children have killed, and some might say that, as such, they
have committed adult acts and should take adult responsibility for
their actions. But are they really adults, or merely children mimick-
ing warped adults, who try to make themselves safe in a society that
does not take care of its children? When should we decide to throw
away the key and not try to rehabilitate a youth? Is there an age, a
type of violent act, a history, a pattern to guide the decision makers,
or will we continue to respond in crisis fashion, as is the current
custom? My own research indicates that we foster family violence by
contributing to the cloak of silence provided by the nuclear family's
closed doors. When victims try to obtain safety through legal or other
appropriate means, they are often unwittingly or even purposely sent
back into the danger zone. Read Dawn's story with particular care.
The judge who forced her to continue visiting with her abusive fa-

ther in the family home's garage could be said to be as guilty of not preventing her father's death as she was.

Why do we tolerate a society that allows a parent's right of access to a child to take precedence over the child's right to safety? "How could a judge or the attorneys be expected to know?" you might ask. But how will they ever know if they won't listen to what makes them uncomfortable?

Dawn's story is unusual only in the ending—she killed him rather than be forced to submit sexually one more time. I sometimes testify before judges and attorneys who try to portray me as a raving mad feminist when I issue the warning that visitation is dangerous to the physical and mental well-being of the child in question. In many of these cases there is obvious evidence of a father's seductive behavior toward his teenaged daughter. He has not raped her, yet, so the danger is said to be all in the mother's allegedly man-hating head. The mother is thought to have hired a psychologist who shares her bias. Why should they even bother to listen when the Children's Code passed by many state legislatures calls for "reunification of the family," no matter how horrendous the abuse?

I am sometimes embarrassed by other members of my profession who are willing to provide opposing testimony, claiming that men who batter their wives do not necessarily pose any greater risk of harming their children. Nonsense, as these children's stories and other recent research demonstrate. Yes, these are the extremes. We know that millions of children are physically, sexually, and psychologically abused each year. Only a small number kill. Many more grow up to batter their wives and children, or continue to be the victims of other people who love them also. We must learn from these few dramatic cases just as we have been learning from the studies of battered women who kill. My associate, Angela Browne, found that the difference between the battered women who kill and those who do not is in the severity and frequency of the abuser's violent behavior. There were no significant traits noted in the women. The children in this book are similar to our battered women who killed abusers in self-defense.

The predominant defenses—mental illness, which excuses (insanity) or mitigates (diminished capacity) the criminal responsibility, and self-defense, which justifies the homicide—are neither well enough understood nor always appropriate for use when women and children kill abusive family members. To be effective we must put the deceased's behavior on trial also. But family violence is too often concealed, forcing a court to choose between faith in a child who has little evidence of a violent act and in a dead father or mother, who seemed like the proverbial person next door. It is critical to demonstrate the reasonableness of the victims' fears and desperation. They are terrified of being even more badly hurt or killed. And, as these children show, they have nowhere to turn.

Finally, there is a sex bias in the courts and therapists' offices that makes it even more difficult for both young and older women to get a fair trial. Are men, who predominate in the system, suggesting plea arrangements to spare children the need to expose their shameful secrets, or to continue to protect other men's misguided sexual behavior from being known? Abuse victims blame themselves for not being better so as to avoid being hurt. Aren't benevolent lawyers simply reinforcing such self-blame by continuing the cover-up?

Psychologist Carol Gilligan has recently found that women and men differ in their moral views about justice. Women, she writes in her book *In a Different Voice*, are more likely to temper justice with an understanding of the surrounding circumstances. The male standard, on the other hand, is less likely to take such a broad look at the whole context of an act. Perhaps the next step is to temper our current system, where abused or mentally ill children do not get enough help, with more of the women's view of justice. Then we will move on to prevention and learn how to raise children in nonsexist and violence-free homes.

Lenore E. Walker, Ed.D., A.B.P.P.
Diplomate in Clinical Psychology
January 1985

# Acknowledgments

I wouldn't have been able to write this book without the help of a great many people.

There were some who were experiencing some of the worst moments of their lives but even so took time to allow me to interview them and ask personal questions and pry into their lives. To them I owe a special thanks.

I also owe a great deal of thanks to Sara Elbert, Sandy Kelman, Elliot and Sue Roberts, M.G., Jane Sufian, Paul Mones, Dimitrios Kamberos, and Margo Hammond.

I also want to thank Rafael Soto, Vanessa Powell, Russ Gunther, Dede Murphy, Naomi Black, Divina Infusino, Arthur A. "Bud" Marshall, Jr., FOIA Inc., the Federal Bureau of Investigation, John Dabrowski, Edward McCarty, Julie Blackman, Karen Butler, Clay Osborne, Ramona Garnes, Darrell Price, Bruce Giffords, Vincent Femia, Tommy Cotter, Sidney T. Farber, Barry Sentig, Dennis FitzPatrick, the Manhattan district attorney's office, the Queens district attorney's office, Tim Maloney, Susan Dodd, the National Institute of Justice, Ed Tobia, Richard Finkelstein, and Julian Jackson and Lieutenant William Mayer and Chief Delmar Leach of the Rochester Police Department, the *Daily News* of Longview, Washington, Kitty Bryon, and the National Criminal Justice Reference Service.

Although in the chapters I have cited the sources that I used as reference material to write *The Kids Next Door*, there were two books that were never specifically mentioned but were indispensable in writing the section on the battered child: *Against Our Will*, by Susan Brownmiller, and *Women Who Kill*, by Ann Jones (which first gave me the idea for a battered child defense).

# Contents

Foreword by Lenore E. Walker         5

Acknowledgments         9

Introduction         13

PART I   The Battered Child         19
   1  Tommy         24
   2  Mary Jane         34
   3  David         57
   4  Lisa         70
   5  Dawn         106
   6  Richie         117
   7  Vincent         120
   8  Buddy         125

PART II   Defending Battered Kids         143
   9  The Battered-Child Defense         145
  10  The Miami Grand Jury         170

PART III   The Mentally Ill                        185
    11   Anthony                                   198
    12   Barry                                     204
    13   William                                   220

PART IV   Matricides, Patricides, and
          Mass Murders                             227
    14   Vic                                       231
    15   Adam                                      242
    16   For the Love of Money                     252
    17   Aaron                                     259

PART V   Garry—A Special Case                      267

Conclusion                                         293

Afterword                                          295

Index                                              297

# Introduction

I was working at *Time* magazine when a west coast correspondent contacted the editors in New York City about an extraordinary murder in Cheyenne, Wyoming. It was a Monday, the first day of a workweek that usually started slowly before it hurtled pell-mell into the frenzy of suddenly breaking news events, rapid schedule revisions, and the inimitable snafus that all timed themselves to crop up at the most unpropitious moments. The weeks began with a sigh and ended in a gasp. Stories occasionally came along, such as the murder suggested by the correspondent, that provided a mild cathartic jolt to a staff trying to shake free of the lingering torpor of a two-day weekend. In the editors' meeting that Monday, the suggestion sparked wry comments from a news staff that regularly eyeballed global cataclysms with droll humor. Its seismic importance, as far as the editors were concerned, rated only a column of about three hundred words. It was slugged "Youth's Revenge."

Later that year, and well into the next, major television networks, newspapers, and magazines would send their staffs to Cheyenne to record chapter and verse of one of the most compelling dramas to be covered by the national media. In the chill of a November evening, when neighbors were nestling in front of their TV sets or sitting down to dinner, Richie Jahnke, sixteen, had staked out a spot in the family garage where he could keep an eye out for his father. He was holding on to a shotgun. When Richard senior appeared, Richie killed him with several shotgun blasts. "I shot my father for revenge," he was quoted as saying. Richie's sister, Debbie, seventeen, was charged with being an accomplice to murder.

*Time*'s news reporting, unlike newspapers', involves four roles: correspondents do the primary interviewing and reporting; researcher-reporters handle the so-called fact checking, gather background information, and do occasional reporting; writers emboss the material in *Time*'s style; and the editors rewrite or rework according to their bent. I was assigned to write "Youth's Revenge" and the researcher who also was working on the story mentioned that *The New York Times* had already published an account of the murder. I told her that I had also read a similar story, and she said she recalled it, but as we talked we both realized we were discussing two unrelated episodes of patricide. I added that the patricides we were discussing sounded vaguely familiar to another story that I believed had been reported during the previous weeks. I was not certain if the victim had been a mother or father, or if both parents had been slain. The researcher said she had heard about or read that account, and then added some additional tales that she was convinced were somehow similar. We could not recall specific dates, times, and details but we surmised that several stories of kids killing their parents had been reported recently. After musing about what had been happening in those families, and wondering aloud why parricides seemed to be taking place, we shrugged off the tragedies and went about preparing for the week ahead.

Although journalists are supposed to expect the unexpected in the news business, it was still a surprise when the editors canceled the story. "The Sunday *New York Times* persuaded us that this family was far from the normal middle-class unit where the children justifiably struck back, that its members were for a long time terribly troubled" was the editors' message to the west coast correspondent. "In light of this the story interests us far less." What they had read in the *Times* was a story of unrelenting familial terror. The father, an unemployed mechanic, had tyrannized his family for years with ax handles, guns, and threats of death. "We were beaten and brutalized," his wife was quoted as saying. The family lived in a rural area, and the wife, who worked as a waitress in a hamburger drive-in, was a former high-wire girl in her family's carnival show. When her son killed his father in the summer of 1981, she helped him bury the body beneath a tool shed floor. It was a respectable family but poor, and in the eyes of *Time*'s editors, the story did not possess the news appeal they wanted for their readers.

But they changed their minds.

"Oops," *Time*'s editors said in a rushed dispatch to the west coast correspondent. "Please disregard our most recent advisory on this story and proceed with reporting for a two-column story closing this week." They had made a mistake: "We in our haste mistook yesterday's *New York Times* story on a similar family killing in Oregon for the Jahnke family in Wyoming." Richie Jahnke and his family were brought back into the *Time* limelight, and Vincent Whatley and his family in Oregon were retired. By then I had been assigned to another story, and "Youth's Revenge" was given to another writer. But a seed had germinated, and when I left *Time* I wanted to know more about sons and daughters who kill their parents.

When I started researching this book, I recalled an incident from my past. One summer day when I was spending a vacation at home with my parents, I was outside spraying water on some friends and neighbors with a garden hose in the backyard. I thought it was funny to see them scurrying to get out of my way, but my father, who was watching my escapade from inside our home, thought it was ridiculous that his college-educated son was acting juvenile. He walked to the back door and announced in a menacing way that he would be coming out and down the rear stairs to go to work, and warned me of the consequences if I sprayed him. Of course, he could have walked out the front door to go to work as he usually did. But something on this day convinced him that he just had to walk out the back door where his oldest son was spraying anyone within reach of the garden hose.

When he walked through the door I sprayed him, and we both squared off. I was going to learn that he would not tolerate that kind of insubordination. He was going to learn that I was not going to be pushed around by him. I picked up a two-by-four and waited for him to rush me.

In that brief moment when we both became trapped and there appeared to be no way to save face and end the showdown, my mother intervened. She chided both of us for acting foolish in full view of the neighbors. When my father walked out of the backyard he was shaking just as much as I was. We both were near tears. It was the first time anyone in my family had ever threatened another member with mayhem. What should have been nothing more than a typical father-son spat almost erupted into a life-and-death struggle. Something had been brooding between us for who knows how long, and we were about to resolve it in a most heinous way. My father and I were not thinking about murder that day in our backyard. But any man brandishing a two-by-four can maim if he does not kill. A few days passed before we talked about what happened, and then we talked and talked, and have talked and talked since, so that something like that could never threaten our home again.

When I recalled this incident, as I started researching my book, I wondered how many times I would come across similar accounts that ended tragically. Father-son face-to-face duels involving guns, knives, clubs, and two-by-fours happen. But they do not show up significantly on the path to murder in the three hundred to four hundred parricides that occur annually in the country. Though the popular belief is that matricides and patricides occur regularly, and some news stories indicate that parricide is on the rise, there is a dearth of published material on the subject. So it was necessary to take to the road. I visited small towns and big cities to interview families and their friends and neighbors, as well as doctors, juvenile agency officials, lawyers, judges, prosecutors, police officers, and many others. When I could not visit I used the phone. I also reviewed news accounts, court records, and transcripts of trials, as well as psychiatric records and medical evaluations when I could get my hands on them. I ended up with more than just a look at the ABCs of why sons and daughters kill their parents. What evolved was a picture of what is happening in the American family today.

The family is the most violent institution, group or setting that a typical citizen is likely to encounter. There are exceptions such as the police or the army in time of war.

—DR. MURRAY A. STRAUS
University of New Hampshire

# PART I

## The Battered Child

There were about 46 million children aged three to seventeen living with their parents in 1975. Between 3.1 million and 4 million of them had been "kicked, bitten, or punched by a parent at some time in their lives," Murray Stevens, Richard Gelles, and Suzanne Steinmetz estimated in their study of violence in the American family. Between 1.4 million and 2.3 million had been "beaten up while growing up." The authors, based on their data, also estimated that as many as 1.8 million kids had been attacked by a parent wielding a gun or knife. "The actual violence children experience is probably much higher than the figures we report here," they wrote in *Behind Closed Doors: Violence in the American Family*. They believed that their figures "only hint at a much more extensive incidence of the abuse of children in the United States."

There are regular news accounts of how children suffer at the hands of their parents, such as this Associated Press story reported in the fall of 1984:

Music was blaring from the second-floor apartment of a building in Auburn, Maine, and even though it was a Friday, when people were expected to cut loose a bit at the end of the week, the noise became unbearable. An annoyed neighbor knocked on the door and asked that the volume be turned down. A voice from the other side of the door gruffly told him to go away. And the music continued well into the night. The next day neighbors heard shouts and clamor coming from the apartment as if there was a big fight going on inside. They also heard Angela screaming.

"Let me out, Daddy, let me out," the four-year-old wailed.

A few hours later that day, an upstairs resident smelled smoke and an unusual scent coming from the apartment. She walked downstairs and knocked on the door.

"Is there something on fire?" she asked. "Is there something burning in the oven?"

"Yes," answered a voice from the other side of the door. "I'm cooking Lucifer."

Later, the thick smoke and pungent smell coming from the apartment alarmed the other building residents and they called the police and fire departments. When the fire fighters and police officers arrived, they broke through the door. Inside the apartment, they found a chair propped up against an oven door. Inside the oven they found Angela. She had been cooking for several hours.

Angela's death was one example of the extreme end results of family violence. Robert M. Bloom, Jr., was another. While people will remember Angela with pity and as a victim of abuse, only a handful who read about Bloom in 1983 will remember him as a victim of child abuse. People will recall Bloom with a shudder.

One day in April 1982, he crept up on his sleeping father and stepmother and shot them both in the head at point-blank range. After slaying them, he shot his six-year-old stepsister and then stabbed her more than twenty times with a butcher knife. He was charged with three counts of first-degree murder, which is punishable in California with death. At his trial a year later he received permission from the judge to argue his own case. His attorney was not allowed to participate.

Bloom, nineteen, argued for his conviction, and the jury found him guilty. In a second hearing to determine his sentence, Bloom again acted as his own attorney and told the jury to sentence him to death.

"This is my father," he said, showing the jurors a picture of Robert M. Bloom, Sr. "He was executed. I'd do it again in the same circumstances. He got everything he had coming."

He could not remember killing the little girl or his mother.

"I don't want to live in your society," he told them. "It ain't nothing but a free ride and a paper moon. Kill me if you got the heart. Don't slap my hand."

If they only sentenced him to prison, he warned, "I'll kill again in prison."

If he ever escaped, he threatened, he would come looking for them.

"Kill me if you got the heart," he taunted. "I deserve to die. I want to die."

The jury deliberated for two and a half hours before giving Bloom his wish.

"There was no reason for a trial," he had scolded them. "You had no reason to interfere in my life. It was a family affair."

In a brief interview, his lawyer said Bloom had been abused all his life.

"This boy was dead the minute his father touched him when he was born," the attorney said. "He [Bloom senior] was a bastard if there ever was one."

Despite research and evidence on how children are brutalized in their families, it is still easy for this society to act and respond to parricides as if they happened for reasons other than the most obvious: physical, psychological, and sexual abuse.

# 1

## Tommy

Loretta imagined herself too independent to lean on anyone, even her husband, but what happened frightened her so much that she did not want to be alone for days. Even after "the fear" left, anxiety lingered on and on for months, hovering over her like an intransigent ghost. Before that night in April 1982, she had believed that she could deal with the inevitable—until it showed up unexpectedly on her doorstep.

"At three o'clock in the morning I hear this pounding on the door, and no one gets in my house at night because I have four kids upstairs asleep, and I'm alone. Well, I immediately thought my husband had come home early and maybe lost his keys or had car trouble or something. So I looked outside my bedroom window and I saw what looked like a pickup truck, and it was a truck that I didn't first recognize and then suddenly I thought: It's Dad's. He's either bought a truck or borrowed a truck and he's over here. And he kept pounding and pounding and pounding and my heart kept beating and beating."

She started to call the sheriff's office.

"I was scared of him. I was just flat-out scared. I was afraid he would harm me and my kids."

But in her panic she forgot the number, so she forced herself to go downstairs to a first-floor window for a closer look, praying it was not one of the nocturnal rampages of the father she had not seen in two years.

"And I saw this medium-height man with gray hair and glasses and a moustache, and I knew immediately it was Dad. And I was shaking so bad that I could hardly get back upstairs. I was weak with fright. I could hear him pounding and trying the doorknob and he just kept being more insistent and kept pounding and pounding. I started dialing again, and my thirteen-year-old son got up and looked out the window and said, 'Mom, that's Denny D—'s truck.' So I ran downstairs and let him in."

Denny was the local fire chief, and Loretta, relieved that he was not her father and now worried about a fire, forgot that Denny was a civil servant who wore two hats. That night he was not chasing fires, and she remembered that he was the local coroner just after he told her that her brother, Tommy, had just shot and killed her father, Eugene, and his new bride.

"My husband stayed home a week from work because I couldn't stay by myself at night. Even though I knew the fear was gone, that Dad was gone, I couldn't stand to be alone. I kept thinking that he would come back."

Three weeks later, after her father was buried, the local prosecutor announced he would seek the death sentence for Tommy.

All the names in this chapter are pseudonyms.

The town where Loretta and her brother and two sisters grew up is smaller than small. It sits in a region of southern Illinois ravaged by the worst plague of bankruptcies and farm foreclosures in the state, an emotional dust bowl of shattered dreams and withering hopes. But it is also an area where more bedroom communities have been sprouting. The new folks sought and found homesteads where doors can remain unlocked without peril, and children can walk along country roads at night without too much worry, and drugs, so far, are a distant menace. They left their big-city fears back in places like Champaign, Decatur, and Mattoon for the bucolic pocket of southern Illinois where Loretta and her neighbors lived.

"Champaign is getting worse with drugs and crimes, Decatur is rough, and Mattoon is a real hellhole," said a resident. "You have to go to a smaller town if you want a better environment. The area has its share of spouse beating and child abuse, but the child abuse has to be blatant to go to court."

How blatant is blatant? If it does not slip into the public eye, it can remain sequestered for years and years behind closed doors. And murder is a rare occurrence. In 1973, a woman, after enduring years

of beatings and threats of death, shot and killed her husband and
then buried his body in a cornfield. A jury found her guilty of manslaughter but she never went to jail. An appeals court threw out her
conviction because her attorney also represented her husband's bank,
a clear conflict of interest. Tommy's double slaying was the first in
memory. The prosecuting attorney's plan to seek the death penalty
also was a first. And because Tommy, who had always seemed taciturn, would not talk to his attorney, Loretta, the oldest and the
strongest of the kids, was compelled to testify in his defense. She had
to reveal things about her father and her family that had gone unnoticed for years. Most people where she lived had never really
known her father.

At her brother's trial, in summing up her testimony, she said that
Tommy "has done us all a great service." Now she and her sisters
could go to bed at night and not be terrified. Their father's death was
the end of a terrible ordeal.

"He never let most people see how he really was until the later
years. Most thought Dad was really a good guy. There are little old
ladies out there who still think he is a nice guy. Mom didn't care
what she said to anybody. Dad always wanted to make a good impression. My grandmother, Dad's mother, did not know what was going
on. She knew Dad drank but she didn't know how bad and the
effects on us children. Dad was just mean when he drinked. It
brought out a meanness and a hatred in him."

In an interview Loretta recalled, when she was three, and Tommy
two, her father picking up furniture and hurling it with enough
force to knock holes in the walls of their home. There were other
nights when Eugene was more menacing.

"I was six or seven when he got out a big machete and said he was
going to kill us all."

They lived under constant threat of a death sentence that was
always commuted. With so many threats of violence, they considered
it a blessing that he rarely touched anyone.

Eugene squeezed his mayhem into a forty-eight-hour period. On
Friday, after work, he would head to his favorite bar and drink late
into the night or early Saturday morning, and then drive home and
resume drinking. Then he would leave, returning late Saturday or
early Sunday morning. On Sunday, he would get up and act like
nothing had ever happened, as if there had been no reign of terror.

"When Dad would leave to drink, we knew what was going to happen. When he came home he was going to be blowing-up mad. We would go to bed at six or seven o'clock at night in the summer to get away from him. If we heard his car pull up in the driveway there were four kids immediately in bed. We just lived in a little two-bedroom house and four of us kids were in one bedroom, and there was no place for us to go. And we were scared. And we would all go to bed, and it wouldn't even be dark out, just to avoid his rage."

He was unpredictable, and no one could ever be certain when a siege would begin or end.

"I would feel this immense relief when he stopped. Everything would be okay for a while, and then he would start back."

When he was not drunk, he was not violent—just mean.

"He would reach into the very core of what made us what we were, and he would just destroy it. He would make us feel that we weren't worth being his children, that he was better than we were, and that we were a big disappointment. We were so ashamed of what was going on, we didn't make a lot of friends at school. People are ashamed when something like this is going on."

Eugene rarely spent much time with the family when Loretta was young, and on the occasions when he did take them out, it usually was just another way for him to go and drink and for them to suffer and wait.

"He would ask if we wanted to get ice cream cones, so we would go out and he would buy us ice cream cones and then go to Arcola, where all the taverns are, and he would go in while Mom and the kids sat out in the car with no place to go, not even a bathroom. Four kids cooped up in a car with Mom."

After he drove them home, all hell broke loose.

"I never knew why he drinked. He always blamed everybody else for his problems. He would come home drunk sometimes and begin to cry that all the neighbors had things and he didn't have nothing. All he had was four kids, and if he didn't have us kids he could afford something."

Later years brought him a measure of prosperity.

"He could always go to the bank and get a loan. His home was paid for, and as long as Mom was alive he always paid his bills. And he could buy a new car when he wanted. I can't find an answer from anyone why he was the way he was. He was never a real problem

with the neighbors; he just brought it all home to us. I don't know if
he knew why he did the things he did."

He cut them off from contact with other families, though the children established some community ties when they started attending
school. But their mother suffered. She made few friends—"She
didn't take to people well"—and turned to her children for compan-
ionship. Her childhood had not been easy either. Her own mother,
unable to care for her, had placed her in an orphanage. She grew up
bereft of love and affection and drifted away from her two sisters and
seven brothers. When she married Eugene, she left one state of un-
happiness and entered another. One night, before Loretta was born,
her father staggered home drunk and in a rage.

"Mom was pregnant with me. He was drunk and started beating
Mom right in the stomach, and they thought she was going to lose
me. I asked Mom why she didn't ever leave him. She said she loved
him and that she didn't have anyplace to go. She did leave him one
time, but she went back. She said she thought he was going to try
better."

He developed better ways of making sure that she would not
leave him.

"He told her if she left him, he would stop her medical benefits—
she had high blood pressure and diabetes for a while. She had to
have medical benefits."

He also berated her for having only an eighth-grade education, and
taunted her that she could not leave because she had no way of
supporting herself.

"Mom and Tommy took the brunt of his anger, Tommy in particular. Dad would say things to us girls but he wouldn't really do
anything. It was Mom and Tommy that he took most of his abuse
out on. Us girls wouldn't take it. Tommy always took it. From the
time I can remember, any kind of relationship between Tommy
and Dad was 'Tommy, you're stupid; you're ignorant; you can't follow instructions.'"

Tommy had a few friends but he was never close to anyone other
than his mother. And she tried to protect him from Eugene as best as
she could. Tommy grew up shy and withdrawn and rarely spoke to
anyone—"It got to the point that he couldn't speak." He started fall-
ing behind in his classes and would never graduate from high school.
One day when he was young, he went fishing with his father and
somehow got entangled in a fishing line. It should have produced a

chuckle but instead brought down a hail of scorn and ridicule. No one who was there has ever forgotten that day.

"Tommy grew up thinking he wasn't worth fifty cents."

Later, when Tommy was a young man still living at home, Eugene tried to commit him to a mental hospital. Tommy was twenty-one when the years of humiliation became too much and he grabbed one of the many guns in the house and told his father to shoot him because he knew Eugene really wanted him dead.

"That's how we always thought it was going to end. With my dad shooting Tommy."

In 1968, Loretta graduated from high school and married—"I always had the attitude that I was getting out of that place as soon as I could. I didn't want to stay there and take it."

Shortly after her marriage, her father stumbled and fell during one of his drunken stupors, smashing his head into a chest of drawers. It was later that year that he decided to take the cure and stop drinking.

"For a ten-year period we had the best family life we ever had."

An inpatient or outpatient of an alcohol abuse center for years, Eugene was also an accomplished musician. And when he eased into his new self-imposed temperance, he often serenaded and entertained his family with the guitar, mandolin, and harmonica.

"During that period when he wasn't drinking, he had a good relationship with my husband and my son and they went on all-night fishing trips together. They had good times. He loved his grandchildren and for the first time he and Mom did things together, and he finally treated Tommy halfway decent . . . sort of."

About 1975 or so, he became a born-again Christian and focused on the salvation of souls and the redemption of the world. He also became an itinerant preacher.

"Sometimes, when he was preaching, it was just like when he was drinking: He would be in a trance."

Eugene persuaded his family to start attending Sunday school as religion became his new passion. About two years later, he fought off a bout of tuberculosis. He was not drinking, and the doctors warned him that he would probably die if he resumed.

"The whole family rallied around him and supported him when he was in the hospital. Someone was always taking Mom and the kids to see him."

After he left the hospital, he started sipping whiskey for a cold that he could not seem to lose. Within months he started imbibing more and it was not too long before "he was back drinking and driving Mom crazy."

She left him.

"When she went back all of her will to live just went. We went over there and she wouldn't even be dressed. She wouldn't even clean the house. She had no will to live. She told me she was praying to die."

In 1980, "she keeled over on the floor dead." Tommy felt responsible. Eugene also thought Tommy was responsible and wanted to kill him.

Three days before she died, Tommy had staggered into a supermarket and made his way haphazardly through the aisles, picking up a razor blade and some other sundry items. He was walking through the check-out line when someone asked him what he was holding up under his shirt. When he showed all of the things he had picked up, he was arrested for shoplifting. The news stunned his mother and angered his father. Eugene and Tommy both believed it contributed to his mother's death.

Tommy had become as much of a lush as his father and, instead of harassing people like Eugene, developed a penchant for accumulating traffic tickets for driving while intoxicated. But he never hurt anyone. When he appeared in court on his shoplifting charge, the judge agreed not to send him to jail and released him on a probation that required him to enter an alcohol rehabilitation program to try to break his drinking habit. He was struggling to cope with his mother's death when his father asked him to come back home. The request almost bowled him over. For years, when his mother had been alive, he had been unable to win his father's approval. Now, at thirty-one, he found his mother's death bringing them together. But Loretta opposed it. She thought that it would be only a matter of time before her father would come home drunk one night and shoot Tommy. She convinced Tommy to live with her for a while, but he eventually moved in with Eugene.

A few days after Tommy moved back home, not too long after his mother died, his father came home drunk one night and brought a woman friend with him to spend the night. Tommy and Loretta, though hurt and ashamed, never said anything. But Loretta began to cut herself off from her father and Tommy as well.

"I couldn't take it anymore. I didn't want my kids to see what I had grown up with. I told Dad and Tommy don't come to my house because I wouldn't let them in."

She was unhappy about the way her father appeared to be dishonoring her mother's name, and she did not like being around Eugene or Tommy when they were drinking. And now they both were drinking heavily. She recalled how ironic it had been that their occasional drinking bouts together formed the first real "father-son relationship that Dad had with Tommy."

After working eight years at a broom factory, Tommy lost his job, and as the tension mounted in the house, that tissue-strength relationship of two "good ol' boys" who could not be father and son to each other fell apart. Eugene was angry that Tommy was not working and carrying his share of the weight, and Tommy seethed with anger over the woman his father had brought into his mother's home. But Tommy never argued, even when his father picked at him.

"It's hard to know what Tommy feels about things. He holds everything in. He doesn't show emotion, just like the very night he killed Dad."

Eugene allowed the woman and her kids to have the run of the house, as if "they were taking over."

"For years, Mom wasn't allowed to have a phone, and when she got a fifteen-dollar phone bill that would set Dad off. But this woman's kids were allowed to call collect, running up a hundred-dollar bill. There were things he wouldn't allow my mother to do that this woman did. And he had preached against living together without marriage, always worried about what other people would think, and here he was living with this woman."

When her father married the woman, things got worse, and they tried to drive Tommy out of the house.

"They weren't letting him eat but once a day, and if they would leave the house, they would come back and check to see if he had eaten anything after they left. And they had changed the locks on the door so that he couldn't get in."

One night in April, after drinking all day in a tavern, Tommy came home and the newlyweds started in on him, criticizing him for not working, not contributing to the family—"and something snapped."

Tommy walked into his bedroom and loaded his 20-gauge shotgun. Both he and Eugene owned several guns. They were not hunters but sometimes they would go to the railroad tracks and shoot snakes or rats. When Tommy came out of his room, his father was sitting on the couch.

"I walked in," he told a court later, "and he got up. He said, 'Hey,' and that's all he said and I pulled the trigger."

When he aimed the gun at his father's wife, she screamed, "No, [Tommy], no," and then he shot her.

His father writhed in agony on the floor. He had been shot in the abdomen. The woman was hit once in the leg. They were both bleeding profusely. Tommy called the police and waited for them to arrive.

When the police arrived, Eugene was moaning in pain and his wife was unconscious. Two ambulances were dispatched, and the crew of the first to arrive decided to take the unconscious woman. For some reason that later was the subject of an intense debate, they did not take Tommy's father. A few minutes after the ambulance pulled away from the house, the woman died. But the crew decided to drive to the hospital anyway and did not return for Eugene. When the second ambulance arrived thirty minutes later, Eugene was dead.

"When the police arrested him, Tommy seemed very calm and very cooperative," Loretta said. "But they said he showed no emotion. He told me weeks after I was visiting him that he was hurting really bad and he told me, 'When they came and got me that night I thought my whole world was over. I thought I had lost everybody.' He in no way ever thought that any of us would ever go to that jail and visit him."

When the prosecutor announced he would seek the death penalty, Tommy's family panicked. His attorney said he could arrange a plea bargain that would require Tommy to plead guilty to manslaughter for killing his father and second-degree murder for killing his wife. With the death sentence hanging over his head, Tommy decided, after consulting with his family, not to go to trial.

"We didn't know if we made the right decision with the two murders. If he went to a jury trial he might have gotten the death sentence or life in prison. And can you imagine what would have happened with the publicity if he had gone to trial—it was enough with the murders."

At his sentencing, the prosecutor recommended that Tommy get fifty-five years.

"The prosecutor insisted that he sat there and let them die," Loretta recalled bitterly, "that he didn't make any attempt to call for help. He hit her in the leg and ripped a main artery. Dad was hit in the abdomen. She could not have lived longer than twelve minutes, depending on how excited she was."

Loretta had talked to a pathologist who explained to her that both her father and his wife had been fatally wounded and it was unlikely that they would have survived even if they had been whisked to the hospital by helicopter.

"The prosecutor portrayed Tommy as a cold-blooded person, but the facts could have been brought out in a trial if he had chosen to go to trial, but we had to weigh the risks. If he hadn't killed that woman he may have only had a five-year sentence. He's not serving time for Dad's murder; it was for hers."

The judge, however, sentenced Tommy to twenty-five years in jail and explained, "I am reluctant to deal out these sentences, but the law says we have to. I sympathize with you," he told Tommy. "I wish you the best of luck."

Tommy will be eligible for parole when he is forty-three.

"Dad didn't destroy the four of us. He wouldn't have been happy that we stuck together. We lost contact with him in the later years. We would have helped him if he wanted us to. But if Tommy hadn't known that we loved him, he wouldn't have been able to take it. We know what he did was wrong but we didn't want to abandon him. He'll be paying for this the rest of his life. We are all carrying scars."

After her interview with me, Loretta wanted a copy of the tape recording to help her prepare her own article about what drinking can do to a family. But she changed her mind. Months later she wrote:

"I feel like since I have talked to you that it isn't necessary to talk or write about what we've been through. My feelings have changed with the passing of time and I think right now that we should all try to let it be."

# 2

# Mary Jane

"I want you to know that I do not like to talk about my past. I am only agreeing to it because it would be wrong of me to sit back and feel sorry for myself if I can possibly help someone else."

Her name, for this account, is Mary Jane.

The first time Mary Jane ran into the kitchen she was going to kill herself, but she ran back into the living room where he was lying on the floor. She quickly ran back into the kitchen. She kept shuffling back and forth between the living room and kitchen, between wanting to live and wanting to die, between staying and escaping, until the sight of blood all over her hands startled her and she scurried into the bathroom. She washed her hands and grabbed a bunch of towels and rushed back into the living room. He was not groaning. Though his agony was over, she tried to stop the blood pouring from his wounds. But there were too many wounds, and she wanted to flee. She dropped the towels and started throwing all of her stuff into a suitcase. She grabbed his truck keys and and some camping gear, loaded the dog into the truck, and fled. But she did not know where she was going and drove around in fear and panic. Her world was disintegrating and she was frantically grasping for the pieces to hold herself together.

When she calmed just a bit, one of the myriad of thoughts racing around in her head broke loose from the tangled cluster of ideas, images, and impressions and breathed some sense into her. She needed someone to help her. She decided to drive to her boyfriend's

house. With no obvious display of the pandemonium ranting inside
her, Mary Jane greeted him warmly. He was heading south to his
father's cabin and asked her if she wanted to go with him. It was one
more thing in the past hour that made sense to her and she grabbed
it. She helped him unload her stuff from the truck into his van. At
the cabin, she thought, she could at least relax and think about what
she should do next.

Their first stop, before taking the interstate south, was to pick up
his pay check. And then they made one more stop, at her gynecologist's office. For a day shaping up to be the worst of her life, she got
good news. She was not pregnant and they both breathed a sigh of
relief, but Mary Jane breathed deeper. It was one less pain that she
would have to worry about.

On the trip, she did not tell him about the body in her living room.
For months she had been holding in things that weighed in on her
and caused her to faint, experiences she had never discussed with
anyone. And she was not about to start now.

It was a pleasant fall ride, and after they reached the cabin, she
fixed dinner. They both drank some liquor and got high and mellow.
They were in bed when the car drove up and she begged and pleaded
with him not to answer the door. But he got up anyway, and when
he opened the door his father and brother walked in and told him
that the police were looking for him and Mary Jane. Someone had
killed her father. And they were suspects. When the three confronted her, she would not talk, and on the trip back she kept to
herself. They drove to the station house of the volunteer fire fighters,
because the town was so small it did not have a local police department. They had to wait for the cops.

They were both charged with first-degree murder, and Mary
Jane's boyfriend almost went out of his mind. He was in a lot of
trouble and he did not know why, and the police did not believe him.
The investigators did not try to take a statement from Mary Jane
because at fifteen she was a minor and a parent or guardian had to be
present before she could be questioned. It was then they learned she
had been living with her mother in an adjacent state before moving
in with her father. She was a runaway. They called her mother, who
told them she would catch a plane as soon as possible.

Mary Jane was not looking forward to meeting her mother when
she flew in two days later. A police officer met her mother at the
airport. She told the officer she did not want her daughter to sign a

statement, but the investigator cagily told her they had mounds of evidence against Mary Jane and said it would be easier on her daughter if she confessed. They had recovered the knife and the gun. Her fingerprints were on both weapons. (Charges against her boyfriend were therefore dropped subsequently.) When Mary Jane's mother arrived at the police station, she told her daughter it would be in her best interests if she told the truth and signed a statement. Mary Jane hesitantly told the police that her father had tried to kill her. That was why she had shot him. They told her she was lying, that her explanation had as many holes as her father's body. And that was when she started screaming. They had not been there. They did not know what had happened.

"I knew what happened—they didn't," she said later.

They could not convince her to change her statement and typed it just the way she told them. Her father had shot at her and she had shot back, hitting him several times. She could not explain, and they did not ask (there was no need for them to ask), why there were no other bullet holes found in the walls or floors. If he had missed, there should have been holes. If she had shot him in self-defense, why had he been stabbed so many times? She signed her statement and was returned to her cell. She was charged with first-degree murder, but was being treated as a juvenile.

Her mother flew back home. They had not talked much, and after her mother left, Mary Jane languished briefly in jail waiting for the court to appoint her an attorney. She was assigned two, and she told them what she had told the police: She had shot her father in self-defense because he was trying to kill her. The attorneys later got her out of the county jail and into a juvenile facility, where she stayed a few days before the court ordered a pretrial psychiatric evaluation at a mental hospital. She was there almost two months.

On her admission, Mary Jane was loath to talk about her past, but she told the resident psychiatrist that she would try to cooperate.

"For an evaluation, I believe that by evaluating me they can make a more fair decision," she told him.

And she gave him as much as she could. Mary Jane had been living with her mother and stepdad when she started running away from home. She had been about fourteen or fifteen. She was eventually placed in a foster home, and she ran away from there and moved in with a girlfriend. It was about then that her father sent her a bus ticket so that she could come and live with him and his new wife. She got along fine with them for the first few months. He helped her to find a job. When she had run away before, she had skipped a lot of classes, but he even convinced her to go back to school. Her dad introduced her to one of his friends who eventually became her lover. In her new home she found more freedom; she believed she had discovered the happiness that had been missing in her life. Her father took her camping and swimming. Sometimes he would joust with her in a roughhouse manner and hit her so hard she would cry. He and his parents would chide her for acting like a baby. But it was just play and she was happy. They also taught her how to shoot a handgun.

But in a few months life soured. Her father lost his job, and though he had always been a heavy drinker, he started lying around the house and criticizing Mary Jane and his wife. His wife would tolerate only so much. Mary Jane, however, took the brunt of his self-pity and anger. After a while, it seemed that both of them started picking on her. He complained that Mary Jane was spending too much time with her boyfriend and not enough time at home. His wife ordered her to do more work around the house to make up for her indolent father. Sometimes when Mary Jane's father was drunk and steeped in self-pity, he came to her and complained about all his problems and expected her to comfort and sympathize with him. That did not stop him from continually criticizing her and constantly putting her down. He restricted Mary Jane to the house and allowed her out only to go to school and work. The tension increased and they screamed and argued more. She also cried more. She told the psychiatrist she wanted a father she could trust. She had learned he was not the one.

"While still loving him because he was her real father, she gradually grew to hate him," the psychiatrist wrote in his report.

Why didn't she run away?

She was afraid he might catch her and afraid of what he might do to her.

Mary Jane told the psychiatrist that she had not planned to kill him. "It was a spur of the moment thing," the doctor wrote. She also said there had been no fight the night before or the morning that he died. Nothing more than usual, she said.

In his report the psychiatrist noted that when Mary Jane was first admitted she had been sarcastic and rude to the other residents of the hospital, and she had walked around the facility with a chip on her shoulder. He described her as "snippy."

"She had refused to discuss the feelings that generated these actions and offered no explanation as to why she had been behaving thus," he wrote. "She was placed on a group plan where she was to confront and self-disclose meaningfully or she would be restricted her next meal."

It was excruciatingly painful for Mary Jane when she did open up to him and bare her soul. Supposedly that was what he and the staff wanted. She did not decide to talk because of any restrictions. She could not hold it in anymore and needed to talk to someone who could help her. When she reached that decision and began to reveal her problems to him, he told her that what she was saying was making him uncomfortable and nervous. He could not help.

The doctor's account was based on what he had seen and learned from Mary Jane and what the other staff members had told him of their observations. When he weighed the importance of what he was told, some observations received greater significance than others. In one sense, the doctor's account was accurate. Mary Jane had been "snippy" and uncooperative in the beginning. But there were things that he left out of his report, information that would have placed what he thought he saw and what some other staff members thought they saw in another perspective. They were either unimportant, in his judgment, or their significance eluded him.

For example, in the hospital Mary Jane was in an alien world. The secured medical facility held a little more than two hundred patients, less than a dozen of whom were women locked up in a wing set away from the rest of the general population. They were inmates from the women's state prison who were either dangerously suicidal or homicidal, or both. Mary Jane was not incarcerated with them. She was placed in the general population, where she was the only female. Her presence created problems for some men and they, in turn, created problems for her.

"A lot of men wouldn't leave you alone and the other half hated you because they were gay and didn't like women," she recalled.

As another example, she was expected to participate in an all-male therapy group. That upset her. Therapy sessions consisted of one person baring his soul and the group tearing into him, trying to

break him down, "until you busted him down and he was crying."
She did not want to be busted down by the men in her group.

"A lot of the men were in for child molesting," she explained.
They had been sexually molesting, fondling, assaulting, and raping
daughters, nieces, and any other little girls they could get their
hands on. She did not want to talk or listen to them, but she had no
choice; though she was required to be present, she refused to participate. That prompted some of the staff to see her as arrogant and
uncooperative. One day after listening to one man drone on for a long
time about how he liked having sex with little girls, she blew up.

"There was this guy who was in for lascivious acts with an eleven-
year-old girl, and he didn't think it was wrong," she explained.
"After an hour I'd had enough of his whining and crying."

She ripped into him. A staff aide, who had befriended her when
she first arrived, interrupted just before she delivered her coup de
grâce.

"Tom asked me," she recalled, "'If you were in the position of that
eleven-year-old, would you have shot him?' Then I shut up." He
pulled her aside and later convinced the psychiatrist to call her, but
she would not go see him at first.

Later she was convinced it was time to talk.

"One day I said, 'All right, I guess if I don't say anything I could
get a life sentence.' There was a time I didn't care. After a couple of
weeks of being locked up, I developed an attitude. At that time I felt
I had lost everything and everybody anyways so I didn't see how it
mattered whether I told them what happened to me or not."

But she now wanted to live and did not want to spend the rest of
her life in jail. She walked into the psychiatrist's office and stayed
more than three hours. For the first fifteen minutes she just sat
there trying to talk. Nothing came out. He sat there patiently while
she stumbled and fumbled. The silence was deafening. She could not
say "rape" so she finally told him her father was forcing her to have
sex with him. The first sentence, by her estimates, took almost
twenty minutes. In the next hour, she managed a few more sentences. She told him her father had forced her to have sex more than
once. It had happened many times. He would just make her do it.

She wanted and needed help and that was why she was talking to
the doctor now. "He told me I was making him nervous, that he was
used to dealing with men, not women," she said. "He didn't know

what to say to me. But I wouldn't leave. I made myself talk to him even if it wasn't everything I could have said. I knew it was important. I talked several hours. Once in a while he nodded."

She struggled through three hours filled with long pauses because sometimes it felt like she was going to choke on every word. After that one meeting, even though he let her know he could not help her, she started participating in the hospital program more and loosened up enough to be friendly and more accommodating to the staff and other patients, but she would not discuss her emotions. She had tried once.

". . . she continued to be quite active in the group, confronting her peers and expressing her opinions," the nervous doctor wrote. "She, however, did not do much self-disclosure and never did very much throughout the rest of her stay. On the unit she was seen as a more warm person, but it was noted she still needed to continue working on her feelings."

Shortly before she was released from the hospital and returned to the juvenile facility, a male patient tried to rape her. He was a "friend" who during recreation outside one day told her he wanted to have sex with her. Mary Jane said no. She did not want to get in trouble or harm her case or evaluation. Later when she was walking inside the hospital, he forced her into a staff rest room. He pinned her against the wall and tried to pull her pants down. She pushed him away. He tried kissing her and running his hands all over her body. She tried to get free but he was too strong. He kept pulling at her clothes, and she kept telling him to stop. Finally she growled that she would scream. He pushed her away and left. Concerned about what the staff and other patients might think about her, she was afraid to tell anyone what happened. All she wanted was for her attacker to leave her alone. But she finally confided in Tom, the aide. The staff started an investigation.

"We're not sure whose story to believe," the doctor wrote.

The male patient insisted that Mary Jane had been coming on to him and walked willingly into the bathroom and then chickened out. It was an explanation similar to the rationalizations used by some of the child molesters in Mary Jane's therapy group. The victims really wanted it.

"Probably they both were correct to some extent but this writer would tend to believe more what [Mary Jane] had to say," the psychiatrist wrote.

After the rape attempt, Mary Jane was escorted to the bathroom by a staff member and warned to stay in view of the staff at all times. About a week later, she was returned to the juvenile detention center to await more court hearings.

In his final diagnosis, the doctor found Mary Jane to be a basically very bright, healthy adolescent female who was nonaggressive but had a "conduct disorder."

"I would note that psychological testing showed some aggressive tendencies but she has not really engaged in any serious or overt aggressive behavior in the past," he wrote.

His recommendations? He believed Mary Jane needed some "structure in her life" and that she was "not ready to live independently."

"I think she realized this herself and is quite scared of the future should she have to live on her own," he wrote. "If she would not have to do time, I would not recommend her returning to her mother. I would recommend some other sort of structured environment for adolescent girls. If she does have to do some time, that will provide some structure."

He cited mitigating circumstances "in regards to her crime," which "consisted primarily of her age and her father abusing her sexually. . . . The actual decision to kill her father was made impulsively with her stating that she decided this was the last time he was ever going to attempt to force her to have sexual relations. I think the decision was made over a matter of seconds or at most a few minutes. I think she was both angry and scared."

But he did not let it end there.

"On the other hand, it would be my impression that she was still capable of understanding the nature and quality of her behavior," he wrote. "It would also be my impression that she was still capable of distinguishing between right and wrong. It is equally this writer's opinion that at the time she had the capacity to form intent consistent with accountability. Her degree of responsibility is a matter which seeks resolution through the judicial process."

The doctor was the consummate equivocator. On the one hand, she had acted "impulsively" and in self-defense when she shot a man who was going to force her to have sex again. She had killed a rapist. On the other hand, he explained, the rapes had not diminished her ability to understand the nature and quality of her behavior. She knew right from wrong. Had she been right in acting in self-defense? Or wrong in shooting a man who was going to rape her again? Perhaps the doctor would not have equivocated so blatantly if she had killed a rapist who was not her father. He was saying that under the law, in his august opinion, she was not insane. But, again, does a girl have to be insane to defend herself against a rapist?

The doctor also bungled his evaluation of her. It had taken her eight months to gather the courage to talk about what had happened to her. Under some special circumstances and with some assistance from a friendly and intuitive aide, she told the psychiatrist what had happened, and he told her she was making him nervous. In his report, he wrote that he could not understand why she then refused to confide her emotions.

It is not rare for psychiatrists to be insensitive or inept in working with patients who are incest victims. "Therapists of both sexes," writes Dr. Judith Lewis Herman in *Father-Daughter Incest*, "are often resistant to the idea of raising questions about sexual abuse with their patients. Most if not all of these resistances reflect the therapists' discomfort in confronting their own feelings about the issue. . . . Most therapists lack the ability to help incest victims because they have never been trained to deal with the issue. In fact, they have been trained to avoid it. . . . If confronted with a patient who insists upon talking about it, the therapists suddenly feel like a novice again."

In her book Herman mentions the testimony of two doctors as examples of how reputable psychiatrists might deal and have dealt with incest victims. She quotes one as saying, "I know I don't want to hear about it. I have no idea what to do with these cases. And I don't think I'm unusual." And another: "When she told me about her father, I didn't know what the hell to do with her. I felt I couldn't help. My supervisor advised me not to open that can of worms."

Mary Jane, after the psychiatric evaluation, was returned to the juvenile detention center to await another hearing in court. Things that she had not disclosed were still struggling to get out when she left the facility. A good chunk of her life and what she had really endured was still sealed tightly inside her. By the time she did appear in court again, the district attorney, after probing her past in her hometown, found she had a police record for running away scores of times. She had also been involved in two stolen-car capers and in shoplifting incidents. It was enough material for a probation

officer to call Mary Jane a "hard core juvenile delinquent," the kind
of incorrigible whom he would like to see behind bars for a long time.
She would be no longer treated as a juvenile but prosecuted as an
adult. The judge did not object. At fifteen, with a first-degree
murder charge lodged against her, Mary Jane was now looking at life
in prison.

"In [this state] life is life," her attorney said in an interview.
"They mean life when they say life. Not twenty years or thirty years,
but life. Life is life. I can't recall the last time a governor of this
state commuted a life sentence."

Mary Jane used to like to take things home with her. Pencils,
pens, jewelry, trinkets, knickknacks of all shapes, sizes, and col-
ors—all were agreeable to her. She took things she did not need and
really did not want. Her grabby little fingers came with invisible
suction cups that would impulsively attach to something before she
realized what she was doing. She was a budding kleptomaniac at five.
It was her way of getting attention. At least that was what a counselor suggested. Mary Jane licked the impulse, except for an occasional backslide, which got her in trouble for shoplifting.

Taking things she did not need to get attention was only one of her
problems. She also developed a penchant for getting into the oddest
jams. When she was older, some kids would practically tie her up
before she realized that she was in trouble, like the time some little
devils, nasty pals of hers, bound her to a signpost with a bicycle
chain and blackened both her eyes. She blundered into perils that
other young kids her age easily avoided, and at home it seemed everywhere she stepped she hit a land mine. She was always in trouble at
home. At fourteen, she and her mother locked horns. If she was ten
minutes late for dinner or curfew, Mary Jane could be grounded for
a week. When she was ordered to stay home, she ran away. Her
mother constantly prowled for the telltale signs of cigarettes or,
worse, marijuana, and when Mary Jane caught her mom going
through her personal things, she flipped out. And ran away.

"I guess I felt at the time that my mother was pushing her beliefs
and values and morals on me," she explains. "See, I had everything.
My mom was pretty wealthy. I didn't want everything, but I didn't
feel that I had the freedom and that was what I wanted. That's how
I came down to [her father's hometown] as a runaway. I was looking
for something new. Freedom."

Freedom?

"Well, I had some minority friends and my mother is very prejudiced. And boyfriends. My mom didn't like my boyfriends. Well, in fact, she never really got to meet too many of them, but she didn't like my going out with guys."

At fourteen, Mary Jane hung out with "boyfriends" who were really men in their mid-twenties. She thought she loved them and they loved her, until she realized there was no love and they were only using her or they started making demands. She would drop one and pick up with someone who was little different from the one she had dumped. When asked to describe them, she said, "Yuck!" and her face twisted in mock pain. Her boyfriends were good for providing crashpads when she ran away from home.

"I ran away from home twenty or thirty times," she recalled. "I probably stayed away for anywhere from a day to two months. I went to school in bits and pieces. I went to an alternative school because I was running away so much. If you run away you can go back and make up your work and they don't really hold that against you." The interludes between escapes were occasions for her and her parents to try to patch together some kind of reconciliation through some form of counseling. It was her parents' idea.

"There was counseling all the time," she says. "Counseling for all of us. It was either me going to counseling or family counseling. I always dreaded going."

By her account, the sessions usually resulted in her being told that she was the cause of the problems between her and her parents: She always wanted things to be her way or she was selfish.

"Which I probably was," she explained. "Most everything I did, if they had let me alone I would have been all right. I probably wouldn't have done it."

The things that she did annoyed her mother solely because of her mother's exceedingly high standards.

"Mostly what I did . . . things that I did weren't up to her standards," Mary Jane said. "She wanted me to be just like her."

And she stated emphatically, "I am nothing like her."

One day when the tension in the house built up a monstrous head of steam, Mary Jane ran away again. When she returned, her mother challenged her to a fight. It started with an argument.

"I started screaming I hated her and she got really upset," more upset than she had ever seen her mother, Mary Jane said.

Her mother dared Mary Jane to hit her. Mary Jane balked. Her mother dared her again. When she refused, her stepdad took off her mother's glasses and ordered Mary Jane to hit her. Hit her, hit her, they kept insisting. But Mary Jane refused.

"Mom wanted to fight, but I wasn't going to hit her back," she said.

So, after her mother belted her a few times, she ran away again. At fourteen, when she was a pubescent little girl who could pass for nineteen or twenty or twenty-one, she noticed that her stepdad could not take her seriously.

"He can't talk to me; he feels uncomfortable talking to me," she explained. "He was really hurt when I went to [her father's home] to see my real dad. When I went to see my real father, he stopped talking to me."

She also had brief encounters with the police over "little problems," things that a probation officer would embroider around his label of "hard core juvenile delinquent."

"It was mostly little stuff," she explained. "Once I took my boyfriend's car when he was in jail. I had one of his keys and I just wanted to go for a ride. I went for the ride and got in trouble. The car overheated and the engine blew. It was a '57 Charger on the biggest street [in her hometown]. I took a bus home."

She left the car where it died, and when her boyfriend's sister filed charges, with his blessings, Mary Jane was charged with a misdemeanor and placed on two months' probation. A social worker and a probation officer believed her problems stemmed from home, and Mary Jane, with her parents' willing consent, was placed in a foster home. For a while it was a good idea.

"I felt a little bit more comfortable because foster home was a little bit looser than it was at home. The rules were better. But then," she sighed, "I started getting into trouble again, started getting grounded, started feeling suffocated."

She fled and stayed with a girlfriend, and was at a watershed when her father slithered back into her life. She had first learned that he existed when she was nine. She answered the phone one day and a man calling long distance asked to speak to her mother. Her mother said it was a friend's husband but later told her the caller was her real father, and he wanted a picture of her. Mary Jane did not think it really mattered one way or another, but when she started fighting seriously with her family, she accepted his offer to come live with him and his new wife. He sent her bus fare, and several hours later Mary Jane met her real father. He brought his wife and Mary Jane's grandparents with him when he picked her up, and she was feted like a homecoming queen.

"I knew living there wasn't going to be anything like living with my mother and stepdad because of what they told me in the car," she said. "I could do whatever I wanted. There were no expectations. They showed me around to all of the relatives. I was shaking so that they got me high. They gave me Valium and some beer. I thought: Wow, this is the life. The second night they did the same thing and I got sick."

She had a great time with her father that summer. Besides swimming and camping, they taught her how to shoot at a firing range. Her father and grandfather kept guns scattered around the house. Her father often flirted with her in that unctuous way he had of concealing it behind his roughhousing with her. It was all supposed to be in good fun and Carol, her stepmother, and Mary Jane's grandparents would tease her if she started crying when he played too rough. Carol was friendly in the beginning but later became jealous because she thought her husband was spending too much time with Mary Jane. But it was still a pleasant summer, even though she thought they spent a lot of time drinking.

"The only recreation we had were two bars, and that was it except for a park," she said. "I played a lot of pool with my dad."

In that small town, Mary Jane's new family had earned quite a reputation. Many of the barflies would leave as soon as they saw the clan approaching. Her father was known as an ornery cuss who had spent time in jail for beating up another man. He had also earned a reputation for beating up women who crossed him. Mary Jane's mother had left him when her daughter was just an infant because of one punch too many. But the bar regulars were equally afraid of Carol, who was as wide as she was tall and just as mean.

"When they saw us coming, half would leave because of Carol," Mary Jane said. "She would hit people with a big stick and once broke a chair over some guy's head."

Her grandfather was too old to mix it up in the bar; his heyday was over. So he contented himself with smoking grass and getting drunk and using other drugs, and, of course, watching his son and his daughter-in-law raise hell. Mary Jane's grandmother occasionally joined them but she did not like to fight. Mary Jane thought they were all a mite strange, definitely not like her mom and stepdad, but no one was hassling her, they all welcomed her, and there was no reason she could discern for her to be worried.

By the time school started, her father was lying around the house drunk and mean. And he started getting upset with Mary Jane because she was spending too much time with her boyfriend and not much time with him at home. He eventually grounded her and ordered her to stay around the house. Her problems with her father made Carol happy.

He eventually got around to what was really on his mind. After a fight one day with Carol, he staggered into Mary Jane's room and started whining. She later remembered him as being drunk and almost crying. He told her how much he loved her and how he had missed watching her grow up. And when he sensed that she was feeling sorry for him, he told her how she could help him. Sometimes, he said, two people help each other by making love. That's how she could help him. It was a normal part of life and anyone could make love, husband and wives, boyfriends and girlfriends, and fathers and daughters. She felt sorry for him and wanted to help but she was confused over how she was supposed to deny him. How do you say no to your father? He was on top of her before she could speak, forced her to spread her legs, and used her while she lay there. When he finished, he got up and left without saying a word.

He was back again the next morning and on top of her before she could rub the sleep out her eyes. After a few minutes he got up and left. Soon he was coming into her room regularly in the morning, and when she resisted or fought him he overpowered her. Sometimes he slapped her, and sometimes he jabbed her so hard she cried.

Mary Jane wanted to run away but this time there was no place to run. She had little money, and there were no boyfriends or girlfriends with crashpads for her to use. She was afraid of him and needed to hide but there was no place to turn. Her casual boyfriend was just a sometimes lover and not someone she could trust in time of trouble. She could not tell Carol. So she started getting up early in the morning and leaving before he could come into her room. That infuriated him. He started screaming at her when she was in the house, calling her a slut and whore and telling her she was no good, and then he would rape her the first time he could get his hands on her when no one else was around. She started having fainting spells.

Her complexion became ashen, and she looked fatigued. When she started missing her period, Carol told her she must be pregnant.

When the district attorney decided to prosecute her as an adult, Mary Jane's attorney hired another psychologist to help prepare her for the ordeal of a trial. She would have to testify publicly about what had happened to her if she did not want to go to jail forever. And what she had disclosed to the first psychiatrist was not enough to help her case. She would have to provide more details. She would have to be able to convince a jury that she had been attacked and that she had acted in self-defense. In other words, the victim would have to prove that she *was* the victim.

In the first meeting with the new doctor, a woman professional who had worked with battered women and girls and women raped by their fathers, Mary Jane talked about her family and her life but not about the rapes. She had already tried once to explain what had happened, and the support she needed had not been there.

In a later meeting, however, many of the details she had held back poured out of her as the doctor reassured her that it was important that they talk. Mary Jane told her about the day she had woken up nervous and afraid. It had been about 5:30 A.M. that fall. She was fearful that her father would come into her room, as well as about an appointment Carol had made for her to see a gynecologist. Mary Jane dreaded the appointment because she could not be sure if her father or her boyfriend was the father of any child she might have.

When Carol left for work, Mary Jane's father yelled to her that she was supposed to tell the doctor that her boyfriend was the child's father and then pack her things and go back to her mother. He told her he wished that she had never been born and accused her of being the cause of all his problems. She was responsible for making Carol angry at him. They started arguing. He told her he was not going to allow her to leave the house until it was time for her appointment. She was going to spend the day with him. He went into the kitchen to get a beer, and when she started to walk outside, he rushed back and pushed her into a chair and warned her not to try to leave. But she got up to leave again. He came back and grabbed her and started trying to kiss her. He wanted sex one more time before she left.

The gun, like so many guns in the house, was nearby. This one was hanging on the wall. She shoved him off her onto a couch, whipped the gun off the wall, and peppered him with shots, handling the weapon just as he and her grandfather had taught her. But then she panicked and began running back and forth between the living room and the kitchen, until she picked up a knife. She was going to kill herself, when she heard him gasp and moan. He was still alive and, in her mind, still dangerous. She ran back into the room and stabbed him until the blood chased her away. She packed quickly and left. Later she learned she was not pregnant.

"The patient is a relatively bright young woman with a high average IQ, and a borderline personality organization," the doctor wrote to the court. "She is quite depressed and has shown a life of chronic depression, experiencing people as either being frightening or rejecting. She has a tendency to act under extreme stress, a situation which is quite typical of a borderline individual. The borderline individual shows poor reality testing under stress situations while showing good reality testing when in non-stress situations. When the reality testing becomes poor under a high-stress situation, they have a tendency to act upon their impulses rather than suppress them."

Though Mary Jane's psychological test disclosed a borderline personality, she in fact had no history of acting violent because she could not suppress her impulses. The extraordinary circumstances in which she found herself trapped by her father would have been enough to cause any other girl or woman to fight back in self-defense by any means necessary.

Although there are several theories about the shaping of a borderline personality, some research implicates an impairment in the mother-child relationship, when the child is as young as one year or less, as a cause of the personality disorder. It can also be brought about through a childhood trauma, but there are indications that chronic neglect and lack of love and attention from an overworked, overburdened mother, or a neglectful and unresponsive one, can be a primary cause.

"Although she had had sexual experiences with other young men there is a big difference between the loss of boundaries in a parent having sex with a child regardless of the age and two peers having a sexual relationship. The child expects the parent to be protective and take care of them and when the parent becomes exploitative, it betrays the trust the child has in them, and it is an extremely anxiety-producing experience," the doctor wrote.

In Mary Jane's case, the extreme anxiety was exacerbated by her belief in her pregnancy and by her father's calling her a slut and telling her that she would have to leave, and then preparing to rape her again. The big man who could not hold a job or manipulate his wife, but thought he could use Mary Jane, pushed too far one time too many.

"It was the contrast between his rejecting the results of his having sex with her and then turning around and having sex with her as well as putting her under extreme pressure that caused her, in her own words, to 'snap,'" the doctor wrote. "Given the borderline personality structure at that point, she would have lost contact with reality and simply seen herself as in need to react to the threat in her environment. . . . The very point that she kept shooting and stabbing and stabbing shows that she lost contact with reality at that point under the stress. . . . Under situations of less stress she probably would have reacted simply by running rather than by reacting in such a violent manner. However, she saw herself, with her poor reality testing at that point, as being in extreme danger and the source of the danger being the father.

"In light of this," she concluded, "I think it will be important for her to have an opportunity to make some kind of payment for the crime but do not feel that it needs to be in extreme. She needs a treatment process to help reorganize her life and help her learn to deal with stress situations, hopefully none as extreme as this. . . . She is a bright and basically sensitive youngster who could be taught to handle things better and be rehabilitated."

Despite the disclosures, and what her father had done to her, her attorneys strongly suggested that Mary Jane accept a plea-bargaining arrangement offered by the district attorney. She recalled later that they had sprung it on her suddenly. She should plead guilty to voluntary manslaughter in return for a possible light sentence that she could serve in a juvenile facility. If she chose to go to trial, she risked getting a life sentence in a state where "life is life."

"They told me I had three weeks to make up my mind," she said. "I didn't want it but I pled. My attorneys' word was the law. It was the only advice I had."

On the sentencing date, the judge said he recognized that this was "a tragic case" indeed.

"We have a girl here only 16 years of age [for] whom I think there is a lot of hope and, of course, there are reasons at least advanced to explain what happened," he said. "I am not saying that the reasons advanced excused what happened or condone what happened, but they do tend to explain them. I think, however, that that has been reflected in the fact that the charge originally filed was murder in the first degree and it was in this case reduced to voluntary manslaughter, which is a substantial reduction. And since we have a homicide here, any question of a probation, I think, would unduly deprecate the seriousness of the offense. The court finds that the maximum opportunity for the rehabilitation of the defendant and the protection of the community from further offenses by the defendant, based upon recommendation of counsel, and the facts as presented to court, which were duly considered by court, will be realized by the below stated order."

He gave Mary Jane two consecutive ten-year sentences for killing her father and using a gun. It was understood that she would be sent to a juvenile facility until she was eighteen, when she could be sent to the state women's prison, but it was expected that she would be paroled if she was still incarcerated then. On her first day in the facility, the officials greeted her by tossing her a mattress and some blankets. She would need them to spend the night on a floor. They told her she was too dangerous to be held in their juvenile facility, and they were arranging plans to transfer her to the women's prison. They refused her plea to call her attorney.

Eight days later, when they transferred her, she was finally allowed to call her attorney. He told her that he would file a motion to have her sentence reconsidered and that she should be out of jail within ninety days because of all the time she had spent incarcerated after her arrest. She had never been out on bail. She called him regularly during the next ninety days, and he kept reassuring her that he was going to file the motion. He had ninety days to file the motion and he never did. She subsequently learned that she would not receive credit for time spent in the juvenile facility now that she was in state prison. She might have to spend three years incarcerated before she could be eligible for parole. Her lawyer said in an interview that though he was surprised by her transfer, he believed the women's prison actually had more to offer her. Lawyers who are negligent in handling their clients' cases can be disbarred. This case begged for an investigation, but who was she going to ask to investigate a lawyer who was supposed to be investigating her case? She let it pass after reading him the riot act over the telephone. He never came to see her while she was in jail.

Her latest attorney filed an appeal, claiming that the "sentencing court erred in imposing terms of incarceration and in refusing to consider mitigating circumstances on the basis that these circumstances had already been reflected in the reduction of the original charge of first-degree murder where the record failed to show the defendant committed the higher crime." She had a strong chance of winning the appeal, but that could take a long time, and it was possible that several parole dates could pass before her sentence was ever reconsidered.

So Mary Jane sat in jail waiting for her date with the parole board to arrive swiftly. She had few visitors; and while she and her mother exchanged an occasional letter, she was not planning to go home when she got out. There was no therapy program, and she did not trust the prison psychiatrist who came around once a month or so. Her counselor, like so many people, told her it was a shame that she was in prison and, worse, that she was growing up in jail.

When her mettle rose, Mary Jane swelled with bravado and felt impervious to the past that pursued her relentlessly. It was during those times when she was full of herself that she fended it off with equanimity, reminding herself—sometimes aloud, sometimes within—that the killing had not been her fault. Her defenses seemed impregnable: He shouldn't have done what he did. He got what he deserved. Don't think about it. It's over and done with. Forget him. Forget it.

"Sometimes, no matter what happened, it isn't right . . . that he did that to me. Sometimes, I feel like I don't care. . . . I try to push it out of my mind."

Her strength would ebb and flow, and as it began to wane, she became a little less sure of herself.

"I do okay. . . . I don't let it really get me down or anything, except once in a while I get really depressed, and I feel real down, like everything in the world is wrong. But most of the time I'm doing all right."

As her energy drained, depression closed in. And the guilt tagged along as its companion.

"It's all my fault what happened. I shouldn't have done what I did. He's not here anymore. . . . I just don't have a dad. I really loved him."

Mary Jane thought that it was not so strange that her mood swayed like a willow in a spectral wind that blew it first one way, then another.

"I have mood swings," she acknowledged.

But there were times when her spirit plummeted precipitously and the past broke through, fulminating with visions, smells, and sounds vivid to the bloodiest detail, and she was snatched back to that day she wanted expunged from her life. It started insidiously, when the thoughts she normally controlled refused to go away.

"I can't get the thoughts out of my mind, and then all of a sudden all these sounds are around me. All of the smells are around me, like I was there. And I'd be there . . . and it was happening all over again."

Gunshots exploded one after another. A dirge of moans and groans gasped resignedly from a body about to die. And the knife plunged and plunged, once, twice, on and on, until the blood frightened her away. She struggled to escape and return to the safety of her jail cell.

"All I can do sometimes is scream," she said.

Her scream chased everything away until the next time she must scream, each episode leaving her more rent than the previous one. It was an ordeal she had to bear alone. There had been times when she discussed that part of her life with those who dutifully listened and expressed astonishment and dismay that she had suffered so, before they dumped her. She did not talk about it much anymore but held it in—but not too close—so that it could not mangle her life any more than it already had. But she knew she would not come out of this unscathed.

"I feel they didn't need to put me here. It's making me a worse person. I think I was a lot more compassionate person when I was first locked up. I was always a pretty quiet person; I was never quite loud about a lot of things. Since I've been here, I have developed quite a temper. It takes a lot to get me upset, but once I do, that's it. When I first got here I got along with everybody. Now, I don't care about a lot of people anymore. I've made it difficult in the past months in purposefully not getting along with people. When I was first locked up, I learned a lot that I wouldn't have learned. It helped me . . . but not anymore. I'm tired of the hassles. I hate this place. I hate being locked up. I hate what has happened to me. I guess, I guess because I'm in jail I'm not supposed to, but I like myself now, which might sound strange after all I've said. But I have confidence now. I believe I can overcome any obstacle. After everything I've been through, nothing can be as bad as all this."

*       *       *

Mary Jane was growing up in a midwestern prison when she was interviewed. Incarcerated a little more than two years, and hoping to be out in November 1984, she was the youngest inmate in the state women's correctional system. She was hoping to be released before her eighteenth birthday. That was the way I had planned to end her chapter.

That ending was rewritten after I made a last-minute check with her about the status of her appeal. The new version reads:

Mary Jane was certain that she would be released in November. Prisoners had to submit proposals of what they intended to do if they were paroled, and she wanted to be released to a halfway house where she would live while she worked, finished college, and tried to determine what she wanted to do with her life. She was counting on the assurance of the staff that it would support her bid for parole, and she hoped to impress the parole board with her achievements. These included working her way into the prison's honor cottage, earning college credits, editing the prison newspaper, and toiling fifty hours or more in the prison kitchen even though most of the money she earned went to the state (prisoners were expected literally to pay for their crimes by reimbursing the state for the costs of their incarceration). With all of this in mind, she was confident she would be released and on her way to something better.

One day the staff informed her about some changes involving her upcoming parole hearing. The good news was that the hearing date had been moved up. The bad news was that the staff would not support her bid for freedom. She was told she had not spent enough time in jail. She felt betrayed again.

"When they said they weren't backing me, I started crying and got hysterical," she said.

When she calmed down, she decided to go ahead with her original plans to submit a proposal. At the hearing the commissioner of the parole board told her she should remain in jail another year. A board member disagreed. He said she should be released as soon as possible because of the circumstances surrounding her case. Another board member had a third opinion. He believed she should wait a while but it should be less than a year.

And they all squabbled in front of Mary Jane and a few other people attending the hearing. The commissioner ended the argument

by saying that Mary Jane would not be considered for parole for at
least a year and that was final.

"I thought I was going to be really hysterical," she said. "I was
really surprised how calm I was. It didn't bother me as much as I
thought it would."

Two things happened shortly after the hearing. She received a
mimeographed letter from the parole board, which said that a parole
would not have been in the best interests of society. And the jail staff
informed her that they were scheduling her for a furlough sometime
in November.

"A furlough, that's unusual," she said. "You [usually] don't get
furloughs until three or four months before your release."

But she wasn't complaining. She was to be allowed out of the
prison for eight hours, and all that time she would be in the company
of one of the volunteers who visited and worked with prisoners. It
would be her first breath of freedom in more than two years. If the
furlough was successful and without incident, she could be allowed
to start taking weekend furloughs. The furlough was beckoning as
strongly as the parole once had.

"I'm trying to hang in there," she said.

There were people who read in the newspapers or watched on
television the accounts of her arrest and trial and the revelations
about how she had been repeatedly raped. For them, the drama
ended when it was announced that she had been sentenced to a juvenile facility, and that it was expected she would be released when
she turned eighteen or, as some were led to believe, within ninety
days. They did not know she was in prison. Her drama has not
stopped. It continues in the prison of her own mind but especially in
the penal world where she lives.

"She needs an advocate," said the director of a local organization
that works with incest victims.

The director remembered her trial.

"That was a mess," she said. "It's another example of ignorance in
the system. The judges don't understand. One of our projects is to
get training to our district judges about child sexual abuse."

The police suspected from the beginning that Mary Jane had been
attacked by her father, this official said. They called her agency and
asked for someone to talk to Mary Jane.

"But she wouldn't talk," the director said. "That's understandable [for an incest victim]. They've had one adult say, 'You can trust me,' and it wasn't true. After they've been betrayed like that they don't trust anyone."

If Mary Jane called her organization now, she said, it would be willing to help her. It could act as an advocate in helping with her problems with the criminal justice and penal systems. But she would have to call the organization. If she did, one of the agency's workers, who regularly visit the state prison, would try to help her.

Why does the agency make regular visits to the women's prison?

"There are a number of incest victims" in the state prison, the director said.

# 3

## David

Andrew and Louise sat on the patio of their ranch-style home, relaxing in the twilight of a fading summer day. Dinner had been uneventful and, except for a trip to a hospital to visit an ailing friend, it had been a typical Sunday. Andrew worked at the National Aeronautics and Space Administration, popularly known as NASA, as a physicist, and Louise held down the home front. They had been married about twenty years and their son, David, a college sophomore, was home for summer vacation. He was upstairs cleaning his room. At nineteen, David could have been mistaken for a high school freshman, but his boyishness belied his considerable achievements as a musician and designer. David had long been judged a child prodigy by teachers who predicted a great career for him in any chosen field. His academic successes were crowned by David's ability to charm everyone but his father. Andrew remained unimpressed by his son's laurels.

As David was moving about his room, he looked out a window and saw his parents talking, and he started reminiscing about all the things that had passed between him and his father. As his mind roamed over past times, a current of excitement washed through him. He began breathing deeper and faster, and felt his body slipping into a strange state, as if, he would say later, it was being lulled to sleep while he was still awake. An ominous feeling "that something was not right" stirred him but he could not grasp what was wrong. Still confused, he found himself walking downstairs and into the kitchen, where he picked up a Julia Child carving knife. He had a horrible foreboding, but he kept telling himself that everything would be okay, that nothing would happen. Even as he tried to reassure himself, the tension swelled, robbing him of his control as he struggled to maintain it. He jammed the big knife twice into a kitchen wall to stem the rage that was engulfing him. Racing to the screen door, which opened to the patio, he slashed its wire mesh. All the time he kept telling himself that everything was going to be okay, that nothing would happen. After he slashed the mesh, however, his control vanished and he stormed through the door. David, who had rarely raised his voice in anger against anyone, bore down on his parents with the big carving knife in his hand.

A bloodcurdling scream rang out. Louise and Andrew looked up just in time to see a figure rushing toward them. Louise saw her son run up to Andrew and then flee back to the house. Her husband clutched his chest, but it was not until Louise saw a knife on the ground near his chair that she realized he had been stabbed. She ran next door and asked the neighbors to call an ambulance for her husband. Then she ran back to the house to look for David. He was cowering on her bed, crying hysterically, and begging his mother not to leave him.

"I did it for you, I did it for you," he repeatedly wailed.

Andrew was sixty-two when he died that night in 1982.

In the Maryland county where David and his family lived, the police department, despite reforms, had an unenviable reputation for incivility. Allegations lingered about police "death squads," vigilante groups that had stalked and ambushed people committing crimes, then blew them away in a hail of gunfire. Through the years, the predominately white police force had maintained an adversarial relationship with a black community that made up almost 50 percent of the country by 1980. For many residents, policemen were barbarian marauders, not servants of public safety. No hearsay accounts or allegations of police brutality were too outlandish to be believed. David's experience, however, did not substantiate the county police department's negative reputation.

"All the cops liked him," said one law enforcement official. "He was meek and polite. Most kids arrested by police are hard-nosed. But he was college educated, communicated well with them, and was not mouthy."

The image of David in custody stood in ironic contrast to the screaming wraith plunging a knife into Andrew's chest. David told them he could recall picking up the knife, stabbing the wall, slashing the screen; but he could not remember stabbing his father. It did not matter. There were enough telltale signs to charge him with first-degree murder. And after charging him, the police fretted about what they could do to protect David from the perils awaiting him in the county jail. Once inside, the young man who had led a sheltered life would meet with all kinds of hardened criminals in the jail population. But the police made sure that there were provisions to protect the "wimpy little kid" while he was incarcerated. The next day he was released on bail put up by his mother.

The police were not the only ones taken with the meek young man they called a kid. A prosecuting attorney in Maryland can seek the death penalty in a first-degree murder case, and in the jurisdiction where David lived, the local prosecutor aggressively sought the death sentence more often than any other prosecutor in the state. His office was so aggressive that he sought to have some cases tried in surrounding counties because he did not believe he could get a fair trial if he asked for the death penalty before a jury in his own county. Not that every defendant charged with first-degree murder faced the death penalty, but the policy augured the tough law-and-order plank to be walked by anyone charged with the state's highest murder charge: a long sentence or the electric chair. Yet after David was indicted for first-degree murder, an assistant prosecutor would say that the case raised questions for him.

"What do you do with a kid who is not a criminal type, led an exemplary life, and has a good future but who did kill his father?" asked the assistant prosecutor handling the case. "I'd like to think I am a reasonably compassionate man too."

He spent many hours talking with David's mother about her and her family. He found her articulate and noted that she wanted the best for her son, who had been brought up with aristocratic pretensions. The family had lived comfortably. Their only real problem in life was Andrew.

David's lawyer originally considered an insanity defense, and that decision was no knee-jerk reaction to a seemingly inexplicable, brutal murder. Such a defense, despite public misconceptions, is rarely raised, and when used, it rarely results in an acquittal. Confronted with a seemingly meek, sensitive, exceptionally intelligent young man who had killed his father in an explosive rage, most people would ponder just how crazy he was at the time of the murder. But David was not mad. At least, not in the legal or clinical sense of madness. A psychiatrist, a psychologist, and a team of doctors, using brain scans and physical and psychological testing, found no brain lesions, no anatomical or physiological signposts pointing to a possible cause of his murderous outburst. He did not use drugs, and he had not been drunk, and he had not argued with his father that day, week, or month. They found no severe personality disorders. What they did find could have been easily misread as uncaring, unfeeling, and unremorseful in the eyes of observers less concerned or sympathetic—perhaps a reporter watching the defendant for signs of regret or emotion, or a prosecutor sniffing for an unrepentant murderer.

"He displays an amazing lack of awareness of what has happened and the possible consequences, though he feels depressed and remorseful," observed one psychiatrist. He saw David several days after he had been arrested. He subsequently noticed that David "became more depressed when the reality of the situation finally hit him." He recommended continued psychiatric counseling, "preferably from an older male psychiatrist," and opined that David was unlikely to commit another act of violence. And he emphasized that David should not be sent to jail.

A psychologist who met with him later could not help but note that David had "the look of a cherubic adolescent. At times, David seemed to be beaming, but there was something superficial about it." David, when he met with her, "would not talk about the relationship between his mother and father." He had known his mother would not leave Andrew, so he "did the best to help her." Her evaluation was that David had a "negativistic, passive-aggressive element and that there is a narcissistic streak to his personality. He is concerned with oral aggression."

It is not hard to imagine that millions of people with nine-to-five routines could be called passive-aggressive in pseudopsychiatric jargon. They walk the streets and ride the subways and buses and shop in supermarkets every day. They do not kill their fathers. It is understandable that David's lawyer at first sought an insanity defense and then abandoned it. What David did could be considered the act of a crazy person but no one could find a psychosis. David was in touch with reality and that was enough to drive him over the edge.

\* \* \*

Andrew's first marriage had lasted only a few years and ended after he committed his wife to a mental institution. But he never abandoned her. Despite considerable financial hardship, he placed her in a private hospital to ensure the best of care. When he subsequently divorced her and remarried, his new wife, Louise, took over sending the monthly alimony checks to her in the hospital.

This second marriage, between the Chinese scientist who was a naturalized citizen and Dutch-born Louise, was rancorous almost from the beginning. At home, Andrew was brusque, taciturn, a demanding perfectionist. Frequently morose and angry, he exploded unpredictably and with sudden malice at the most inconsequential things. He did not want children, and was annoyed when Louise told him she was pregnant. But after David was born, he became very protective, lavishing extraordinary attention on his son. He became very possessive of young David, especially so when Louise left Andrew, as she did two or three times.

Occasionally Andrew's picayunish and enigmatic ways would disappear in a sudden burst of generosity. At times he would praise David, not to his face but privately to Louise. There were times when he exuded happiness about his luck in marrying Louise, but again he did not directly praise her—he told their friends.

As David got older, Andrew became even more aloof and excruciatingly critical of his son, and David, at any moment, at any time, without warning, could be buried in vitriol. They rarely laughed at home, and Andrew frequently told his wife and son to shut up because their dinner table conversation "was not intelligent enough." He also liked to use David as a pawn to torment Louise, frequently denying his son something because he knew it would upset his wife. David began to see his father as a "powerful" figure with an aura of strength about him. His father had never physically hit him but found other ways to torment him without touching him. One day Andrew picked up the family's puppy and threw it against the wall, breaking its leg. The dog lay on the ground until Andrew left for work before Louise could summon enough courage to take the animal to a veterinarian.

Although his schoolwork remained excellent, except for one marking period where he got three Bs, David began to ponder killing himself and frequently struggled to shake bouts of depression. His father had isolated the family from close contact with neighbors and friends, and David, though ingratiating, was rarely close to anyone outside his home. In his teens, he became incensed about his father's despotic attitude toward Louise, and often begged her to leave home with him. But Louise always insisted that they wait until he finished his education. She did not want anything to thwart plans for David's college education, and at one point, when her husband threatened to stop setting aside money for David's studies, Louise withdrew all the money from a special account and set up another with her and David's name on it. She concealed this from Andrew for about a year, until one day he confronted her and threatened to stop contributing college money if she did not reinstate the old account.

When David graduated from high school and started college some of the pressure was relieved, but when he came home for the summer his father picked up where he had left off. During the summer after his freshman year, David purchased a stereo with money he had earned, and planned to take it back to school with him that September. Andrew decided that David would be paying too much attention to his stereo and not enough to his studies, and ordered his son to leave the stereo home when he left for college. In the past, Andrew's demands had usually met with meek compliance, but this time David erupted in anger. He screamed at his father, and then asked his mother to pack her belongings and leave with him. Andrew's feelings were hurt and Louise was astonished. It was the first time that David had ever attacked his father, and it was also the first time that either parent got a good glimpse of the depths of David's feelings about his father.

Louise started fighting back about the time David started attending college.

"In the beginning, I was probably like David, I didn't speak up," she would testify later. "I didn't speak up. But eventually I realized I probably could fight him and I would talk back on occasions. I no longer took it as much anymore. And I didn't have to worry about David anymore. I knew he was . . . safe in school. He didn't have to live in that kind of atmosphere."

But he had to return home during the summers, and that day in June, memories of past events with intimations of continuing abuse swept him up in torrential frenzy. He had only been home a short time for vacation when he walked out of his room and went downstairs into the kitchen.

*　　*　　*

There were enough mitigating circumstances, in the eyes of the assistant prosecutor, to consider reducing David's first-degree murder charge. David's scars from years of living with a brutal father, his impressive academic record with no taint of violence or crime, and the prospect of a brilliant career once David made up his mind what he intended to do, all made the prosecutor willing to accept a plea to second-degree murder.

"I wasn't looking for a long jail term but some incarceration as a signal to the community that killing an abusive father would not be condoned but that justice could be tempered with compassion," the prosecutor explained.

When David accepted the plea through his attorney, he was no longer looking at life in prison but ten years or less. The plea-bargaining arrangement, however, had to be accepted by Judge Vincent J. Femia, who was presiding over the case. And he had many, many questions. David's former teachers had beseeched him to be lenient, and a pastor had virtually parked himself in Femia's chambers on behalf of David. The doctors had insisted that David was not dangerous and that he should not go to jail because it would be harmful, but they did not adequately explain why he had killed his father. Femia was not satisfied, and for a long time felt that there were things that he was not being told about the case. Shortly before he called another hearing, a police officer tipped Femia off about something he thought the judge should know. That prompted Femia to place David's mother on the stand.

"I have been saying, since the very first day that the prosecutor walked this case into my office, that there is something wrong in this case," Femia said that day in court. "There is something in this case that I'm not being told. I think you have heard me say it before. This totally bizarre aberrational conduct, it just doesn't fit in the pattern of the young man that we know through the doctors . . . through the letters I have received. Something is wrong. Now, you are his mother. And one thing I know about mothers universally, if there is something wrong, the mother knows. The wife may not know, but the mother knows. I am very deliberately putting you on the witness stand and under oath, because I want to know what's going on in this case that nobody is telling me," Femia said.

"Well, what I have said was really the truth," Louise replied. "David always was a fantastic child, very easy, very easy going. We never had any trouble. We originally lived under an enormous pressure."

"What were those pressures?" Femia asked.

"Domination," she said, "and I never realized it as much as now, now that it is gone. We lived a secluded life. We had very few friends. I don't know. It was a strange life, now that I look back at it. During the holidays, the Thanksgiving holiday, I was visiting the [pastor] . . . and a lot of people and singing, and they had a good time. And it was very strange to me. We never laughed at home. I never saw David laugh. David laughed just recently. . . . And when Andy came home it was like something came over us. He was so domineering, it became frightening. He was moody."

Femia asked what she meant by "domineering." Had her husband beaten David or her?

"No. Maybe things bothered him and he would come home from work, he . . . you could tell from the way he looked up, you would say, better be careful, he might just blow up. And he would sit at the dinner table, look, and something might not look right to him, and he would blow up. There was no communication, very little communication between the two of us. While his niece was living there, and we would talk, he would sometimes tell us to shut up because the conversation was not intelligent enough."

After talking briefly about her family, she gave more anecdotes to describe her husband's tyranny.

"I got punished like a child," she said. "He would take the car keys. I couldn't use the car. So, finally I got a second set of keys. I mean, I'm not . . . I don't feel I should be treated that way. I have a right to . . . any time that he took care of the money, he would withhold the household money till I would say, you better go to the store, otherwise no food. One time he was repairing the car and David had to go to piano lessons, and he refused to fix it. And he said to David, 'I'm sorry, you can't go because your mother is being punished.'"

She talked on about other incidents, about the day he had broken the dog's leg, and she was so "afraid to pick up the dog and take it to a doctor. I had to wait till he went to work before I could do something."

Femia asked her questions as she testified, but it was not until she was almost finished that he started zeroing in on what he really wanted to know.

"What was, if you know, different about your husband's life in June of 1982?" he asked. "What had changed in his life? Other than the fact that David was away at school, and apparently David has almost been a straight A student. Obviously, he didn't dare bring home less than a B, but I have his high school record here, he did once get a B, in 5th year French. And he once got a B in physical education. And he once got a B in English. But the three Bs were in junior high school. It should have happened to me. Other than the fact that David was away, what was happening in [his father's] life that might have made him different?"

"I don't really know," she said. "He was a hard worker. He would go to work, he would stay later than the average person."

"What kind of work did he do?" Femia asked.

"He was a physicist. But then later on they called it staff engineer, I think. I know very little about his work because it goes above my head. So there was no contact there, either," she said.

"Was there something going on at work that was bringing pressure to bear, that you're aware of?" he asked.

"Oh, I'm sure. He had a lot of pressure, of course, with him being Chinese. I think he always felt that they . . . what is the word?"

"Suspect?" Femia asked quickly.

"No. No, no. Discriminated against him," she said.

"Did he ever say anything to you about this discrimination?" Femia asked.

"Yeah. He mentioned it once," she said. "One time he wrote a paper and it had to be presented in Paris. And somebody else was sent down there to present it because they felt he did have an accent. Even so, he went to school here, he still had the accent. And he was quite hurt by that. And I think he felt they did discriminate."

But it was not discrimination that Femia had in mind.

"Are you aware of any other pressures that he might have been under?" Femia asked.

"No, not really," she said. "He never would say anything about his work."

"Have you any idea whether or not he might have, at the time this happened, been under investigation?" Femia asked.

"No. Although he worked for the government, so I think they do investigate on occasions. He had worked for the Navy and the Army, and he was with NASA for the last, maybe, eighteen or nineteen years. I'm not quite sure how long," she said.

"Did you ever have any conversations with him about, or are you

aware through others, about his being investigated by the FBI?"
Femia finally asked.

"No," she told him. "The only thing that I know that he was
briefed in 1977, because he was going to China. Now, I don't know
if he was briefed before or after. Because he went on a visit to
China. That was his first visit."

"But you are not aware of anything in 1982?" he asked.

"No," she said. "No, sir."

"Through either him or others?" Femia asked.

"No, sir," she said.

Femia was trying to determine if David had slain his father because Andrew was under investigation by the FBI for espionage.
David and his mother had not known about the investigation. Femia
had only learned about it when the police officer tipped him off.

A few days after David was arrested, FBI agents had walked into the
office of the assistant prosecutor who was assigned the case. Andrew
was under investigation for espionage, and the agents did not want the
prosecutor to interfere in their investigation. He told them he did not
want them interfering in his murder investigation. The assistant prosecutor said later that though the FBI was "very concerned" about
Andrew, he did not know the extent of the investigation. He also said
Andrew's dilemma with the FBI had in no way influenced his decision
to allow David to plead to a lesser charge. Femia, who was tipped off
almost a year later, at first thought perhaps David had killed his father
because he suspected Andrew might be a spy.

"That may have compelled his conduct," Femia said later. "I tried
to scrutinize if they [David and Louise] were aware of it. I was told
that an indictment was imminent and that they [the FBI] were ready
to go out and arrest him. It's possible he [the police officer who
supplied the tip] could have been misinformed. He made no pretense
to have firsthand information."

Under the Freedom of Information Act, the FBI can withhold information but it must release an index of the material it has on a case
when a request is filed. Sometimes when it does release the index,
the disclosures may amount only to blank sheets, which are only good
for allowing one to estimate the extent of the investigation. But when
a request was filed in this case, the FBI forwarded photocopies of
newspaper stories on David's arrest and sentencing, and refused to
release any other information, including the index. The FBI claimed

that it was withholding the information "in order to protect materials which are exempt from disclosure by the following subsection of Title 5, United States Code, Section 552: investigator records compiled for law enforcement purposes that the disclosure of which would (a) interfere with law enforcement proceedings." The investigation, which did not involve David and Louise, was still continuing.

Femia sentenced David ninety days after his last hearing. He did not make up his mind until the morning of the day that David appeared in his courtroom. His decision was in no way influenced by the FBI investigation, he would say later.

In the early sixties when he was a juvenile court judge, Femia's handling of cases attracted national attention. But it also made him the bane of liberals at a university, where he taught a course in juvenile justice. As a result, he lost his teaching job. And although he has garnered a reputation as a tough law-and-order judge, he has irritated conservatives as well.

Femia does not shy away from controversies. A flap erupted between him and the local public defender's office over Femia's rejecting the state's psychiatric testimony that a man had been insane when he raped and strangled a woman. Femia found the defendant guilty of first-degree murder and rape and gave him life plus thirty years, which means he must serve the first thirty years of his sentence before he can be eligible for parole. In a magazine interview, Femia said it was obvious that the defendant had known what he was doing because he had hidden the woman's children in closets before strangling and raping her. He had also thrown away his shoes after the murder. "Those doctors are no more qualified to interpret the facts than I am," he was quoted as saying. "Those doctors have no stake in this other than the fee they're paid. . . . But I do have a stake, to see that justice is done."

In another case, he told a man convicted of first-degree rape that it "bothers me to sentence you." Femia believed that the prosecution's case was weak and that while the jury had voted the defendant guilty he would have acquitted the man if he had sought a nonjury trial with Femia, as judge, deciding the verdict. Nevertheless, Femia gave the man thirty years in prison. His attorney complained and filed an appeal but Femia's decision was upheld.

"I don't get paid to do what is popular, but what the job demands," he said about the case. The jury had found the defendant guilty, and rapists who appear in Femia's court do not get less than thirty years.

"The first impact you get as a judge is that you have been given awesome power," he said, recalling his first day as a judge in a land-lord-tenant court. "This is a scary experience. You now have power over human beings' lives. You're sitting up there with a couple of hundred people who are being put out of their homes. And here I was having a devastating effect. Not adjudicating great law cases but having a devastating effect . . . having a devastating effect on people. There I was the first day calling balls and strikes."

When a defendant strikes out in the big cases he now adjudicates, and comes before him for sentencing, Femia will have considered several criteria in reaching his decision. Is this a defendant who needs to be incapacitated, rehabilitated, made an example to the community, or sentenced for vengeful purposes? (He said that the last criterion "is something that judges don't like to admit.")

When David appeared for sentencing, Femia could have given him a "light sentence" of one or two years and no one would have blinked at his decision. The prosecutor would have been satisfied with a work-release program, which would have allowed David to spend part of his time at school or work during the day, and in the evening return to jail. Such programs offer a judge a good deal of sentencing flexibility. It is rare for a judge, however, to consider such an option for a homicide case, especially one in which self-defense was never an element.

Femia's decision? He sentenced David to ten years, then sus-pended the sentence and ordered him to spend eight hundred hours teaching reading, writing, and arithmetic to prisoners in the county jail. David would not spend one day in jail. And Femia's decision was based on solid legal turf.

"How would the community view this?" asked Femia, speaking rhetorically of one of his concerns. "Was I by my sentence saying that patricide is countenanced? It could be perceived that way but I had to weigh this against the consequences"—aggravating a family tragedy and creating another by sending David to jail. "I felt it served both the interest of the family and the community. . . . The best solution was probation. Probation is within the ambient of the court's power in second-degree murder. Criminal law presupposes when probation would be countenanced. If there ever was going to be a case that applied . . . this was the case. I saw no social interest gained by incarcerating him. To lock him in prison would have been a terrible injustice. There is nothing that I as a judge can do to bring [Andrew] back to life and make this case one wit better."

Incapacitation?

David was not dangerous, and the chances of his ever committing a serious crime again were "virtually nonexistent," Femia decided.

Rehabilitation?

"Obviously rehabiliation doesn't apply here," he said. "He is a brilliant young man with a brilliant career before him."

Make him an example?

"He was not a bank robber. . . . A long sentence would have served as no example to anyone," he said.

Revenge?

The community did not cry out for revenge. It was hardly aware of the case.

It was an extraordinary decision, but hardly anyone raised an eyebrow. The local papers gave it only moderate coverage, and except for a squalid story by the *National Enquirer* (SON BRUTALLY KILLS DAD—BUT SOFT-HEARTED JUDGE FREES HIM) and a few crank phone calls, there was hardly a murmur. Good kids who have endured rapes and beatings and threats of death regularly go to jail for killing a tormentor, even when the evidence discloses that the shootings and stabbings were in self-defense.

"I've only done it twice," Femia said.

A few scant years before David appeared in court, a devoutly religious, God-fearing woman killed her husband. They had been married for more than twenty years and had seven children, and every Saturday night, for as long as he had been married, he would come home drunk and beat her and the kids.

"Beating them was his wont," Femia said.

One night he was beating his pregnant daughter, and his wife picked up a knife and warned him to stop. He charged her and, in the words of her attorney, "became stabbed." At forty-three, black and poor, she was looking at a long time in jail.

"It was the same old situation," Femia said. "She would get a warrant from the police, and a judge would be lenient and cut him loose, and he beat her worse the next week. I just wasn't going to put her in jail. There was nothing to be accomplished socially or otherwise. He had been beating the family every Saturday night, beating everybody in the house. I'm surprised it didn't happen sooner."

# 4

# Lisa

Nine months after Judge Vincent J. Femia sentenced David to eight hundred hours of community service, Emilio, a forty-five-year-old hairdresser, was attacked in his home, bashed unmercifully on the head with a makeshift club, and stabbed in the heart. When his wife, hearing a commotion, rushed to help him, she was stabbed but was able to stagger outside and alert neighbors for help. She and her husband, childhood sweethearts who had been married for almost twenty years, were rushed to the hospital. She lived; he died. The police arrested the couple's daughter, Lisa, fourteen, her boyfriend, Daniel, thirteen, and their buddy, Fred, twenty. The trio was charged with first-degree murder in what police called a contractual killing. Lisa was singled out as the brains and the bankroll behind the murder. The police said she had offered Fred five thousand dollars to kill her parents. The judge presiding over this case would be Vincent J. Femia.

The attorneys for Daniel and Fred, according to *The Washington Post*, said their clients had entangled themselves in a wry version of *Romeo and Juliet*. On the day the two pleaded guilty to first-degree murder in a plea-bargaining arrangement, the prosecuting attorney, Joseph Sauerwein, said in court that Daniel, Fred, and Lisa had planned the murders for three weeks. Lisa and Daniel wanted her parents dead because they were "obstacles" to the teenagers' seeing each other. On the night of the murder, Lisa hid Daniel and Fred in her bedroom and then called her father in, supposedly to fix her television set. He was attacked at the top of the stairs with a table leg that had metal weights taped to it, and then stabbed in the heart with a knife. His wife, hearing the struggle, ran upstairs and Fred stabbed her in the shoulder. The *Post* said, "The plot was only partly successful: [Emilio], 45, was fatally stabbed . . . but his wife survived a stabbing."

Sauerwein told the court he did not know which conspirator had stabbed Emilio but he was certain Lisa was not the one. Stories in the *Post* and the county newspaper, the *Prince Georges Journal,* explained that the parents, both hairdressers, had been planning to sell their house and move to another home in order to break up Lisa's relationship with Daniel, and that the family kept a safe in the basement containing several thousand dollars. When Fred's and Daniel's attorneys described their clients' participation in the murder as similar to *Romeo and Juliet,* Femia's riposte was blunt: "This is a delusional, contractual ambush. We've come 180 degrees from *Romeo and Juliet.* We're not talking about suicide but patricide. We're not talking about an emotional outburst." When Lisa's attorney suggested that his client's culpability was less serious because she did not kill her father, Femia retorted: "This is to suggest that Hitler never hurt any Jews because he didn't personally gas them." The local newspaper quoted a friend as saying that Lisa's mother was shocked that "her daughter showed no emotion as her father was being killed." In that same story, it reported, "Those who knew the family said there was a terrible familial struggle between the father's values and Lisa's contemporary attitudes."

"He believed," a family friend was quoted as saying, "the daughter should listen to the father 100 percent. Lisa wanted to date, to think for herself. That girl never missed nothing he could buy for her, but Emilio was too possessive. I said to him a few days ago, That girl's a human being. You can't keep her in a show window like a statue. You can't have her all to yourself.'"

According to the paper, the father had left Italy in the early 1960s and spent a couple of years in Canada before moving to Maryland. "He married a local woman who had been raised in the Italian tradition, and they had a daughter, an only child." Lisa's attorney, Joseph Vallario, at first rejected a plea-bargaining offer. "Then it was expected," the *Post* wrote, "that Lisa would go to trial in December and that [Fred] was expected to testify for the defense." But Lisa later pleaded guilty to conspiracy to first-degree murder and was sentenced to fourteen years. Sauerwein said in court, according to the *Post*, that Fred had been involved in the slaying for money while Daniel had apparently been participating out of love. "The bizarre tale unfolded when the boys gave their statements to police," the *Post* said. "Because of the seriousness of the crime, [Daniel] and Lisa were charged as adults."

"The tragic murder of [Emilio] stunned the Adelphi community and puzzled many in the county courthouse in Upper Marlboro who watched the two young lovers blow kisses to each other during a bond hearing a few days after the incident. Vallario asked Femia to send Lisa to Patuxent Institute for further mental evaluation and treatment." Femia refused: "I'm not about to send a 16-year-old girl to an all-male institution."

Patuxent is a rare species. It is a hybrid institute with features of a mental health hospital and a correctional institution with rehabilitation as its goal. It lacks the harsh ambience of a penal institution. After Daniel and Fred were sentenced, they were eligible for parole the day they walked through the gates. Patuxent has its own regulations for how long sentences are served. Not that the facility gives quick releases to inmates convicted of serious crimes, but the promise of an earlier freedom is one of the carrot-and-stick incentives of the institute's rehabilitative program. Because there are no juvenile facilities for girls and no Patuxents for girls or women in Maryland, Lisa apparently received the toughest sentence. At sixteen the youngest inmate in the state women's prison, she could be out of jail in eleven years if she got credit for good time served.

The attorneys kept their clients from getting life sentences, and the prosecutor secured stiff penalties, but there was a great deal of dissatisfaction in the end. Sauerwein, for one, did not wrap up the case as neatly as he would have liked. Five persons had walked into the bedroom. One had been fatally stabbed and died before he could identify his murderer. The three co-conspirators, he said, would not "cop to much of anything" and would not reveal who had killed Emilio. Lisa's mother had not seen her husband slain. Fred, who was willing to testify against Lisa, was not considered a really reliable witness. Lisa's mother, even in the agony of knowing that her only child was implicated, would not testify against her daughter. Sauerwein could not prove who had stabbed Emilio in the heart, and there were other questions that nagged him, other missing pieces to the case that baffled him more than was indicated in the newspapers. He would say later that though he had achieved some of the things he sought in prosecuting the trio, the case still lacked a "certain finality." Later, he would also discount some of the reasons he had offered in court to explain why Emilio and his wife had been attacked. It had had little to do with a girl's yearning to be with her boyfriend, he would say.

Vallario's position was no less exasperating. Lisa's mother, who would not put up bail for her daughter, was adamantly opposed to cooperating with the prosecution but was also reluctant to testify for the defense. Lisa confided more in the chaplain of the local jail than in Vallario. To prepare her defense, Vallario needed the help of the chaplain, who provided him with information but also disliked being a middleman. Because of the confidential nature of his relationship with Lisa, the chaplain did not tell Vallario everything Lisa had discussed with him. There were other frustrations as well. Vallario wanted Lisa treated as a juvenile, but Femia refused his motion. He was equally frustrated that he could not get her out of the county jail and into some other facility. No one ever posted the thirty-thousand-dollar bail for her. Even after Lisa pleaded guilty and was sent to the women's jail, Vallario was still hammering away at her case. No one was paying him a dime.

It would be fair to say that Fred and Daniel—two mercenaries, one involved for cold cash, the other reportedly for love—were bit players in this drama, even though one plunged a knife into the heart of a man who had never harmed him. In this case, many things publicly revealed and portrayed as facts were not as accurate as they were made to sound.

Joseph H. Vallario, when he was defending Lisa, was a veteran Maryland state assemblyman, a Democrat, who had been in office for ten years, a practicing attorney for eighteen. The walls of his comfortably furnished office in southern Maryland were covered with memorabilia. On one wall, framed behind glass, a newspaper article told about the acquittal of a man in his forties who had been charged with a double murder. He was accused of setting afire the home he had shared with his mother, sixty-six, and father, seventy-two, who were both killed in the fire. Vallario convinced the judge that the man's confession had been obtained under duress. The confession was thrown out and the man subsequently acquitted. In another part of the office, there was a picture of Vallario and Femia, both smiling in the dazzle of a European holiday with their families. They had been good friends for years.

Before I visited his office, I first talked to Vallario about Lisa in the hallway of the courthouse where she had pleaded guilty. I caught him in between cases, and though he was polite, he was less than enthusiastic about talking to another journalist. He gave me a thumbnail sketch of the case, and also said that Lisa's mother, after a great deal of anguish, was beginning to visit her daughter in jail. I told him I wanted to talk to him about the case and to speak to Lisa as well. We agreed to meet at his office later. Vallario had poured an enormous amount of time and effort into the case even though he knew he probably would never be reimbursed. Though he did not mention costs, friends who followed the case and his efforts conservatively estimated his expenses and time on the case at twenty-thousand dollars. At his office, I asked him how Lisa had gotten in trouble.

"Lord knows," he said. "It was a snowball that developed into a volcano. She was overly impressed by the individuals she met in her life. She's made one mistake, and she is going to pay dearly. It couldn't have been a worse mistake. It was a mistake she made. On her own, by herself, she's not capable of this. . . . She's never missed a curfew. When she was told to be home, she was there. We've all missed curfews."

She also had never been in trouble with the law or caused any problems at school, where she was an average student. Vallario said that "there is no malice in her" and that she was a "good girl" and "vulnerable." In his eyes, she was an ingenue who had never been in trouble before for anything in her life but allowed herself to become involved in a heinous crime. As he spoke, I was turning over in my mind Femia's riposte to Vallario's plea that Lisa was less culpable: "This is to suggest that Hitler never hurt any Jews because he didn't personally gas them." And the prosecutor considered her a Jezebel, a manipulating siren, spoiled rotten and made contemptuous by overly indulgent parents.

When I asked Vallario how he had gotten involved in the case, he said a fellow state assemblyman, who had been contacted by someone who knew Lisa and her family, had asked him to help represent her. He eventually took over the case.

"There was a little girl who reminded me of my own," he said. "I have a daughter exactly the same age as she is. I saw her out there with no father, he had been murdered, and the mother torn between deep left field . . . and then I got involved."

It is not unusual for newspaper headlines, and the promise of media exposure, to lure lawyers to cases of children who are charged with their parents' deaths. But when I thought about all the money he was expending, that he was not getting paid, that he was providing services that other lawyers in similar cases had not even considered, I decided to take his word.

"I wanted to help her," he said. "I knew we wouldn't get parole. Here you have a little kid out there . . . they don't know what the law's about. This was a child who really needed to have something . . . and I tried to explain it to her."

He did not say exactly what she had not understood about the law or what he had explained to her.

Even though Lisa was now serving time, he was still irritated that he had been unable to get her bail reduced from thirty-thousand dollars to get her out of jail.

"It was more than a reasonable bond, under the circumstances," he said. "There was no likelihood that she would run. Where would she run? Her mother was more than unwilling to put up bond because she didn't think [Lisa] should be out at the time."

It made sense. Lisa's mother, according to evidence introduced in court, had been the target of a murder conspiracy. Her only child had been involved in her husband's death.

When Lisa was in jail, Vallario said, the chaplain and "all of the guards in the women's section kept an eye on her. They saw she was a child, and put her right next to the chaplain's office. They kept Lisa in a room normally used by the trustees and guards."

He was very candid about Emilio. "He didn't want something to develop," Vallario said. "The father was adamantly opposed to any relationship with his daughter and this guy. Adamantly opposed. They [Daniel and Fred] were dropouts, real bums."

Vallario described how Emilio, after he decided to move his family out of the neighborhood to get Lisa away from Daniel, had flipped through the real estate ads in a newspaper and, when he read about something he thought he might like, dialed the number listed and offered to purchase the house sight unseen. He was ready to make a down payment that day.

"Can you imagine, he bought the house sight unseen," Vallario said. "He signed a contract to purchase a house unseen so he could move from this area. His wife saw it and liked it."

But Emilio never did. From Vallario's description as well as other accounts, I imagined, while sitting there in the office, that Emilio had been very possessive of his daughter. My mind flitted back to a neighbor's comment: "That girl's a human being. You can't keep her in a show window like a statue. You can't have her all to yourself." So I asked Vallario if there had been anything more to Lisa and her father's relationship than just father and daughter. I was beginning to think that perhaps Lisa's father was much more covetous of his daughter than had been publicly revealed. When Vallario understood what I was asking, he gave me a puzzled look as he said no.

Vallario's efforts to help Lisa had not stopped after she was sent to the women's prison. He filed a motion for reconsideration of her sentence with Femia. It was possible, Vallario said, that in three, four, or five years the judge might consider reducing her sentence. When he expressed that hope I could not help but recall Femia's description of Emilio's death. He had almost roared.

"That was cold-blooded, contractual, choreographed murder," he had snapped in an interview. "The thought of probation never entered my mind."

The judge also said he had not seen any remorse when Lisa appeared in his courtroom. I knew that Vallario had a strong practice and a good reputation, but I thought his optimism was unjustified.

I learned later that besides an appeal to have Lisa's decision thrown out and the case referred to juvenile court, Vallario filed a lawsuit against the state. He was charging it with sex discrimination in the correctional system, where there were no facilities for girls and no Patuxents for women or girls. One state assemblyman, who served with Vallario, said the suit would prompt the legislature to find funds for temporary facilities for girls until permanent residences were built.

Vallario and I talked for a little more than an hour, and near the end of the interview, I mentioned that I thought the prosecutor was very incensed at Lisa. Before I interviewed Vallario, I had met briefly with Sauerwein to arrange a suitable time to talk to him, and in a fifteen-minute discussion he mentioned that Lisa had glared contemptuously at him during her courtroom appearances. That had infuriated him. But I never mentioned to Vallario specifically why I thought the prosecutor was incensed and couched my question in terms of "resentment."

"There was resentment towards this child" was all that Vallario would say.

I also knew that Vallario and Sauerwein had feuded before a plea-bargaining arrangement was made and that the two attorneys, who had been friends before the case started, felt less than amiable about each other after it ended. As part of Lisa's defense, Vallario had introduced a psychiatric report that said that Lisa and her father had been locked into a "symbiotic relationship" and that she was being smothered by it. A "symbiotic relationship" basically means that a child is forced to live out the expectations of a parent and to feel only that parent's emotions, a process that is harmful to the child. It is a form of psychological abuse, and the doctors who examined Lisa said it had been generating considerable unexpressed hostility in her. Vallario believed that his client was as psychologically abused as David, the brilliant college student who killed his father but was not sent to jail. Femia, however, rejected the doctors' psychiatric report on Lisa, deciding that all they had proved was that Emilio had been a doting father. He also disregarded their opinion that Lisa had become involved in the murderous plot because she was "immature." Immaturity was not a sufficient explanation for a teenager accused of the "choreographed" murder of her father.

Lisa had met Daniel one summer afternoon after a dip in the community pool. A girlfriend, who also was one of Daniel's pals, introduced them. He was sitting on the back porch of his home when the girls, after they finished their swim, walked into his backyard, which faced the pool. It was not a big meeting. There were no fireworks.

"I thought he was a nice guy, just a nice guy," she later recalled. "I didn't even know anything about him."

Peer group pressure took over and ignited a slow-burning fire.

"A month after I met him, everyone was trying to get us together."

At the time, she was dating an ex whom she still saw occasionally, and she continued going out with her buddy while she waited for Daniel to ask her out. Some of his friends, however, told her to forget him because he was not good enough for her. Daniel, they told her, was a wiseass. But she thought he was "nice." He was also a reluctant suitor, however, and some exasperating moments, which seemed like several lifetimes, passed before he made the big move and asked her to go steady. When he did, she stopped seeing her old boyfriend. Lisa and Daniel were now officially, exclusively, boyfriend and girlfriend. Her father, who did not know they were dating and thought he was just one of the neighborhood kids, sometimes cut his hair. Not only was thirteen-year-old Daniel nice and respectful, he was someone who needed Lisa. He could not get along without her. She was convinced that his parents neglected him and all he needed to be turned around was someone who cared for him. Like her.

"He could go out any time of night . . . and do almost anything he wanted," she said, describing what she considered the mark of neglect. "I tried to get him to go back to school, quit drugs . . . I tried to help him. We had fun. When I first met Daniel I thought he could be changed . . . he could be different."

When I asked her why she was dating a boy a year younger than her, she blurted, "He's built . . . pretty well built. He looked about sixteen when I first met him."

It was a bumpy road for them, and they broke up several times only to patch it back together. There were days she really liked being with him, and other days when she never wanted to see him again. She claimed she could not recall all the reasons they kept breaking up. Her memory might have lapsed because I was treading in a sensitive area, but she said one reason she had wanted to stop seeing him was because her parents wanted her to call it off.

"I was not going to argue with my parents on something like that," she said emphatically. "This is a no-win situation."

But because she didn't fight them did not mean she wouldn't use a little subterfuge to see Daniel surreptitiously, even though there were times when, after she had schemed to see him, she wondered why she had ever made the effort. One day she told Daniel it was over and she meant it this time.

"I won't forget that day as long as I live," she said.

They were talking on the phone, and he told her if she stopped seeing him he would kill himself. She told him good-bye. That night, a girlfriend crept up to Lisa's house about 2 A.M. and knocked on the window.

"She said that Daniel overdosed and was at the hospital," Lisa said.

He was held overnight, and when he was released they got together again. Once Daniel and Fred started leaning on you, she said, there was no way to get rid of them. She had first met Fred when she was eight, and introduced him to Daniel years later when she started dating him. The three of them linked up with three others, so that there were Lisa and Daniel, Fred and Sharon, and another couple who were friends of Lisa's. Fred had street smarts, Lisa believed, but no brains. He also was down on his luck and without a home.

"His parents didn't care for him. . . . They abused him," Lisa recalled. "They kicked him out of his home, and Fred moved in with Daniel. Daniel needed an older brother, and his parents thought Fred looked like Rick," Daniel's older brother, who had been killed in a motorcycle accident about a year before Emilio died.

When I first talked to Lisa, she was hoping she would not have to spend a long time in jail. An appeal, a lawsuit, and a motion for reconsideration of her sentence were in the works, and she was hopeful that one or all would bring redemption or a shorter term, at least. In the meantime, she was learning to survive as a girl in a prison for women, noting the irony of the way the jail staff kept a protective eye out for her.

"I'm a juvenile charged as an adult," she said. "They put me in an adult facility and treat me like a juvenile."

Friends?

"You don't have friends in jail, you have associates. Every time you think you know someone they turn around and hurt you," she said.

She had received her high school equivalency degree at fifteen in the county jail and was starting college at sixteen in the women's prison. She was planning to study computers, an idea suggested by her father, who had been considering buying her a home computer when the fracas erupted over her seeing Daniel.

There are several ways to conduct an interview. I try to engage people in conversation and lead them in the direction I want to go, or follow them in the direction they want to lead me. But I frequently do both, leading and following. Sarcasm, sympathy, and anger are part of being as open as I can when I interview. Journalists who are honest with them are usually the only reliable visitors these young people have in prison.

Before interviewing Lisa, I read news accounts, flipped through court records, talked at length with Vallario and briefly with Sauerwein and Femia. Vallario, in her defense, said Lisa had been "involved" but incapable of malice. Femia, based on the information before him, said she had "choreographed" her father's death and had been unremorseful when she was in court. And Sauerwein, in prosecuting the case, had found her personally contemptuous and manipulative and the architect of her father's death. Lisa had not cooperated with the police after the murder and had stymied their efforts to get her to incriminate herself and Daniel and Fred. In the eyes of the police and prosecutor, she had demonstrated a certain maturity, a savvy that they would not have expected in a fourteen-year-old girl.

When Lisa and I first introduced ourselves, I explained I was writing a book about parricide and asked her why she had consented to an interview. She said she wanted to help someone else who might get into similar trouble, and when I asked her how, she could not answer. So, after a few other initial questions seemed difficult for her to answer—she nodded but would not talk—I asked why the prosecuting attorney "hated your guts." I think Sauerwein felt more contempt than hate, but "hate" sounded stronger. This is rarely the way to begin an interview, but I wanted to see how she would respond. She looked surprised and said she did not know why, so I reiterated the point and added that if he did not "hate your guts" he at least "definitely didn't like you," and quickly asked why she had glared at him in court.

She had not glared. She had just stared at him.

"Naturally, I was upset at him. He was saying all those things. I was looking at him. You can feel people [when they don't like you]," she replied. "Know what I mean?"

She had stared at him because she did not like what he was saying and because she thought he did not like her. I nodded to her that I understood and wished, to myself, that I had been there to see this great staring-glaring contest. I might have thought she was being contemptuous. I would have at least thought it was unusual.

I asked her to explain how she had gotten in trouble.

"I didn't kill my father," she said, as she lowered her head.

Was she responding to my description of my book as an investigation of sons and daughters who kill their parents? Was this some kind of psychological denial? Or were we going to spend a lot of time splitting hairs? I certainly did not want to waste time on this, so I reminded her that she was not accused of killing her father but had pleaded guilty to conspiracy.

"No one said you killed your father but only that you planned it," I told her.

She did not answer.

"Look, even your lawyer said you were involved," I said.

She grimaced and tried to conceal her reaction in a smile.

"Did he say that?" she asked.

"He said that you got involved in something that you couldn't stop, that it was a snowball that became a volcano," I said.

She did not like hearing that Vallario had told me she had been "involved." She forced a soft chuckle over his use of mixed metaphors, but she still was unhappy about what he had said. She was insisting that she was innocent, but she did not want to discuss it, so I decided to ask her some other questions. But I knew I would be coming back to her being "involved." I asked her to talk about the night she had been arrested (and later it would be phrased "the night your father died," "the night you got in trouble," "the night it all happened," or "the night it all fell apart").

"That night I remember very vaguely. I was in shock that they told me my dad was dead. . . . I wanted to go home," she said.

I asked what had happened at the police station.

"They wrote down statements that I gave them," she said, adding that one detective had ripped up the statements one after another.

"I guess he just didn't believe me," she sighed in an affected manner. "One detective was doing a little yelling. He wanted me to give him something so they could write the way they wanted [the statement to read]."

She was not giving me much detail either, so I told her I wanted to talk to her about school. After a brief stint in public school, her parents had sent her to a private grade school and then a private high school. They chauffeured her back and forth to school. She was just an average student but she enjoyed high school, where there were small classes of eight to ten students and everyone spoke of going to college.

"I passed eleventh grade in county jail," she blurted.

So we talked about jail life.

"I was spoiled in the county jail. The officers and my chaplain took good care of me. I was in the trustees' quarters. I had television, a big television set . . . a bathtub. The officers were great. . . . They let me walk around," she said.

Lisa has a very charming way of flattering people and ingratiating herself. She wants to be liked. She also has learned to conceal herself behind that persona of charming exuberance. It helps to keep people at a distance. It was during one of her strolls around the jail, when, I would guess, as she was smiling broadly, probably flattering some guards, and talking and acting very upbeat, that someone from the prosecutor's office, visiting the jail on business, saw her. In those eyes, she was a strutting, swaggering vamp, sashaying around the jail as if she owned it. It was a scene indelibly etched in a memory forming a picture of a contemptuous and manipulating fourteen-year-old vixen.

We had talked about two and a half hours when the prison staff asked us if we wanted to break for lunch. We both said no. The conversation was flowing smoothly and we did not want it to end. We dallied with the mundane—she played the piano, shot hoops for sundry basketball teams—and talked about the things she had done before she got in trouble. She had been an average student, she explained, because she had studied only enough to pass. She did not want schoolwork interfering with her having a good time. She liked to party. There were no curfews.

"As long as they knew where I was, they wouldn't get upset," she explained. "It was understood that if I went to a dance or party I had to tell them when [I was going]. I could stay at dances as long as I wasn't home past midnight. My parents had to know. It wasn't like I could just get up and go."

Had she ever gotten high?

"I never got high," she said.

Tempted?

"Sure, everyone is tempted. I've been asked this question a million times," she laughed. "I know when it's coming. Most people in Adelphi get high. I had no desire for drugs. I have friends in the neighborhood who did drugs. My friends in private school were straight. Private school kept me out of it."

What about peer pressure to take drugs?

"I always felt I could make my own decisions," she replied. "You can't tell me to do it [take drugs] if I don't want to. I just had no desire for it, so I didn't do it."

So-called straight preppies at purportedly the finest finishing schools in the East, I thought, use drugs. But what was more significant than whether she used drugs or not was that she described herself as someone who could not be persuaded to do something she did not want to do. That sparked some thoughts. How had she become so "overly impressed" with a chronic dropout who needed her more than she needed him, and a twenty-year-old man who was often called a boy, that she involved herself in "a snowball that developed into a volcano"? I thought I had time to come back to this, so I asked her who had stayed in touch with her after she was incarcerated. Some friends wrote her frequently, she said, and her mother and an aunt visited regularly. She was also close to her chaplain, a psychologist, and a lawyer. When she had first been arrested and placed in jail, she had had marathon crying jags that frightened her attorney and the jail staff enough to convince them she might commit suicide. She could not stop crying, and when she turned to someone for help, the chaplain was there. They became very close, and she confided in him.

"He really knows me," she said.

She trusted him more than she trusted anyone else. She indicated in a childlike way, but did not say, that she trusted and confided in the chaplain and did not conceal herself from him as she had from her lawyer and the doctors who examined her. So I picked up the gambit and told her I wanted to talk to the chaplain, asking if it would be okay to tell him that she had given me permission to talk to him. She agreed but said he probably would not talk to me anyway. The case had received a lot of news coverage, and he did not want to be exploited. It was unclear what she meant by exploitation, but if he was someone who knew more about her than her own lawyer and doctors, and perhaps more about what happened than she was telling me, I wanted to try to talk to him. I eventually rolled the conversation around to ask why Fred thought he could get money from her "for anything."

"Fred needed money. He knew we kept money in the house. He robbed us. Fred was in love with Sharon. So he needed money. Daniel liked my dad. Fred didn't."

I asked her to explain more about Fred and Sharon, and the money.

"Fred asked for the money," she said. "He had [parking] tickets he wanted to pay on his car. And he wanted to marry Sharon. I had loaned him two hundred dollars once before."

I asked her how a fourteen-year-old girl got her hands on two hundred dollars to loan to a friend. She said it was simple. Her parents had kept the money in a safe in her home. She had had access. She wanted to know why I was surprised.

"He wanted two thousand dollars for the car tickets," she continued, "and also wanted to marry Sharon. He was jealous of us and hated my father."

Fred had written her two letters in prison, apologizing for all of the trouble he had caused her, but she refused to answer him. She had also received letters from Daniel. She had read the first one but turned it and Fred's letters over to her attorney. I asked her about the night that got her into trouble.

"I came upstairs. The lights were on when I walked downstairs. The lights were off when I came up. Fred was behind my father. I ran into my mother on my way out."

I wanted more details.

"I don't like talking about it," she said.

So we talked about how she and her mother were getting along.

"We get along great. I know she has a lot of questions still, but I just can't deal with the answers right now," she said.

She also said that her mother would have been willing to testify against Fred but not against her. So I asked her why everyone had ended up in her room that night. Daniel, she explained, had called her up and wanted to come by. He and Fred were celebrating someone's birthday. When she let them in the house she discovered they were drunk, and when she asked them to leave they refused. She called her father to make them leave. The police, I told her, said that had been part of the plan, to get her father to come into the room. She denied that she had planned anything, and when I tried to ask more questions, she refused to talk. And then she changed her mind. Lisa said she would tell me everything that happened that night on condition that I agreed to tell her lawyer everything that she told me, and that I agreed not to write about it if Vallario said it would cause legal problems for her, or get her into more trouble.

I said no. I had already told Vallario I would be willing to discuss my interview of her with him. But I was unwilling to allow anyone to tell me what I could and could not write.

We were both flustered. She wanted to talk but only on condition that I would not write anything that Vallario thought could get her into trouble. After a few moments, I said there were probably things she did not want to or could not talk about, but we could find some middle ground that accommodated what I needed to know and what she could say comfortably without getting into trouble. I did not really believe that there was anything that could get her into more trouble than she already was in. But she thought so. We agreed to try, and I asked her again about Fred and the money. "How did Fred or anybody get around to talking about your parents dying or being killed or whatever?" was how I phrased the question.

It all started as a joke.

Lisa and Daniel, Fred and Sharon, and two other friends were sitting on a picnic table near Sharon's house. They were just talking. It was not too long after Emilio had learned that Lisa and Daniel were going steady. Fred wanted her to give him two thousand dollars to pay off his parking tickets and to marry Sharon.

"Something was said about my parents," she explained in a subdued manner, "and Fred said he could get rid of him for money. Daniel said, 'I can spend more time with you.' . . . We all laughed. We were just sitting on the picnic tables and talking."

That was three weeks before her father was killed, which, according to the police and Sauerwein, was about the time when the conspiracy was hatched. Did the conspiracy commence with a joke or was it a joke that got out of hand? Was this the "snowball that developed into a volcano"? Lisa would not talk more about the day on the picnic table or the days following. So we changed topics and talked about the news coverage of her arrest and plea, and while both of us were chortling over an easier subject, I blurted out, "How can someone in as much trouble as you, with fourteen years staring you in the face, be so bubbly?" That stung her.

"What am I supposed to do?" she asked.

It was not a rhetorical question, but I did not answer.

"Sit here and cry all the time?" was her follow-up.

My question was a cheap shot because I had been prompting laughter and trying to get her to relax, and when she did, I zinged one at her. But I had to see how she would respond. I expected her to get angry. Someone else would have been angered. But she did talk briefly about how she felt about jail. She was always depressed. And when it felt as if the walls and floors were really beginning to close in on her, she would try to retreat to someplace where she could be by herself. There no one paid her much attention, and she waited for the depression to pass. If it did not pass fast enough, she forced herself to dress it up with an upbeat, smiling, amiable facade. The kind that keeps everyone at a distance. I wanted to talk about remorse and guilt, but changed directions and returned to the scene of the crime. I asked her who had called the police.

"My mother was yelling and screaming. I ran outside and told a neighbor to call the police and an ambulance. I can't remember what happened next," she said.

But she recalled that later in the evening she had been sitting in a neighbor's house waiting for the police to take her statement. When she was arrested several hours later and was waiting to be booked, a "detective brought me and Daniel together after I had said specifically that I didn't want to see him. I made him get him out."

She fumed that the whole idea about her wanting Fred to kill her parents so that she could be with Daniel was stupid.

"If I wanted to be with Daniel, we could have left the state," she said.

It was a foolish statement, and I planned to come back to it later, but I had another question. *The Washington Post* in one story had reported that Daniel and Lisa were blowing kisses to each other during a hearing in court. It sounded foolish as well as contemptuous, and I wanted to know why they would have pulled such a dumb stunt.

"I was just sitting there. . . . Vallario told me not to even look at him. I was just sitting there," she insisted. "He was blowing kisses. I didn't."

I believed her and wanted to talk more about the night she was arrested, and as I started asking some questions, she started hitting the side of the desk with her foot. She wrapped her arms tightly about her and started squirming in her seat. She wanted to end the interview but would not say so. I ignored the soft thumping against the desk for a minute or so and then asked her if she was sending me a message. We both laughed. On a Richter scale measuring the merriment in our laughter we would not have rated 0.1. There was no joy and nothing to celebrate, but the laughter cut through some tension and made the awkward a little less difficult to bear. And even as she laughed, it was obvious she still wanted to end the interview. But she would not say it. Instead, she pouted and wrapped her arms about her and kicked the side of the desk. She was submitting and resisting, all in one movement.

"What were some things," I asked, "that you did that made your father angry?"

"If I wanted to go somewhere . . . or was too tired to go with them, and they wanted me to go" was all she offered.

"Was your father too protective?"

Her eyes said yes before she did.

"He was overprotective. . . . He was mothering me, sort of," she said. "He gave me everything I wanted, and he wanted me to find a perfect guy to marry. In Adelphi there is no perfect guy."

I asked her to talk more about her father.

"He worked all the time. . . . I saw him at night. The relationship with my dad was special," she said.

I wanted to know more about the special relationship, but I suddenly asked about remorse because I thought the interview was coming to an end. She was still kicking the desk. "Sauerwein and Femia said they didn't see any real remorse when you were in court," I said.

"They don't know me," she said resolutely. "They haven't seen me outside of court."

But she had been seen outside of court. She was walking around the jail one day, and in one pair of eyes the image was formed of a little tart sashaying about as if she owned the place.

"Why do so many people think you're spoiled?" I asked, though I was posing a question based on the impressions of only a few persons.

"I've always been spoiled. I didn't have to ask for anything. My parents never had anything when they were young. They were poor, and they wanted me to have everything. I would never ask for anything . . . but only because they never had anything they tried to give me everything," she said. "I would do anything for them."

Her foot started swinging against the desk again. But I asked her why she thought the prosecutor was so harsh in his description of her.

"A daughter supposedly hired a man to kill her father," she replied. "Sauerwein is a man. What do you think he's going to say?"

"One of the newspapers," I told her, "said that your father wanted to raise you in the old tradition. What's that mean?"

"Kids always listen to their parents," she said. "But they weren't that bad, basically. They were too overprotective. I knew they cared. If they let me do everything I wanted I'd start to worry."

"Why do you keep saying that you can't remember anything when I ask you about the night your father died?"

"I don't know. Maybe I'm scared. Maybe I don't want to know. I don't know," she said resignedly.

Her foot was hitting the desk with a little more vigor, but I had more questions and there were several that I had to ask over again, so I did not want to end the interview. I wanted to know more about her "special" relationship with her father. What did she mean by "special"? I was afraid that once I broke off contact she might not want to talk again.

It would not have been the first time that someone changed his or her mind because the interview touched upon unresolved personal conflicts or sensitive areas. One youth who had killed his father showed up for the interview to tell me he would rather talk some other time, even though I had flown a few thousand miles to see him. He was so nervous that as he talked he was kicking the table— much harder than Lisa was—and shaking his keys and reminding me every so often that he had left his car running in the parking lot. I conducted a brief interview and after meeting fifteen minutes with me, he fled to the safety of his car.

In another case, I caught an early morning train to talk to a lawyer whose client had shot her father nine or ten times in the head, back, and neck. With the aid of a psychiatrist and a shot of Amytal, the lawyer had been able to get her to reveal a dozen different occasions on which her father had raped her. We talked for a half hour, and then he asked me to have a seat in his waiting room while he finished up some business. It was the second time I visited his office, yet he kept me waiting three hours. He had changed his mind about talking any more but he would not tell me. He thought if he just ignored me I would take the hint and leave.

One young man who had killed his mother, his brother and sister (ages two and three), and two other toddlers who happened to be in his home at the wrong time changed his mind after contacting his aunt and telling her that he wanted to talk to me. The day that we would have talked was within just a few days of the anniversary of the family massacre. And there were other incidents of people who abruptly changed their mind about talking because they could not say what they thought they wanted to tell me, or felt they had said too much and, therefore, did not want to say any more.

So I was reluctant to let Lisa go. But our interview did not end that way. She was relieved when I said we could stop talking if she wanted. But she agreed to talk to me the next day.

\*   \*   \*

I asked Lisa to describe her "special relationship" with her father the second time we met.

"He worked most of the time . . . and since I didn't see him so often I tried to see him as much as possible," she said. "I would go out to breakfast with him or go fishing. Dad did a lot of fishing. He was a real good dad. Me and mom never wanted for anything. He was there for me; both of my parents were there for me."

I was about to ask another question when I saw Lisa suddenly tense as if she had just been stung. I heard a soft gasp and she dropped her head slightly. She was about to cry. Her body clenched, and I stopped looking directly at her. After a few seconds I said, "Maybe we should move on to something else."

She did not answer. After some moments, her body relaxed, her head popped up, and she started smiling. It was over but I suspected that it was still lurking beneath the surface. We both acted as if nothing had happened. But I changed the direction of the conversation and it rambled a bit, with occasional non sequiturs popping up whenever Lisa thought about something she considered more important than what we were discussing. At one point, she talked about how her parents often made an effort to meet her friends and take them out after basketball games. Then she switched directions and started talking about a drawing book her mother had recently sent her. She was sending her drawings home to her mother. We also talked about Fred and Daniel.

"I really didn't feel sorry for Fred that much," she said about the problems he was having. "Now, I don't feel sorry for him at all, him or Daniel."

After we talked about Daniel for a little while, I asked her again about her special relationship with her father.

"He always tried to get me into everything, typing, horseback riding. He wanted to get into computers," she said. "He was always saying that he wanted me to have a good life. His mom died before I was born. Grandpa [Emilio's father] lives in Canada. He [her father] wanted to be closer to me than his father was to him."

Her parents, she said, were married seven years "before they had me." They took frequent trips, visiting Canada and Italy, where she had relatives living in a small town near Palermo, and Monte Carlo.

"Oh, we had good times, great times," she said, then switched directions.

"I've been reading a lot of jail books about how a lot of other people deal with it," she said about surviving in prison. "Not too many successful ones do."

She had read a book written by singer Johnny Paycheck, who "tells you what to look for, what not to do . . . lets you know what's the worst thing that can happen to you. There's good advice in that book."

I asked her how her father had discovered that she and Daniel were going steady.

It was about 1 A.M. and her parents were waiting up for her when she came home from an evening out with some friends whose parents had taken a bunch of kids to an amusement park. Her parents were upset, not because she was coming in late—the trip had been prearranged with their consent—but because she had cut her typing class to see Daniel.

"Dad asked if I liked him. He said it was up to me [to decide if she still wanted to go steady with Daniel], but I knew they wanted me to break it off," she said. "That's when I was going to break it off."

She did and Daniel overdosed and they were back together within a day or so. Lisa said there had been a "heated argument" with her parents for about an hour that night she came home from the amusement park. I asked her to explain what she meant by a "heated argument." She was just sitting there while her father scolded her.

"I would never scream at my dad. No sense in trying to tell him in that moment," she said.

She sat there for more than an hour while her father raged about her going out with a boy he considered a bum. He had warned her that there would be boys who would only be interested in sex and who would be no good for her. Daniel was a prime example. When I asked for more details about that night, Lisa would not talk. I pulled bits and pieces out of her. She did not use the word "rage" when she talked briefly about her father's anger that night. I decided to use it because it was the best way to characterize her father's reactions. She indicated but would not say that there had been other occasions when he had become incensed at her. That night was not unique.

"My father didn't talk to me a couple of days," she said. "Then I apologized and then everything was all right. He put his foot down. . . . He thought it was over."

But she continued to see Daniel on the sly, and her father, after some minor altercations with Daniel and Fred, decided to move.

"I agreed to move," she said. "I wanted to move. I was a total mess. Daniel wouldn't leave me alone. I wanted to make my dad and mom happy. I still liked Daniel. If we moved, I didn't have to make a decision. It was already made for me. When all of this stuff came down, [Daniel's] idea was that we were going down to South Carolina where his uncle was. He thought I was going to leave home. I wasn't going to leave home."

When she first started explaining about her father's plans to sell the house and move, she thought I did not believe her. But I did, and I believed that she had been "a total mess." I could not get her to talk about her mother's role in all of this, so I asked her why she had not talked to someone about it, like a counselor or teacher or someone she could trust.

"I could have discussed it, but I usually don't talk to people about things," she said.

So we grappled over her not confiding in anyone and hiding her feelings. I understood her unwillingness to confide everything to *me* and her insistence on concealing her feelings, but I thought that it gave *others* the impression that she was unfeeling and felt no remorse.

"They weren't with me twenty-four hours a day, not with my chaplain, not with my friends," she replied tersely.

In jail, Lisa said, she had been angry, hurt, and lonely.

"I was so angry that I didn't know how to deal with it," she said. Why?

"My uncle died," she said. "That immediately brought back memories of my dad. I just couldn't believe it. A lot of times I thought my dad was still alive. It was hard to believe he wasn't there anymore. It still is."

She also was angry and hurt because of what Daniel and Fred had done, exclaiming, "I couldn't understand it."

I was about to ask her what she could not understand when I asked if she ever talked to her mother about what had happened.

"We really don't talk about it that much," she said. "Both of us get upset."

Her foot had been hitting the side of the desk for several minutes, so I told her I only had a few more questions. I wanted to talk about what had happened that night.

When she realized the boys were drunk, she said, she asked them to leave. She was afraid they were going to make too much noise and get her into trouble because they were not supposed to be in the house.

"I called my father upstairs to get rid of them," she said, and insisted that she had not called her father upstairs to fix her television as had been reported in the newspapers and mentioned by Sauerwein.

"What did you say to him?" I asked.

"'Oh, Dad,'" Lisa said, "'could you come here for a minute?'"

When she went out of the room to get him, the lights were on. And when she returned, the lights had been turned off. As her father walked in, she tried to pull him out of the way. (She was talking fast.) The last thing she saw before she ran out of the room was Fred sitting on her father's chest. She did not see him stabbed. She ran past her mother, down the stairs, and outside. She heard her mother's screams but she just stood there and did not move. Her mother came outside and alerted a neighbor, who called the police and an ambulance. This version of the story differed from her previous account, in which Lisa said *she* had alerted a neighbor to call the police. She was kicking the side of the desk when I asked her for more detail. Had she seen who had hit her father in the head? Why had she just stood there? Why hadn't she screamed? She would not talk. I again used Sauerwein as an ogre who was going to tell me all sorts of hideous things about her. I suggested that she at least tell me enough to balance what Sauerwein would say. She said that just before she pulled her father out of the way, she had noticed something in Daniel's hand. The police, she explained, "made a big deal" out of Daniel and Fred's showing up at her house with knives on them. But she explained that they "always carried knives on their sides." They kept the knives in sheaths.

"I never paid any attention to the knives," she said.

And that was it. She was not going to talk any more or answer any questions. When I tried to use the Sauerwein apparition again, she told me to go talk to Sauerwein and then come back and "talk to me." The interview was just about over.

"If I hadn't let them in," she offered, "none of this would have happened."

I asked her why she had pleaded guilty to conspiracy if she was innocent.

"The only reason I did was because Vallario told me to," she insisted. "I sat up there [in court]. . . . I couldn't say I was guilty. I

heard my mother crying behind me, and my knees were shaking . . .
if the judge had asked me questions about what had happened, because if he did I was going to tell him the truth," she said, visibly
shook up.

What was the truth?

She would not speak.

There were holes in Lisa's explanations and descriptions of the
night her father had been killed. I also sensed a great deal of denial
when she was talking to me. I needed more information. I wanted to
know more specifics about her relationship with her father. Had he
frequently exploded in anger when he disapproved of something she
did? Or had that been an unusual outburst the night of "the heated
argument"? When I was talking to Lisa, she indicated that it had not
been so unusual but refused to say anything more. I also wanted to
know more about what had happened that night in her room. I
thought the chaplain might be able to throw some light on my questions, and so I tried to reach him by phone. When I contacted him, I
introduced myself and explained that I had already talked to Vallario
and interviewed Lisa for several hours. I told him Lisa had said it
was okay for me to talk to him. I heard him take a breath, and even
though I was on the telephone, I could sense that he was bracing
himself to muffle an acerbic comment. He said, with strained po-
liteness, "I do not want to talk to you. I believe all of you are exploit-
ing a helpless young girl."

"All of you"? I guess he was talking about reporters but I am not
sure. He stayed on the line for a few seconds while I unconvincingly
tried to disassociate myself from "all of you." I later met with Vallario
in the courthouse and told him that the chaplain did not want to
talk. I also told him that I needed to talk to him about my interview
with Lisa. Vallario had said earlier that I did not have to let him
know what I got out of the interview, but I thought it was important
for me to talk to him. When we sat down, he listened briefly, asked
me who was publishing the book, and then looked upset. He got up,
extinguished his cigar, and walked out before I could say anything
else. I believe Lisa said more to me than he had expected, but what
actually worried him I never learned. When I left the courthouse, I
was hoping that Sauerwein would not be strike three.

Joseph C. Sauerwein had been in private practice for a year and a half before he became a prosecutor in 1966, climbing the ladder of power in the state attorney's office steadily. He got stuck on the second rung, and after several years as the number two man, he decided to resign and return to private practice. In his seventeen years as a prosecutor, he handled "a couple of hundred cases." He won his first murder conviction against a father who had decided to teach his daughter a lesson after she went to Annapolis without asking his permission. The father cut his daughter down with a shotgun. Sauerwein was in private practice when Lisa, Daniel, and Fred were arrested. The state's attorney brought him on the case as a special prosecutor. I thought it was ironic that his first and last murder cases involved daughters and their fathers. I noticed when I talked to him this time that some of the acrimony toward Lisa had dissipated. Perhaps, I thought, that was because the litigation was several months old, and he was now engrossed in his practice.

"When she first came into contact with the police, she was not a suspect," Sauerwein said. "She gave an ordinary witness statement but did not identify [Daniel] and [Fred]. The police thought she might have let them in the house but was not involved in the attack so they let her go home. Several hours later they brought her back to the station house and asked more questions. She was brought back . . . and gave them a couple of other statements. Each of the statements amounted to nothing more than a product of answering questions to what the police already knew. The questions that she answered showed a developed mind to give the police absolutely nothing in terms of incriminating herself . . . and steering herself and them [Daniel and Fred] away from showing that they were part of a planned murder. The second time the police talked to her she was technically arrested. They had put handcuffs on her but they let her go home with her aunt with the condition that maybe they wanted to talk to her again. That night the aunt found her in the bed, huddling under the cover, saying she was not coming back. Why? Because she knew the boys were being interviewed."

The police had found Daniel's jacket in Lisa's bedroom, and they were able to identify the two attackers after they interviewed Lisa's mother in the hospital. When Fred and Daniel came to Lisa's house that night, Fred had been carrying the club that was used to smash Emilio over the head. "[Fred] carried the stick because of an earlier confrontation with the father," Sauerwein said. "He had found her with the boy [Daniel] in a smooching position."

It was not until the police questioned Fred that they were told about a conspiracy to kill Emilio for cash.

"Only after that were we able to reconstruct bits and pieces of what happened," Sauerwein said. "The only person who shed a tear was [Fred]. He was the oldest, supposed to be the baddest-ass."

Fred was also the dumbest. By one account he was borderline mentally retarded. And he had every reason to cry, and remorse did not have to be one of the reasons. The conspiracy had called for him to kill Lisa's parents for money, and it was believed that he had stabbed Lisa's mother. Lisa's mother could identify him. Fred was a hitman, a hired gorilla who was going to kill so he could have money to pay off parking tickets and marry his girl. He was not so dumb, however, that he could not realize that he was looking at thirty years or more in prison, if the prosecutor did not ask for the death sentence. I could imagine a lot of people crying if they were in similar situations. But Sauerwein believed that Fred felt contrition for what he had done, while Lisa showed no remorse.

"Lisa," he said, "didn't shed a tear."

His impression of Lisa, when he first got involved in the case, had been that "she was just mean or insane." Now? He used an analogy. He could never imagine her sitting on the back of a motorcycle and clinging to some guy if she was a member of a motorcycle gang. Lisa, he explained, wanted to lead, wanted to ride in the driver's seat. It was a sniggering aspersion, a quantum putdown frequently used by men to describe an uppity woman who did not know her place, or thought she "had balls," or was an ungrateful wench who wanted to act like a man, or, worse, did not act the way some men wanted her to act. When the doctors for the defense examined Lisa, they had described her as "immature" and opined that she had been trapped in a pernicious relationship with a possessive father who was smothering her. Femia had rejected the testimony.

"What she planned with the others," Sauerwein said, "and what she did and the moments following, being a witness to murder, was to handle the police with a great deal of maturity. The doctors don't know what is in her head. Immature, shallow. Absolute definitions of nothing. There is no correlation between maturity and planned murder. She is no three faces of Eve but knows how to manipulate people to her own design or advantages."

Daniel was one of the victims of Lisa's manipulating wiles, he said.

"She could turn him on and off in a second and threatened to break up with him a lot. He said she tried to make him commit suicide. She came on to him one moment and then 'I never want to see you again' in another," he said.

Lisa could not make up her mind either. Some days she wanted him, and at other times she could not stand him. That is not too hard to understand. They started dating when she was fourteen and he was thirteen, at ages when pubescent adolescents are swamped with budding sexual yearnings and desires and confusion. It is still expected that boys will sow their wild oats. Young girls, though the advertisements remind them that "you've come a long way, baby," still must navigate between the Charybdis of going too far and being labeled a whore, and the Scylla of being called cold and frigid. Those are the external pressures. Girls also have to deal with their own inner feelings of yes-no-yes-no. If they waffle too much for some guy's tastes, say, they are cockteasers. Lisa waffled, and Daniel was probably flipping on and off like an incandescent light. So was his girlfriend.

Sauerwein, however, had more to offer. On the day of the murder, he explained, offering another morsel of incriminating information, Lisa phoned a girlfriend and told her, "Wish me luck." The implication was that Lisa told the girl to "wish me luck" in pulling off the murders of her parents.

I asked him if he had ever prosecuted any case similar to Lisa's.

"At seventeen, no, not at that age, not like that," he said.

But he offered a story that, he believed, contained similarities though it involved two men in their late twenties. The story he told, and several things that he said after the tale, caused me to forget to remind him that Lisa had been fourteen when she was arrested and sixteen when she was sentenced. His account concerned two men, with no criminal records, who "felt life would be better without their wives." So they conspired to kill each other's wives. With the insurance money for his wife's death, one husband, who also had his child killed because he did not want to pay child support, bought his girlfriend in Texas a bronco. The second husband, with no children, just wanted the $200,000 of insurance money from the policy on his wife. They were anticipating new lives with clean slates. They both are still serving sentences in jail. Lisa, Sauerwein explained, preferred life "without her parents."

The two men wanted money, no obligations, and new lives, all tangible items, though the means of obtaining them were despicable. Lisa, according to Sauerwein, wanted to kill her parents because she wanted them out of her life. What happened to Daniel? It had been reported that her parents were to be killed so that the two lovers could be together. But before I could ask questions, Sauerwein had moved from the anecdote to something more important.

"There are some strange unanswered questions in this case," he said. "One, I don't understand why [Lisa's mother] wanted the child back immediately. She has to know and be totally aware of her participation. Who knows about mothers? I don't think she saw her child as a sick child. With Italians, the family is first, the government second. Attack the family and all deals are off. Two, the involvement of [Fred] and [Daniel]. There is a great deal of uncertainty on who did what. I didn't have to prove who killed [Emilio]. So many people go into the room; one is dead; the one not arrested was stabbed. [Fred implicated] the other two and then there was corroboration of that [he did not say how it was corroborated] . . . but it doesn't really mean who stabbed [Emilio]. . . . He was beaten severely by a table leg filled with lead and wrapped at one end. They beat him to silence him, but it didn't work that way. He fell and made a loud noise. I don't think they caused this so that they wanted [Lisa's mother] to come upstairs. The reason for her coming up there was that she heard a loud noise. . . . I don't think they were interested in that, stabbing her. It just happened. Which is why she is alive today. Little Lisa, who ran past her mother who was stabbed, she ran past her mother into the yard. Did she cry or scream? No. Her mother went screaming outside for help. Our theory: She didn't want to go back into the house because she was uncertain whether Momma was going to be alive or was dead."

My initial questions were based on the prosecution's believing that both parents were to die and one luckily survived. Sauerwein had been quoted in the newspapers as saying that the conspiracy had been to kill both parents. Now I was being told that Lisa's mother had blundered into an attack purportedly planned to kill her husband. So I asked Sauerwein why he believed that the father had been the intended victim and not the mother.

"If they wanted to kill the mother, they were in a position to stab her more than once," he said. In addition, "She is stabbed in the shoulder," he pointed out, demonstrating how she had been attacked, while "the aim to the father" had been deliberate.

He had been killed with a straight thrust to the heart.

"They wanted to kill the father," Sauerwein said. "But what about the mother? She came because of the screams."

What would have happened if she had not come? If she was not an intended victim, how would Emilio's death have been explained? I had many questions that I had not even asked. But Sauerwein was unable to provide many answers other than to say that Lisa's mother was not supposed to be in the house when Emilio was to be killed. She just happened to come inside without being noticed.

"The police never got the straight answers out of them," he said. "They never really copped to them [the police]."

And he was not satisfied with his results because the case lacked a "certain finality."

"As a prosecutor, you have to realize that the results of a case is dependent upon wanting to obtain some certainty of conviction rather than any possibility of any one individual being found not guilty, particularly Lisa," he said.

Vallario had counseled her that she would be better off pleading guilty to a lesser felony with a lighter sentence than facing a trial, with the possibility of being convicted of first-degree murder and going to jail for thirty years or so. But Sauerwein had worried that if she went to trial, Lisa would have a strong chance of winning an acquittal. And there were good reasons why he had worried.

"[Fred] was going to be a witness," he explained. "If [Fred], who might have reason to lie, wasn't going to tell the truth, and he was the star witness in your case . . . you're in damn serious trouble."

He had also anticipated problems with Lisa's mother as a witness for either the defense or the prosecution. He could not afford to appear before a jury with the mother testifying for the defense. And he did not want to risk calling her as a witness for the prosecution when it was obvious the mother still loved her daughter.

"You couldn't trust a witness like that. . . . You couldn't trust having her on a witness stand," he said. "What would the jury think?"

With the plea-bargaining arrangement, which, as he talked,

sounded to me like a high-stakes poker game, he had at least won some measure of tough sentences for the trio.

"They all got technically the same sentence," he said. "Vince [Femia] knows too that the sentences that were imposed in this case were something to ensure against any unjust result of any one of them walking away from this thing."

Lisa was the one he was most concerned about, so I asked him what had been involved in the planning, and told him that Femia had said that Emilio's murder was "choreographed." He would not agree to "choreographed," but what he did say sounded equally damning.

"She was the primary reason for it, and drafted the blueprint on how it was to occur," he said. "They discussed different plans, different methods, choice of location, and the method and manner of how it was to occur. It was Lisa's idea. She was the one who called her dad in to fix the TV. She let them in the door when her mother wasn't going to be there. What they didn't plan on was the mother being there."

Much of what the police and prosecution had learned was based on "bits and pieces" they gleaned from Fred and were able to draw on from other "corroboration." But, if Sauerwein was worried that his star witness might lie before a grand jury, that Fred had flaws serious enough to make him an unreliable witness, it was not hard for me to imagine that perhaps the other corroborating evidence was less than solid as well. It was also possible that the friend Lisa supposedly told, "Wish me luck," would not have been a good witness either. Lisa could have been asking for good luck for all sorts of reasons that had nothing to do with murder. Sauerwein was convinced that Lisa had been contemptuous of both of her parents and out of that enmity had come her plans for her father's death. I was not so sure. I needed more time to think about everything I had been told.

Sauerwein talked for several minutes about his return to private practice. He was putting in long hours, and though I appreciated the time he took to talk to me, I did not agree with his characterization of Lisa. As I was leaving his office, his last words were:

"I'll be defending the Lisas of the world."

I wrote to Lisa a few weeks after I left Maryland. During the interview, we had discussed plans for me to come back and meet with her again, and in the letter I outlined what I wanted to discuss.

It was two and a half pages sprinkled with impressions of our talks and some general questions I wanted to raise. I suggested, or at least indicated, how we could go about discussing what I wanted to know. I did not say anything about the interview with Sauerwein. She also had agreed to ask her mother to meet and talk with me, and she was to provide addresses and telephone numbers of some friends who she had mentioned were still supportive of her. I wanted to talk to them too. I had telephoned one youth but the call was intercepted by his mother, who was less than enthusiastic about having her son talk to one of those journalists spreading scandalous tales about a "poor young girl." To contact him, I realized, I would have to write to him.

Nothing, however, ever materialized. Lisa never answered the first letter nor the second. Maybe the questions I wanted to ask bothered her, or her attorney had warned her not to talk to me again. I am not sure. I wanted to focus more on her relationship with her father. Though at times she claimed ignorance or poor memory in our interview, she had discussed some circumstances and some of her actions on the road to "the night it all happened." But she resisted talking about problems with her father. She described him as a wonderful father and husband who had provided for her and her mother. But she clammed up when she started talking about the time it was discovered that she had cut a class to be with Daniel. In the interview, she at first said it had been a heated argument, and then later disclosed he had been arguing heatedly while she just sat there. Why was she so defensive about talking about her father?

During the early part of my first interview with Lisa, I had tried to give her an idea of what type of research I was doing and the kind of book I was trying to write. She had looked bored and uninterested as I was talking. So I started talking about some of the different ways the murders had been committed just to see how she would respond. I talked about ax murders, shootings, and stabbings, but she remained unimpressed and was still looking bored. So I started talking about some of the underlying motives for parricides. I gave anecdotes about mental illness and schizophrenia and I described some cases of child abuse, but when I mentioned incest she winced and tried to act calm, as if the remark had made as little impression on her as all of the other things I had said. But the startled expression on her face— embarrassment and confusion—had lasted much longer than she wanted.

Later, when I thought we had established much better rapport, I asked her if her father had ever talked to her about sex. She remained very still and looked straight at me and nodded her head. I asked her if he had ever told her that no man would ever be good enough for her and that what any man would ever really want from her was sex. She nodded again. She was sitting perfectly still in her chair. I asked the second question again but in another way, and again she nodded. I wanted more than just nods; I needed verbal answers. So I decided that I would come back to this area later and try a different approach. I never got the chance.

I would have liked to talk to her mother too. Though Lisa had made references to her parents, she said little about her mother. She had had a "special" relationship with her father. How special was the relationship with her mother? And what was her mother's role when Lisa and her father were locked into their fatal *pas de deux*?

All the questions I indicated in the letter, and all the questions that would have been spawned from those questions, were important because there was no clear motive for Lisa's involvement in her father's death. Vallario said it had been a snowball that became a volcano. He did not say in the interview what had gotten the snowball rolling but insisted that Lisa had not been gripped by malice. As part of her defense, he introduced the results of psychiatric examination, which said she was "naive" and a victim of psychological abuse. Femia roundly rejected the findings. He said all they had done was to convince him that Emilio was a doting father. Perhaps the abuse Vallario tried to introduce as evidence would have been more persuasive if Lisa's mother had testified for her daughter. But she did not. The chaplain, who Lisa indicated knew her better than anyone else, said she was a "helpless young girl" being exploited. Because all the parties in this case were struggling with bits and pieces and vague impressions, maybe that impression should have been offered in court.

Lisa had plotted the death of her parents, Sauerwein said in court, because she wanted to be with Daniel. Months later he said the plot had called for the father to be slain; her mother had blundered into it. The motive? Lisa had been contemptuous of her parents. Where had this irreverence and disrespect come from? He was not really sure. Maybe, he shrugged, it was because her parents were hairdressers. But she was obviously the kind of girl who was not content riding on the back of a motorcycle and wanted to be in the driver's seat. For him, that said it all.

Hate and contempt can be some of the emotional factors in par-ricide, but there are substantive motives that explain why sons and daughters kill their parents. Money is one. A district attorney in Utah convinced a jury that Frances Bernice Schreuder, a board member of the New York City Ballet, had ordered her teenage son Marc to kill her multimillionaire father. She believed, according to the prosecution, that her father was disinheriting her. A district at-torney in Westchester County, New York, convinced a jury that nineteen-year-old Richard Winkler had paid an acquaintance to kill his father. The motive: money. Winkler, the prosecutor argued suc-cessfully, wanted to get his hands on a $150,000 inheritance and to take over his father's business. A few days after his dad's funeral, Winkler walked into the dead man's Wall Street personnel company and announced he was taking command. A security guard threw him out, and the police arrested him a few days later. In New York City, the Queens district attorney won a conviction against a thirty-three-year-old man for hiring an acquaintance to kill his mother. The motive: to get her money, house, and other possessions. I don't think there's any doubt that the defendants were contemptuous of their parents, but the underlying motives involved material gain.

Steven Hayden, fifteen, roiled with hate for his mother. When she had his father arrested, he told her Dad would kick her out when he returned. She told him to straighten up. "She pissed me off, man," he told a police investigator later. "She went to her room, so I went to my room and got me a .44 Magnum, man. Understand? I loaded it and cocked it, man. I went into her room and pointed the gun at her. I blew her fucking head off, man. Understand? I blew her to pieces."

Sounds like contempt, but there is more to the story. His younger brother, Dennis, helped him to stuff their mother's body into a card-board box and bury her behind a barn. Dennis, for his part, was sent to a juvenile facility.

Several months after his sons' arrest, Roddy Hayden killed an eighteen-year-old girl. She was one of several young girls who had run away from home and stayed with the Haydens, with free room and board. She and the rest got all the drugs they wanted too. All they had to do was sleep with the Haydens anytime they demanded. Roddy killed her because he believed she had ratted to the police about the drugs and sex at the house.

But there is more to the story. Three years earlier Roddy had killed a thirteen-year-old boy who had run away and was hiding out on some Hayden property. He thought the boy was an intruder. Roddy received a three-year suspended sentence and was placed on probation. Roddy frequently abused his wife. Even without knowing the specific pathology, a layman could see that fifteen-year-old Steven's hate for his mother was just one part of a horrifying family environment suffused by violence.

A thirteen-year-old boy took his father's favorite gun and blew his mother away during an argument about his going to school. The judge did not hesitate in accepting the boy's plea when he pleaded guilty to the maximum under the law. According to neighbors who knew the kid from the time he was born, he had been physically and psychologically battered from about the age of two. It was never mentioned in court, not by his father or by the attorney, who had been hired by the father.

In all of these cases, there was something more than just a feeling of contempt to incite some son or daughter to kill. Sometimes the motive involves sexual abuse. One fifteen-year-old girl who is serving a sentence in jail killed a father who had been raping her. It took her eight months to talk about what had happened. In a case we will return to later, a seventeen-year-old girl in upstate New York, who had repeatedly been sexually abused by her father, killed him one night when he came to visit her in the family garage. Because of frequent attacks on her divorced mother and sister, as well as herself, plus threats that he would burn down the house and everything in it, he was not allowed inside the house. His visiting rights were restricted to the garage. It took a shot of Amytal plus a "third-degree" session with a psychiatrist and two lawyers to get her talk about what had happened to her. She was a wreck when she took the stand. She had been abused, but not raped, the jury decided when it found her guilty of manslaughter. The pressure of her parents' divorce plus some apparent abuse, maybe sexual but definitely not rape, had caused her to kill, the jurors concluded. Her mother learned about the abuse the same day the jury did.

I do not think anyone would have held it against Sauerwein if he had considered that maybe something incestuous had happened between Lisa and Emilio, and that perhaps it might have been a reason for the conflict between a doting father and his daughter. An insidious form of child abuse that virtually enslaves a daughter, incest can be overt or covert. Overt incest includes rape, sodomy, fellatio, grabbing the breasts, and any other physical, sexual contact. Covert incest would involve a patriarchal father acting seductively toward his daughter. Such fathers often appear to be doting or possessive.

Writes Dr. Judith Lewis Herman in *Father-Daughter Incest:*

> We define seductiveness on the part of fathers to mean behavior that was clearly sexually motivated but which did not involve physical contact or a requirement for secrecy. For example, some fathers constantly talked about sex with their daughters, confiding the details of their love affairs and ceaselessly interrogating their daughters about their own sexual behavior. . . . Still others courted their daughters like jealous lovers, bringing them presents of flowers, expensive jewelry, or sexy underwear. Although all these behaviors stopped short of genital contact, they clearly betrayed the fathers' intrusive sexual interest in their daughters, which was a form of covert incest. . . . Like the incestuous families, families with seductive fathers had an ordinary appearance. They were often prosperous and highly regarded in their communities. Whatever private troubles they had escaped the detection of friends or neighbors and were certainly unknown to social agencies or the police. . . . As seen by their daughters, many of these fathers were quite authoritarian and intimidating. Certainly they had the capacity to rule their families by force, but in contrast to the incestuous fathers, they rarely used it. . . . The seductive fathers were able to control their families less by intimidation and force, and more by withdrawal and unavailability. . . . Like the incest victims, the daughters of seductive fathers experienced their relationships with their fathers as privileged and special. Unlike the incest victims, these women [as girls] did not have to bear the burden of secrecy about the relationship itself, for their fathers generally made no effort to hide their favoritism. Within their families, the daughters were often known as "Daddy's princess" or "Daddy's special girl." . . . Like the incestuous fathers, the seductive fathers often reacted intensely to their daughters' increasing sexual maturity. Many [in the study] became extremely jealous and attempted to restrict or monitor every aspect of their daughters' social lives.

Perhaps some of the fathers in Herman's five-year study considered at one time moving out of their neighborhoods in order to break up their daughters' relationships with undesirable or threatening suitors.

Of course, Sauerwein was a prosecutor. Five people walked into a bedroom; one was slain and one was stabbed and the other three were indicted for first-degree murder. He said he did not have to prove who did the actual stabbing, but he was definitely wary of going to trial against the girl whom he and the police had identified as the bankroll and the brains behind the murder. She wanted them dead because she wanted to be alone with her boyfriend, he said in court. Just reading the accounts in *The Washington Post*, I considered the possibility that a young girl—a decent student, someone who had never been in trouble—might be just dumb enough to want her parents murdered so that she could be alone with her boyfriend. At least, I could read the story without flinching noticeably. But one would have to be peculiarly simpleminded to believe that a girl killed her father solely because she was contemptuous of her parents and wanted to be in the driver's seat. Vallario believed there was nothing incestuous between Lisa and Emilio, though he introduced a psychiatric report that talked of symbiotic relationships, psychological abuse, about a young girl being smothered by her father. It was not convincing and was roundly rejected and she got fourteen years. But the report, as poor as it must have been in Femia's opinion, could not have been any worse than Sauerwein's later explanation for Lisa's wanting her father dead.

During the interview in jail, when she was relaxed, there were times when Lisa had the look of a whimpering cocker spaniel. Her eyes were filled with sadness and pleading. Then she would erase her old look and replace it with a new glance of defiance. She would sometimes cover one eye with her left hand and stare straight at me or hold her hand palms up in front of her and peek around them. Then she would melt and look like a young girl in the middle of a job interview. I still do not know if Lisa's shifting emotional responses were simply caused by her incarceration or whether they were the result of long-term abuse crowned by imprisonment. She will be in jail for a long time, though it is shorter than a life sentence. Her father was brutally murdered. And a price had to be paid. But is she paying the right price?

# 5

## Dawn

On a chilly evening in November 1982, G. Alan drove up the driveway of the sumptuous twenty-two-room mansion that he had once shared with his family. No longer the man of the house but an unwanted visitor, G. Alan returned to the estate once a week on Monday evenings to see his daughters, Dawn and Theresa, who would not have minded if he had forgotten to come or changed his mind about showing up, or if his car had run off the road and into a ditch that would swallow him up forever and ever. His weekly visits were reminders that they could not escape him, that he would always be inextricably involved in their lives. They had pleaded with the lawyers, when their parents decided to separate, that they did not want him visiting them. G. Alan, however, prevailed. But his visitation rights were confined to one sliver of opportunity. He could only meet them in the three-car garage and only for an hour. The real estate magnate, whom fortune had made a millionaire, was not allowed in the house, not on any pretext, not even to relieve his bladder. And if he stayed one iota longer than an hour, the police could be called. And they had raced to the big house in Ballston Spa, thirty miles northeast of Albany, New York, many times. Tonight G. Alan was only meeting with his oldest, Dawn, seventeen. Theresa was away at private school and Jean, his soon-to-be ex-wife, was off picking up jumper cables for Dawn's van. Jean had left her daughter alone in the house reluctantly, only after Dawn assured her, "I can handle Daddy."

G. Alan parked the car outside the garage where he was to meet

Dawn. When he walked inside he was carrying pizza and Coke, which they were going to share. Two bites and several minutes later a rifle shot killed him so fast that he did not have time to spit out the mouthful of pizza he was chewing. All that he might have said, if he had known he was doomed, or any regret that he might have expressed for all that happened in the past, perished when the first bullet smashed into the back of his head. Eight more bullets ripped into his body as it sprawled insensate on the garage floor. Even in her frenzy, Dawn was shooting with grisly accuracy, perforating his head, neck, and back. Shooting, ejecting a shell, and shooting again, as fast as she could, one shot after another, she was trying to pulverize him with a .22-caliber rifle. It was only when she saw the crimson rivulets forming a bloody pool on the garage floor that a surge of revulsion and horror dampened her fury and made her drop the gun. Swamped with fear and panic, she raced to a telephone in her home and dialed an emergency number.

"Is this the police?" she asked.

"Sheriff's office," the voice said.

"This is [Dawn] in the big house on [road name]. I just killed my father."

"You what?" the voice asked.

"I just killed my father," Dawn said.

Almost seventeen minutes passed before the first patrol car arrived, and during that time, an astonished sheriff's deputy tried to soothe a sometimes sobbing, sometimes weeping high-school senior over the phone. She spewed out bits and pieces of an excruciatingly painful family drama, a familial Grand Guignol, that would be whipped into one of the most sensational murder stories in the upstate New York area in years. During the conversation, which was being taped and would be played and replayed several times later, Dawn intermixed directions to her home with cries of pain.

The sheriff's deputy asked how she had killed him, and when she told him "with a gun," he again asked her to repeat her name and telephone number and tell him what had happened.

"I can't stand him anymore," she said. "It's . . . it's not fair."

The deputy responded by asking for more directions.

"It's a great big house, but you can't see it from the road. I'll turn the lights on," she told him.

"All right," the deputy said. "Uh, uh, were you arguing?"

"He, he does this to me every Monday night. My parents are getting a divorce and they [inaudible] . . . he's on [inaudible] just leave me," she cried.

"And you shot him?" he asked again.

"Yes," she sputtered.

He asked for more street directions, and in one breath she poured information over the phone to guide the deputies to her, and in another breath shards of pain and anger followed the street directions given to an invisible deputy with a homicide on his hands.

Tell them to keep an eye out for a stone driveway with a black mailbox, she told him, before sobbing again.

"My . . . the police have been here several times. My father has beat up my mother," she said, crying.

". . . Listen, you said you shot him. Is he dead or did you just hurt him?" the deputy asked.

"No, I don't think he's hurt," she replied.

"You don't think he's hurt?" he repeated.

"I think he's rather dead," she said.

He tried to calm her and reassure her that help was on the way.

"He's hurt me before," she said.

"I know. Okay. Okay, Dawn, just hang right onto the line," the deputy said.

"I don't want him to hurt me anymore," she moaned.

When Dawn told the deputy she had shot him with a .22-caliber rifle in the back and head, he asked if G. Alan had been leaving the garage when she shot him.

"He was . . . He was walking over to the garage, the garage door to down stairs," she said. "He said he was cold and he was tired of seeing my sister and I in the garage, and he said he was going to go in the house and I told him I didn't want him in the house."

A sheriff's sergeant got on the line and asked her father's age.

"It is G. Alan [last name]. Um, I think he is 41 or 42. I don't know. He's been bothering us so long," she said.

"I see, and was it his .22 rifle?" the sergeant asked. "Was the rifle loaded in the house?"

"No, it wasn't loaded," she told him.

"You loaded it?" the sergeant asked.

"Yeah. He's . . ."

The sergeant, concerned about other weapons, asked if there were any more guns in the house.

"I just don't want to be hurt anymore," she said, after telling him there was only one gun, the rifle her father had purchased for Theresa and had taught both daughters to shoot.

"Okay, Dawn, just hang right on, okay?" he said. "Now don't get excited when my cars get there, now, and go grabbing that gun or anything."

"No," she assured him.

"Where is your mother?" the sergeant asked.

"She went to get jumper cables for me for the winter," Dawn told him. "We've been made by the lawyers to see him. We don't want to see him."

The sergeant, trying to get more information on what had happened, asked Dawn if her father had tried to force his way into the house and "you wouldn't let him, was that it?"

"No, he was . . . there is a door going down in the garage, down from the garage, down into the cellar, and he said he was tired of being in the garage and he was going to get someplace warm and he said my mother wouldn't care. He knew my mother wasn't here and he said my mother wouldn't care if he went into the cellar, and I said, 'Mom would care,' and he said, "No, I'm tired of being in the garage!'" Then she broke into tears again.

When the sheriff's deputies finally arrived, the sergeant was greatly relieved.

"Is he 1079?" he asked one of the first deputies on the scene.

The reply was immediate: "Oh, yeah, man, he's deader than shit. Pool of blood a mile long out here. We didn't know what the hell was going on."

Dawn guided the police to her on a road paved with self-incriminations. The police and the prosecutor knew she had shot her father in rage. She had admitted it on tape. She had loaded the gun and shot him many, many times in the back and head. She had hated him. He was always hurting her and beating her mother. Dawn was charged with second-degree murder, and the judge ordered her held without bail. An attorney who sought to have her released told the court she was severely depressed and suicidal and should be freed on bail. If she was that depressed, the judge said, she was better off in jail. What the judge did not say, although it was generally known, was that in Saratoga County unwritten law dictated that defendants in felony murder cases be held without bail. A few weeks later, Dawn's mother hired two other attorneys, John McMahon, a local lawyer, and Stephen Gaits, of Albany.

"As soon as we got in the case, there was an impending grand jury, and our decision was to fight the grand jury and get her out on bail," Gaits said later.

But first they asked the judge who had denied the bail to disqualify himself from the case. They had strong grounds for that request. Just a week before his death, G. Alan and a bunch of Saratoga's finest had flown to Las Vegas on one of their occasional junkets to the gambling Mecca of the Northern Hemisphere. McMahon was on the plane. And so was the judge, a man for whom G. Alan had once performed some work as a surveyor. Dawn's attorneys, basing their request on an apparent conflict of interest, convinced the judge to remove himself from the case. And they got her out on bail after appealing to the state appeals court. It was the first time ever that a defendant charged with second-degree murder in Saratoga County was allowed bail. But she was not freed without a fight. The district attorney asked for $500,000 bail. Her attorneys argued successfully for a significantly smaller bail. Dawn's mother put up the money. As soon as she was released, her attorneys set up an appointment for her with a psychiatrist.

Seventeen of the twenty-two rooms in the family's big house were offices. The rule of the day, week, month, and year: business. Dawn's mother's family had risen out of the Albany Irish ghetto to become among the area's largest real estate developers. Charming and ingratiating and equally ambitious, her father was an engineer who wanted more than just a sip of the good life. G. Alan wanted to bask in it.

Though born into affluence, Dawn was infused with ambition and a work ethic that would awe even the hardest workers. She held a part-time job that involved working two or three nights after school and on weekends. Dawn and her sister also operated a thriving worm farm that supplied bait stores throughout the Adirondacks. Her share of the profits was reinvested in the business as well as used for what leisure activities she squeezed into her busy schedule. Because her B average did not come easy in school, she stayed up as late as 3 A.M. Four or five hours of sleep was all that she allotted herself. At school, she was a model student and a leader. Always impeccably dressed, she was a teenager whose hard work and drive were enough to make any parent beam with pride.

Except someone like G. Alan, who wanted sons and not daughters, and frequently reminded them that if he had had a choice Dawn and Theresa would have been males. A strapping six-footer with blond hair and smooth-shaven good looks, G. Alan frequently beat his daughters and pounded on his wife. Dawn and her sister were hammered for spending too much time on the telephone—only five minutes was allowed—or for not polishing their shoes or dressing properly for dinner. He expected them to polish his shoes as well. The beatings had started as early as Dawn could remember, but she would not cry. When she was about six months old, she was trained and encouraged not to cry. As she got older, she learned to suppress her emotions.

When Dawn met the psychiatrist, she talked about her father's numerous extramarital affairs, which he had flaunted at home, and the two mistresses he had been supporting in the apartments of his large apartment complex. G. Alan was not above taunting his wife about his affair with a nun who had visited the house. Everybody screws his wife two or three times a week, he once told Dawn's mother, to keep her happy so that he can then do what he likes outside.

Despite being battered as a young child, Dawn still thought she loved her father and sided with him in family arguments. Even though he was now dead, she told the psychiatrist, she was still afraid that he would come back and hurt her. "She cannot understand how such a frail person like herself has been able to stop him since no one else ever has," the doctor wrote in his report. Dawn saw her father as omnipotent and herself as weak and insignificant.

When Dawn was three, and her sister one, her mother walked into the bathroom while her father was bathing the young girls and caught him stimulating Dawn's nipples. Almost twelve years later, one night when she was in bed, her father walked into the room and sat on the bed and began talking to her. Without warning, he whipped off her nightgown and began to fondle her body. He sucked on her nipples and hurt her. She pleaded with him to let her go but his bulk was too much for her to struggle against. He left the room without raping her. She later complained to her mother, who did not believe her. Dawn recalled the incident at the grand jury hearing before being indicted on second-degree murder charges.

Despite the disclosures of sexual abuse and the beatings, Gaits and McMahon believed that Dawn was holding something back. The trial date was approaching, and they still were not sure what specifically had triggered the shooting in the garage. When they tried to talk to her after the indictment, she kept saying she "didn't want to be hurt." G. Alan was dead. They could not make sense out of her fear of being hurt again.

"So we went back and we start dancing around the subject," Gaits said. "She was very defensive when talking about her father and at times would not mention his name."

When she continually refused to talk about her relationship with her father, the attorneys assumed that "something sexual had happened" between them. Gaits tried another approach. He invited Dawn to his house one day, and he and his wife offered her coffee and snacks, and then after a little small talk Gaits got serious. He "worked her over" with questions. Why so tense? What's so terrible that you don't want to talk about it? Let's assume that there's more here than you would like to tell me, something that you don't want to talk about. If you're holding back from me, how can I present your defense and advise you? She would rather have gone to jail than talk about it, so he started "bartering" with her. He assured her he would not tell her mother anything she confided in him. He promised her it would not be made public.

"It was an awful obligation, an awful decision to make," he recalled.

Though she agreed to talk she still could not speak about what she was withholding. McMahon and Gaits set up an appointment with the psychiatrist to give Dawn a shot of Amytal, a drug that induces a state of consciousness similar to hypnosis in which a person is able to relax and concentrate. When she received the shot, they found they still had to give her "the third degree" to get her to talk. But what she said shocked even them.

About sixteen months before he was to die, G. Alan had met Dawn at the boutique where she worked after school. He had been forced to move out of the house after he broke his wife's neck, and they were in the middle of divorce proceedings. He dropped by the store to tell her that he had gifts for her and her sister. He wanted her to meet him at a vacant apartment at his housing complex where she could pick up the presents. When she later showed up, she had no sooner entered the apartment than he grabbed her and pushed her down on the floor; then he undid his clothes and hers and raped her.

That was just the beginning. G. Alan ordered her to meet him again. He would drop by the boutique or call and tell her the apartment where she was supposed to meet him. They always met after her work, and Dawn took precautions so that her mother would not know. Dawn would come home after school, change clothes, and tell her mother that she was going out, and then head over to an apartment building to meet her father. Sometimes he slapped her, and he frequently hurt her when he raped her. And the fear was always there of what he might do if she did not do what he wanted. He would hurt her mother or her sister or even her. He might destroy the house, force them to leave school, or sell their possessions. The threats and fear were not new. She had heard them before she and her sister were required to meet him in the garage for one hour once a week. It was a cruel assignation that only a father could get away with: forcing an emotionally troubled daughter, one who had been trained at six months not to cry and to suppress her emotions, to submit to repeated attacks of painful intercourse.

Under the Amytal and the lawyers' and doctor's third degree, Dawn gave accounts of about a dozen attacks. They assured her they would not tell her family or publicly reveal the information. They would file a motion to have the new evidence submitted to a grand jury. They were willing, in order to keep her accounts confidential, to have her plead guilty to manslaughter and be treated under the state's youthful offender statutes, which would ensure her confidentiality. It was also possible, they reasoned, that she would be placed on probation.

When they made their move, however, the prosecutor strongly protested. He said it sounded as if the rape accounts had been fabricated. He vigorously opposed a new grand jury. The judge, in his decision, cited the inordinate amount of press coverage of the murder as one of the reasons for refusing the motion for a new grand jury hearing. The attorneys' disappointment did not match Dawn's shock when they told her she would have to testify in court. She still preferred going to jail to talking to anyone about what her father had done to her. Just to talk to her attorneys and doctor about the attacks, she had needed a shot of Amytal, the third degree, and their assurances that they would never reveal what she told them. Now they were telling her she would have to testify, with as much detail as possible, before a jammed courtroom about things she had never discussed with her mother. And when she took the stand, her mother shuddered at each account, and the jury did not believe her.

The prosecutor contended from the beginning that Dawn had ambushed her father at the garage when he came to see her that night. The motive: hate building up from the pressure of a tumultuous divorce and property settlement. Her attorneys argued that it had been self-defense. She had been repeatedly raped by her father, and the night she shot him she believed he was about to attack her again. Soon after her father entered the garage, he started arguing and criticizing her mother and sister. Then, according to the testimony, he grabbed her and tried to embrace her. All the time, he had been pushing to get into the house or basement where it was warm. But when he grabbed her, she broke free and ran into the house and upstairs to a bedroom where the gun was kept. She loaded it and rushed back downstairs. G. Alan was near the basement door, according to her attorneys, when Dawn started shooting.

However, the prosecutor insisted that G. Alan had been running for his life when he was cut down. The district attorney also hammered away at discrepancies: Dawn's accounts of what had happened between her and her father had expanded after the grand jury investigation. He insisted that the shot of Amytal and the third degree by her attorneys and doctor had only helped her to fantasize about being raped by her father. Another inconsistency: The doctor testified that the shot had helped her to overcome her unconscious repression of the attacks, while Dawn testified that she had always been conscious of what had happened to her but could not talk
about it.

On the witness stand, she was defensive, uneasy, and "just barely holding together." The jury found her guilty of a lesser charge of first-degree manslaughter. A few commented to reporters on the reason for their verdict: On the first vote they decided that she had intentionally killed her father. . . . It had been calculated. . . . It had been an ambush. . . . The testimony had expanded after the grand jury. . . . It appeared the father had been a terrible man and he might have been a miserable husband and father, but that did not give her the right to take his life, unless it was necessary to protect herself. . . . She never warned him; she could have fired a warning shot. . . . They could not believe she would refrain from discussing the rapes when she was facing such a serious charge. . . . G. Alan had been a meticulous man, scrupulously groomed, a perfectionist who demanded cleanliness—"That's not the kind of man who's going to commit a rape on a garage floor."

The consensus, one juror said, was that she had been abused but not raped. It had been apparent when she took the stand that she was in need of psychiatric help. They hoped she would receive such help in jail. Even the district attorney conceded to a reporter that she was an abused child, but claimed the rapes were fantasies. The judge, who could have treated her as a youthful offender, chose instead to give her an indeterminate sentence of two and a half to seven years in the state penitentiary. McMahon and Gaits argued successfully to have her released on $50,000 bail pending the results of an appeal. This time, the district attorney, who conceded she had been abused, asked only for $250,000 bail.

The case was the first time that Stephen Gaits ever worked with an incest victim accused of killing her father. And the insidious nature of incest demands special attention to preparations for a plea of self-defense. Gaits was not critical of the jury's verdict. He said there were things that could have been done to make the jury more comfortable with the nature of Dawn's defense.

"Dawn was not able to bring up the full thrust of what she felt when he grabbed her," he said. "She still masks feelings of fear and her emotions very well. She does not like to be touched. She was just barely holding together on the stand. We didn't walk her through each attack."

If she had been better prepared, he believed "we could have hit the jury with more details. They would have felt more comfortable with the nature of the defense. They didn't get a chance to walk in her shoes. . . . If they had, she would have been acquitted."

G. Alan, he reiterated, had been visiting the garage for a year. All the attacks took place in different apartments of the housing development. Dawn assumed that she was safe at home. When he started pressing to get in she felt threatened.

"Our strong suit now is that she might be given time to think about it," he said. "She is seeing a psychiatrist regularly." She was also handling the books for her mother, who had taken over the ownership and management of the housing development. Though it was heavily in debt, and she could have chosen to take a chunk of G. Alan's estate without assuming any financial liability, Dawn's mother had decided to assume full responsibility for the development.

Gaits also said that if they won a new trial he would pay more attention to jury selection the next time around.

"We should have asked more questions, because people automatically reject thoughts of incest," he said. "Some of the jurors [in the first jury selection process] flippantly said yes, that talking about incest would not have bothered them."

But he still insisted, "It was the kind of case that should have gone back to the grand jury. A grand jury would have cleared this all up. Some were more interested in publicity than justice for Dawn."

# 6

# Richie

This family tale has been retold over and over and over again. Every major newspaper and newsmagazine in the country printed a story. And millions upon millions of TV viewers watched the interviews on morning and evening news broadcasts and on programs like *60 Minutes*. Most can recall pieces of the tale even if they cannot remember the name of the family. For many, the guns stood out: shotguns, rifles, handguns of all calibers, and semiautomatic weapons with the sinister, necrophilic look of the machine guns in El Salvador, Nicaragua, and Lebanon. Countries at war and under siege. So was the family in Cheyenne, Wyoming. It lived, year after year, with slow torture and under the ubiquitous specter of an untimely death. It came to the attention of a mesmerized public in November 1982. It is a story that needs to be told over and over and over again, not because it is unique but because it is a paradigm.

Richard Jahnke, Sr., braced himself for the bone-chilling cold that would seize him as soon as he got out of his car to open the garage door and put away his Volkswagen. Jahnke, a special agent for the Internal Revenue Service, and his wife, Maria, were returning from one of their rare nights on the town. They were celebrating the day they had first met, twenty years ago.

Inside the garage, their sixteen-year-old son, Richie, waited nervously, clutching a 12-gauge shotgun. Inside the house, his sister, Debbie, seventeen, huddled in the living room. She was cradling a semiautomatic weapon.

While their parents were out celebrating, the teenagers had plotted an ambush and set about their task with meticulous care. They tied up the family dogs in the basement to keep them out of harm's way and then turned the house into a combat zone. A high-powered rifle stashed in a corner. A handgun placed under a bed. A shotgun placed here and a rifle left there. The teenagers were poised to kill. If the ambush went awry or something inexplicable happened—if Richie missed or his gun jammed, if their father miraculously survived a hail of gunfire and stormed the house or shot his way inside—they would fall back on their grisly farrago of pistols, revolvers, shotguns, and high-powered rifles strategically placed about the house.

But not a drop of blood soiled the Jahnke home that November evening. When Richard Jahnke got out of his car, he stepped into the sight of the 12-gauge shotgun. His son whipped off six shots, blasting quarter-sized holes in the plywood garage door and hitting his father four times in the chest.

At his trial, Richie recalled years and years of abuse. He told about a father who had been beating him and his mother and sister as long as he could remember. "He hurt me so much," he told a jury. "He'd only stop when his nose began to bleed; he had high blood pressure." Richie's father beat his wife while sitting on her and "pounding away, her mouth foaming with blood." He also abused his daughter: "When my sister got acne, my dad accused her of not washing. He dragged her into the bathroom and scrubbed her face so hard she began to bleed." Nor did he like the way she brushed her teeth, so one day he showed her how: "He scraped her gums so hard they bled." Richard senior frequently fondled his daughter and put his groping hands down into her pants in front of his son, and when he tucked Debbie into bed at night sometimes he would climb on top of her. He went to the bathroom with a gun strapped to him, and he walked around the house hoping for the day someone foolish would try to break in so he could kill.

The children had no grandparents, aunts, uncles, or cousins to whom they could turn. The neighbors or friends who suspected the pain and suffering happening in the Jahnke home did not want to interfere in another family's personal business. Richard senior, some thought, was too strict, but a man's home is his castle. Richard showed up at school with bruises and marks on him. He once complained to a neighbor that his father beat him. When it became too much, he filed a complaint against his father. The social worker who came to the Jahnke home was impressed by the nice, comfy middle-class home of a modern nuclear family.

Richie and Debbie were left to their own defenses. They chose life, and when Richie shot his father, he was saving lives. But he was not acquitted on grounds of self-defense. The jury found him guilty of first-degree manslaughter, and a judge, who was concerned about other battered kids, sentenced him to an indeterminate sentence of five to fifteen years. Richie was to be an example. The criminal justice system was as insensitive as Richard senior had been all of his son's life. When his appeal failed, a groundswell of public sentiment, expressed in a petition with thousands and thousands of names, convinced the governor to commute the sentence. Richie would only have to spend two years in jail—or maybe less. But he should never have been sentenced so harshly in the first place.

The news stories about the Jahnkes riveted people to their TV sets and made for provocative reading. And the extraordinary attention paid this unfortunate family might make many consider it an anomaly. That too would be unfortunate.

# 7

# Vincent

His first year of high school, with all of the specters of defeat encircling him, easily could have been his last. His gauche manner overlay shyness and did not readily endear him to his classmates. With a crooked ridge for a nose and a half-inch scar under his eye, Vincent Whatley seemed unable to avoid walking into doors. His bent for skipping classes, when boredom or frustration whispered escape, did not enamor his teachers. A seemingly slow learner, he said little in class and found innumerable reasons for not doing his homework. "Dropout" was stamped indelibly in the minds of the pedagogues who first came across him in their classes. "Loser" was his surname. Nice kid, just dumb.

A little athletic ability might have softened those impressions. Tall enough at six feet to play basketball, he was too short for forward and too slow for guard. Center was out of the question. Basketball calls for an agility that was distinctly lacking in this gawky young man who seemed too mild-mannered even to throw an elbow or stiff-arm an opponent breaking for the ball or to the hoop. And football, well, at 150 pounds and lacking a killer instinct, Vincent would have been better off trying something else. But he was so poor in school that his academic record held him back from the tryouts that no one would have expected him to get past anyway. This kid had no natural ability. Or so some thought.

But running seemed to be in his blood and by his sophomore year that passion, fused with an indomitable sense of self, began to make everyone who met him realize they had formed the wrong impression. Beneath his subdued demeanor pulsed the heart of a winner. By the end of his first year, Vincent's grades rose perceptibly. In his second year, he had muffled the whispers that said escape and shackled the rabbit that made him flee classes.

He came to the track team with no obvious talent and no expectations from the coach. He was just eager to run. Vincent trained harder and longer, moving inexorably from the back of the pack to the front as a leader. His family came to track meets and cross-country events, a reporter later wrote, in T-shirts with WHATLEY inscribed in black lettering on the back. His father, an exercise zealot who could lift heavy weights hundreds of times with one arm, would train with his son. Chuck Whatley frequently bragged about how well his son was doing in school and running. But he would also tell his listeners that his forty-year-old legs could keep up with Vincent, though the boy pulled ahead of him going up hills.

From their father, Vincent and his brothers inherited a taste for hard work and fixing cars. But Vincent was more than just a great mechanic. He was an artist who pumped life into piston-driven derelicts and resurrected them from the dead. A Volkswagen coupe that he rebuilt was named "Car of the Year" at his high school.

After classes, when he was not running, Vince labored at his family's farm. He cut wood, one of his chores to help earn money for the family.

Chuck, in his own way, imbued Vincent and his two brothers with a work ethic that any parent could envy. On occasions when he thought his sons were not working as hard as they could, and to remind them that he was the boss and head of the family, he would discipline them lest they forget. The reminders, for example, showed up as red marks around Vincent's neck where he had been choked. Scars, bruises, contusions, and knots pockmarked his head, face, and body. The crooked ridge of his nose and the scar under his eye dated back to a day in his early teens. Sometimes, a reporter wrote, just to emphasize a point Chuck would fire a shot in his sons' direction.

Living in rural Oregon, where families were separated by miles and miles of trees, bushes, and small roads, the Whatleys were pretty much isolated. So it was not surprising that when Chuck Whatley died in June 1982 his death was treated as a family affair, that only a son saw him die, and that he and his mother were the only ones who saw Chuck buried. And only a handful knew about the body in the ground under a shed where, Chuck had made it known, he wanted to be buried when his time came. Every time some neighbor or acquaintance asked about Chuck, they were told that he had left for California. One day an in-law, who had noticed the tension building up in the Whatleys and was suspicious about Chuck's four-month foray to the west coast, wheedled out some information and called the authorities. When they found the body, Vincent was charged with second-degree murder and his mother was accused of being an accessory and hindering the prosecution. Chuck Whatley had died one day when someone one day started shooting in *his* direction.

It was a day not much different from a lot of others that had come and gone: Chuck hit Vincent on the head with an ax handle, according to a news story, and then resumed working with a chainsaw to cut firewood he planned to sell. Vincent crept into the house as his father worked and took two weapons, a 12-gauge semiautomatic shotgun and a lever-action .30-30 rifle. The guns had been used by the father to shoot dogs poaching on the family's livestock. Vincent stepped up behind his father and squeezed off five rounds of buckshot, the kind the military uses. The shots hammered his father to the ground. He was probably dead before he hit the earth but Vincent, to make sure Chuck would not rise up and kill him, shot him one more time near the neck with the .30-30 rifle. When she heard the report of the gun, Donna Whatley rushed outside and what she saw stunned her. Chuck was on the ground dead. Six shots ended a reign of terror that had brutalized everyone in the family, but the sudden and brutal slaying at the hands of a son too mild-mannered to throw elbows or stiff-arms compounded her bewilderment. She and Vincent buried Seyborne Jones "Chuck" Whatley as he had once requested and then "sent" him to California.

Several days after the arrests, despite being charged as an accessory, she could not stop talking.

"Everybody says I shouldn't talk to anyone, but this has got to come out," she told a reporter. "We were all beaten and brutalized. The kids were just terrified of him."

Why didn't they run away? They tried twice: once to Missouri, once to Iowa. Chuck found them and brought them back to Oregon after he threatened to kill the people with whom they were staying. Shortly before he killed his father, Vincent threatened to leave the farm, and his father warned him if he tried to go the whole family was going to die. In her unabashed account of life with Chuck Whatley, Donna also talked about times when he was not threatening death. He had kicked her out of a moving pickup truck because she criticized him for stealing fence posts stacked alongside a road. He swiped candy bars and hid them in the house so that no one else would eat them. He sometimes refused medical care for the family when he did not want to spend the money. The kids could go to school but not to church, school dances, or family picnics. They were not allowed to have close friends. Anyone threatening to leave was asking to die. In the few years before his death, the violence was escalating. And the day that Vincent was struck in the head, it looked as if Vincent's choice was life or death, him or Chuck.

Eight months after her arrest, Donna went to trial. She was facing a maximum of five years in prison for being an accessory to her husband's death when the judge declared a mistrial. One of the jurors had shown up drunk. Six weeks after that, she testified in her second trial that she had been shocked by what had happened. She had helped bury Chuck's body under the shed because that had always been his wish. The one-day trial ended in an acquittal. Vincent had already been sentenced.

Vincent's court-appointed lawyer, Stephen B. Peterson, was convinced he could win an acquittal. He lined up more than a dozen witnesses to testify, and recruited a psychiatrist, Dr. Hugh Gardner, who would testify that Chuck had been a dangerously paranoid case sinking deeper into paranoia. It would have been only a matter of time, the doctor would say, before Chuck barricaded himself in his house and started shooting at any moving target. Vincent just plain burned out after years and years of physical and psychological battering. But Peterson took extra precautions.

"In court cases there is a presentencing report prepared for the judge to assist him in making a decision," Peterson said later. "I talked the judge and the prosecutor into a pre-presentencing report. The probation guy said he [Vincent] would never do it again. I had a good idea of what to expect because the report was recommending eighteen months. I thought I had a good shot of getting him on probation and no jail, but he decided to accept a plea bargain."

Peterson said the prosecutor had not been pushing for a harsh sentence.

"The prosecutor was indifferent" in Peterson's opinion. "He

wanted something—a sentence or some time spent in jail—because a crime had occurred, but he kind of let me do what I wanted to do. He didn't take a strong position in plea negotiations. He did recommend some time, but he didn't say or didn't scream that it was a bloody murder. He felt some sympathy toward the boy himself."

When he announced a sentence that required Vincent to spend about eighteen months in jail, the judge said, "I have to give notice to the world that people cannot essentially go about assassinating people."

But Vincent had acted in self-defense. The judge attempted an adroit balancing act: a light sentence and a gruff verbal riff to deter other battered youths (and maybe some spouses too) from assassinating some murderous husband or father.

Though many in the community lined up behind Vincent and his mother—their lawyers had numerous letters of support to prove this—Chuck had his sympathizers too. "I just can't believe he was the type of guy that would just beat his children," an acquaintance wrote to *The Daily News* in Rainier. "The thing that Chuck was most guilty of was that he wanted his boys to grow up and be hardworking, good citizens. . . . No one can say that Chuck Whatley did not love his family very much, and his death was a poor reward for what he was trying to achieve. I raised five children and lived by the old rule, 'Spare the rod and spoil the child,' and Chuck had the same philosophy."

# 8

# Buddy

Every day after school, Buddy junior rushed to the local supermarket and staked out an area where he waited for the shoppers to exit from the store. As soon as they walked out of the door, he approached them and tactfully asked for their sales receipts. He was no street urchin badgering them for their loose change but a budding entrepreneur plying his trade, which at this moment was collecting supermarket receipts. Somber in manner, impeccably dressed, with not a strand of hair out of place, Buddy made it difficult for them to refuse. Shoppers rummaged through their bags or fished patiently through their pockets, wallets, and purses to turn over receipts to the little businessman with the fair skin and hazel eyes. That commercial stakeout was an important part of Buddy's daily life, and he would have stayed outside the market morning, noon, and night if it had not been for school and his parents' insistence that he come home early. Many of the store's regular customers, accustomed to Buddy waiting outside for them, became his regular patrons as well, leaving the supermarket with their receipts in hand ready to be turned over. When he had amassed $200 in receipts, he walked into the supermarket one day and purchased two sets of dishes that had been offered in one of those bargain specials that encourage customers to horde stamps, receipts, or coupons and exchange them for selected gifts. Buddy gave one set to his mother and the second set to one of her friends.

"It was cute the way he did it," recalled the friend and neighbor much later. "He was about nine or ten years old, maybe nine, and such a cute kid."

Buddy's mother, Peggy, and this woman had been collecting different sets of dishes, and when he came across a style they did not have, he made purchasing the two sets his number one priority.

"He and his mother were very close," the friend recalled, waxing nostalgic about the mother and son with anecdotes and remembrances to which only a few in the neighborhood were privy. "He was a very concerned kid as far as some are about their mothers, very helpful with his mother. There were things he did that you wouldn't expect from a young boy. He didn't have too many friends but he was close to her. When she came over to visit he would be there behind her in five minutes. He followed her around like a shadow. She almost died having him; she had a heart condition . . . and was in bad shape when she had him. They were very close."

Growing up, Buddy was a "good kid" with a bad temper, fussing intemperately even as a toddler.

"He didn't cry much," the neighbor remembered. "He cried less than most kids. He showed a temper instead of crying. Something would bother him and he would get angry. He had a temper ever since he was a baby, even more so than most babies. At three, four, five, he would pick up a stick and throw it at some other child if they tried to play with his toys. Even when he was very little, he'd come up to his mother and sock her in the leg, and she ignored him. Everybody ignored it. She was always very calm and understanding, and made excuses about it and tried to hide his childishness from his father. She was a buffer between them. She sheltered him a lot from his father when he was young. She told me. She thought the problem was with the father but she would work it out with her son. Buddy senior is obsessed with being a disciplinarian."

The friend, who had known the family for almost twenty years, thought the son had picked up his anger from Buddy senior. She never fully considered how Buddy junior at three, four, five could have picked up such a rage that he attacked in situations that would have caused other youngsters to cry. When Buddy was about eleven, twelve, or thirteen, it appeared he was always running away, hopping on his bike and riding "all over the place." The police, after so many trips to return him home, became an inconspicuous part of the neighborhood ambience.

"I saw him that Thanksgiving morning," she recalled about a brief visit to Peggy's kitchen. "He was acting like a little child. He'd untie Peggy's apron bow and tell her, 'You have to tie it again.' Everything looked normal. Buddy, like a child, kept pulling at the bow, giggling. He looked happy. Everything looked normal."

Yet today, if she saw him riding his bike on the street where he once lived, she would not welcome him in her home.

"I would be terrified to see him. I wouldn't want to see him, not today. I don't hate Buddy. I've no idea why he did what he did. Who knows? Peggy was a private person. . . . Things happen in the home, no one really knows why. I have suspicions that he was on drugs a long time. Drugs screwed up his mind. There were rumors of drugs all over the place," she said.

All of the names in this chapter are pseudonyms.

On an early morning in December, shortly after Thanksgiving, Peggy walked into the kitchen and discovered her son eating breakfast. Buddy was supposed to be in school, but there he was cutting classes again. Peggy was beside herself. They argued and she told him that if he did not go to class she would call the psychiatrist whom Buddy had been seeing and tell him that her son was acting up again and refusing to go to school. Buddy did not budge and warned his mother not to call the counselor. They argued again until Peggy, exasperated, walked to the telephone and started to dial. Buddy screamed at her not to call.

"I am because you're very violent," she said.

"I don't want to go," he screamed.

"I don't care," she said. "This is the best thing to do."

When she continued dialing, Buddy bolted upstairs to the second floor and pulled down the folding staircase that led to the attic. He found a black case, opened it, and removed his father's favorite gun, a Smith and Wesson .41-caliber Magnum. He then rushed down to his parents' bedroom and opened a gun cabinet where his father kept his rifles and shotguns and ammunition. He loaded the handgun with four shells of soft-point ammunition. He ran downstairs and stopped in the doorway of the kitchen and warned his mother to get off the phone or he would shoot. Peggy, who had already called her husband at work, was leaving a message on the answering machine of the psychiatrist when Buddy walked into the kitchen. She refused to hang up the phone. Buddy shot her once with a gun powerful enough to kill an elephant or wreck the engine block of an automobile. The bullet slammed through Peggy's abdomen and crashed into a door molding. Peggy crumpled to the floor. Buddy unloaded the gun and walked back to his parents' bedroom. He returned the unused cartridges to the ammunition box and walked upstairs to the attic, where he replaced the gun in the case. He went back downstairs and was passing through the kitchen when the phone rang. It was Buddy senior. He was angry because Peggy had called him at work and complained about Buddy junior. Buddy senior wanted to know why his son was not at school.

"What the hell is going on?" he demanded.

"I just shot mommy," the boy said.

Buddy senior told his son to call the police, and then raced to his car. Moments after his father hung up, Buddy junior dialed 911.

"Can I have the police? I just shot mother," he said.

Buddy gave his address and told the 911 operator to "send somebody quick" and that he shot his mother "in the mid section of the body."

Buddy hung up the phone, headed out the door and was walking briskly out of the driveway when the first police officer drove up and grabbed him.

Stanley Kosinski, on the day he interviewed Buddy junior, was a twenty-two-year police veteran with the last twelve years as a plainclothes investigator. He had worked on more than five hundred cases, including sixty homicides, none of which had gone unsolved. Some of his investigations brought him before the network cameras of NBC and 60 Minutes. When he was assigned to Buddy's case, he drove to the family home to canvas the shooting scene. By the time Kosinski arrived, Buddy's mother was already in the hospital. As the investigator moved through Buddy's home, a comfortably furnished two-story frame house in a posh neighborhood, other police officers were already in the attic taking pictures of the gun case that held the .41-caliber Magnum. In the closet in Buddy's parents' bedroom, they found more than a half-dozen boxes of cartridges for rifles and shotguns and 210-grain soft-point bullets for the Magnum. On one box of ammunition, printed in bold letters: KEEP OUT OF THE REACH OF CHILDREN.

Kosinski did not stay long. He familiarized himself with the layout of the home and talked briefly with some other police officers there.

When he drove to police headquarters to interview Buddy, he remembered that Peggy was an old schoolmate.

The investigator met Buddy in an interview room at police headquarters. He told the boy that his mother was in serious condition and that she might die. He then advised Buddy of his legal rights and asked him if he would like to talk. They talked about how much he disliked school and how he did not like the psychiatrist his parents had insisted that he see.

Why didn't he want to talk to a doctor who might be able to help him? Kosinski asked.

"Because," Buddy said, "he told me that to get rid of my frustrations, I should go get laid. It embarrassed me. . . . I didn't want mother dealing with it."

The psychiatrist had embarrassed the boy by asking him questions about sex: Have you ever had sex with your girlfriends? How many girlfriends have you had? Have you ever seen your mother naked when she went to the bathroom?

While Buddy was being questioned by Kosinski, a second police officer walked into the room and asked the investigator to step outside. Kosinski left the room while Buddy munched on pizza and guzzled Coke. When the investigator returned, he calmly told Buddy that his mother had died. And as calmly as the police officer had told him about his mother's death, Buddy asked, "Can I have another slice of pizza?"

Later that day, an attorney, who was a neighbor and family friend hired by Buddy senior to represent his son, showed up at police headquarters. Before he left, he told the police not to question his client anymore. He also said, "I don't believe this case is ever going to trial."

After his arraignment, Kosinski accompanied Buddy junior to the juvenile facility where he would be held without bail while his case proceeded through court. As they rode in a van and were chatting, Kosinski asked Buddy why he had shot his mother with a .41-caliber Magnum. Kosinski told him that his father had other guns in the house, and asked why he hadn't used some other weapon, like a shotgun or rifle. Why, he asked, go up into the attic and choose the big handgun? Buddy told him he could have used a shotgun, but he might have killed his mother right away when he shot her. He used the handgun and shot her in the stomach because he wanted to make her suffer.

Buddy's explanation was another savory morsel of information to be heaped on a mountain of collected facts, allegations, and impressions that would portray him as a remorseless, cold-blooded killer. He was thirteen years old. In a local newspaper the next day, Buddy senior was quoted talking about "fisticuffs" and increasing violence from his son days before he shot his mother. Buddy senior said the shooting had been "premeditated." He told a reporter that he "had hidden the gun in the attic and had hidden the ammunition" in a completely separate part of the house. His son, he said, must have searched the whole attic. He also complained of drugs. "Whether he's so bent out of shape from drugs, I don't know," Buddy senior said. "It got to the point where he had no emotions in him whatsoever." Buddy junior's attorney was quoted as saying that his client did not realize "what death is." The police later contacted the boy's doctor, a professor at a local college, but he refused to talk to them about Buddy. He told police that his discussions with the boy were privileged doctor-patient information. He also said that he had destroyed the tape of Peggy's call to his office the day she was shot.

At forty-three, Kosinski was a portly, soft-spoken police officer. He had a broad nose, brown hair streaked with gray, and an avuncular manner that made it easy to talk to him. In an interview, he showed class photographs of himself and Peggy in grade school and high school.

"I knew her father and mother well, and we all went to the same church," he said. "She was a pleasant girl in school."

Buddy junior, he recalled, was a troubled youth.

"He had a lot of problems emotionally," he said. "I don't think he knew how to cry."

Kosinski thought the problems stemmed from the boy's not wanting to go to school. Although Buddy had shot his mother, Kosinski believed Buddy's real problem was with his father. Every time Buddy senior appeared in court for his son's hearings, the security guards and bailiffs were instructed to keep him under tight scrutiny, Kosinski explained. The police and the district attorney's office were worried that he might try to harm his son. Kosinski did not believe that Buddy junior's problems had been caused by drugs. He reiterated that the boy's emotional turmoil was connected with his father. Of course, that did not explain why he had shot his mother.

In custody, Buddy was mild-mannered and accommodating. When Kosinski took the young boy to one of his court hearings, some bailiffs were concerned because Buddy was not handcuffed.

"The policy of the department is that everyone [under arrest] is handcuffed, but they give you your own discretion," he said. "Buddy never hurt me, and I didn't want any problems. Why make a person violent if he isn't?"

Once when the youth was handcuffed, he demonstrated to the police how he could get free by picking the lock and removing the cuffs.

For several weeks after the arrest, Buddy senior called the prosecutor's office, but not to discuss his son's case. He wanted to know when his guns would be returned to him. On the day of the shooting, the police had confiscated the .41-caliber Magnum and all of the other guns in the house, even though Buddy senior had registered every one. After his son was sentenced, Buddy senior, a member of a gun club, again requested that his guns be returned. The police told him that they would hold on to his guns until after his son's appeal. It was departmental policy. Buddy senior wrote a letter stating that in order to get his guns returned he would not file an appeal. When the police received the letter, they returned the guns. This was also the main reason that Kosinski was allowed to be interviewed.

"Guns used in murder-suicide cases, people rarely want the guns back," Kosinski remarked. "It's unusual, unusual. It's his gun. He has a right to it. But I wouldn't want the damn thing back if my kid had killed my wife with it."

Buddy senior did not want to be interviewed, but there were others who remembered Buddy junior. Some neighbors remembered the young boy as a wild little demon who was always fighting with the neighborhood kids when he was growing up. There was nothing, as far as they were concerned, that he could do right. In school, he was the bête noire of his teachers when he was not cutting their classes. There were others, however, who saw something more than a pint-size rogue. For one teacher, he was a sensitive young boy with a nice artistic touch.

"He was always very gentle, always well dressed and his hair was

nicely combed. He was always set apart from the rest," she recalled.
"There were some kids who were unruly. He wasn't rude; he wasn't
conniving."

But he was the class pariah.

"He didn't get along with the rest of the boys and seemed to be
oblivious to their abuse. He liked to sit with the girls; he got along
with them better."

There were times, however, when he infuriated her.

"I would get angry with him at times. He would be hopping along
in class. It would look like he was in a daze. He wasn't involved but
he never got angry when I scolded him. There's more freedom in the
art room. It's less regimented, and then I only saw the best part of
him."

However, this teacher noted that other teachers constantly had
problems with him in class. There was also one big contretemps involving Buddy in her class. It was a day when Peggy came to school.

"She was complaining that one of the students deliberately
smeared Magic Marker on a custom-made shirt of Buddy's," the
teacher said. "He was always impeccably dressed, with his hair crop-
ped close and not a strand out of place. Anyway, evidently one of the
more rambunctious little boys in the class had put three small drops
of Magic Marker on Buddy's shirt, and his mother complained that
she had tried to have it washed out and couldn't and now wanted to
be reimbursed. I called the boy in and the whole class was for the
boy. She was livid, and she was so embarrassing, making it an issue.
The mother of the boy came in and asked to take the shirt home. She
returned the next day and had washed or rinsed the ink out of the
shirt."

She remembered that Buddy, during this entire episode, always
had a "blank expression on his face. He showed no emotion. He was
oblivious to what happened, even though the kids were complaining
against him."

"He was such a nice boy," she recalled. "Always well dressed and
his hair was nicely combed. I don't see how he has a chance now.
It's almost impossible for me to believe he could make it even with
help. How can he ever be rehabilitated? Even under ideal conditions,
how can he ever be released?"

There were others who worried about his rehabilitation. They had
witnessed his passage from cradle to jail, and they were wracked by

confusion and ambivalence because they had not helped him when he needed it most.

"I was in their house one time at Christmas," said a neighbor who had lived in the area for almost twenty years. "I always gave them a Christmas or birthday gift, so I came in to give the baby a gift. He must have been about two years old at the time. He was a toddler. He was excited about the present and was grabbing his father's pants leg to get his attention while the father was talking to me. His father picked up the kid with one hand, say his left hand, and socked him with the right and the kid landed across the whole length of the living room on top of the staircase. Cracked him right across the head, and the kid went flying through the air and landed on those two steps that start the staircase. I gave out a scream. I can remember it like it was yesterday, and Peggy rushed over and picked up the kid and saw that he was all right, and of course the kid was screaming. And I said, 'I can't stay here to watch this stuff,' and I walked out. I came home and cried. I was just so upset and inconsolable that a kid could have to go through that stuff from those crazy bastards."

It was the only time she ever saw Buddy hit, but on other occasions, on summery evenings when she sat on her porch, she would grimace from the sounds emitted from the house.

"I could hear outside what was going on in their house," she recalled. "The screaming and carrying on. You knew the kid was being hit."

How could she be so certain?

"You could hear it—you could hear the smacks," she said.

When?

"Well . . . those early years, two to ten," she said. "That's only sitting on the porch, which was coincidental."

Why didn't she speak up for Buddy or call the police or at least report the beatings anonymously?

"Do you understand . . . the fear? I really and truly love little Buddy but my fear is greater than my love. Scared. Scared out of my mind that the father would come after me with his gun. To this day, to this minute, afraid to open my mouth. Why should I step in and jeopardize my family, my life, for those people who are really strangers to me? I'm scared to death of that man and his guns."

When the family first moved into the neighborhood, Buddy senior, a skilled craftsman and engineer, made a sign and placed it in front of his home. He painted it white, with black letters with the family name on it. The day that Buddy junior was arrested, the sign attracted the electronic eye of TV news crews covering the shooting. Neighbors complained to Buddy senior that he should take the sign down. It was drawing too much attention. People were driving down the block looking for the house where the murder had been committed, and the sign was a beacon that told them they had found it. The sign was a cherished icon: It was his wooden likeness of a gun. But it finally came down.

Several years before that, Buddy senior had tired of the pranks played by some of the neighborhood youths who traipsed down the block on Halloween and grabbed pumpkins from front porches and smashed them in the street.

"Big Buddy had enough of that," the neighbor recalled. "He was going to fix those kids and teach them a thing or two. He tied a string on to his pumpkin and he sat in the chair right in front of the front door in the living room where he wasn't really seen, and as soon as he felt them tugging on the pumpkin he jumps up with a big gun and goes tear-assing, chasing them down the street. The kids ran into the woods when they heard him hollering and shooting the gun. I came running out of my house when I heard the gunshots. He was shooting at them for stealing the pumpkins."

No one was hurt.

"How do you stand up to a guy with a gun in his hand?" she asked. "He used a big rifle. You get scared, so you ignore it. Years later when I mentioned it, when I had enough nerve to mention it to him, when I had enough nerve to say anything about the whole incident, he said, 'Ah, ah, it wasn't real bullets.'"

She did not believe him, but despite her fears, she tried to help Buddy junior.

"I begged the lawyer at the funeral chapel to call me," she said. "I gave him my business card with my business phone and home phone. I told him to please get in touch with me. I wanted to discuss the case with him and help little Buddy."

The lawyer never contacted her. She hoped that the newspaper or TV reporters would return to do follow-up stories. She had been away from home during the early part of the day when Buddy was arrested, and did not get in until after the police and reporters left.

But no one ever returned, or if the reporters did make one last sweep through the neighborhood, they did not stop at her house.

"My husband is one of those guys who says don't get involved, stay out of it, mind your business," she said. "I was surprised he agreed to let me talk to you. I put it in such a way that we wouldn't be just helping little Buddy, we would be helping so many other kids. He couldn't refuse me."

She had been in touch with Buddy several times, and the first time they talked after his arrest, she asked him why he never ran away instead of shooting.

"Why didn't you get on a train and go to New York?" she remembered asking. "He says, 'I've never been into New York. I wouldn't even know how to get there. I've never seen the city. Besides which, I would have to use my bicycle because I would be afraid to use the money on a bus.' I said, 'What do you mean? What are you saving it for? When you're running away, you don't look to save money.'"

That frugal clinging to pennies, imbued by parents who, she said, insisted that Buddy contribute to his food and clothing, might have saved his life. New York's bright lights lure runaways like flames beckoning moths. Buddy would have had just as good a chance of eluding his parents and surviving on his own if he had dashed down a throughway express lane at rush hour. With luck, some driver might have stopped to offer a lift, or at the very least called the police to remove his body. Someone in New York might have offered to help too—a policeman, for example, who would have returned him home, or some dapper, smooth-talking, sweet-smiling pedophile. This breed sweeps the train and bus stations and sidewalks for runaway children as well as any of New York's finest. Buddy, who was not faring well in school or at home, would not have survived on the streets of a big city. He had never developed street smarts in his own neighborhood. At thirteen, his parents did not give him permission to ride his bike any farther than the block where he lived. He was bound to them body and soul. He found his freedom in skipping classes or in riding away on his bike, ignoring the injunctions to keep on the block or in front of his house. When he was not peddling away from home, he worked for pocket money.

"That kid use to cut my lawn," said another neighbor, who described Buddy as "good boy. He was conscientious about money. He always did a good job."

Just talking about Buddy's industriousness or his "niceness" prompted neighbors to share vignettes. This neighbor too had known Buddy from the time he was born and thought his parents were "too strict . . . too severe."

"One day I saw them in the driveway. It was Saturday. Buddy had lost the keys to the garage door, and his father was so enraged . . ." said the neighbor, who then faltered and stumbled as he tried to explain what he had witnessed.

Buddy senior was cursing his son, but it was worse than cursing. His threats conveyed unimaginable harm. The neighbor gesticulated in an awkward pantomine of Buddy senior's gesticulations that day. The neighbor, who claimed he was not afraid to say what was on his mind, who also talked about having a good-size temper himself, who was not above cursing his own son, said he had cringed from what he saw and heard that day. It defied description.

"He acted like a maniac" was the way he finally summarized Buddy senior's actions. "[Buddy junior's mother] protected him because of the father. When she called him a son of a bitch, it wasn't the same. I'm not out to hurt his father or get my name in the newspapers or a book. But I do feel that there is an injustice being done to this boy by the father and the law."

Kids as young as thirteen can be charged with second-degree murder and prosecuted as adults where Buddy lived. Buddy junior was indicted but he never went to trial. He pleaded guilty to the maximum and received the maximum sentence. He was sent to a juvenile facility where he could be held until he was twenty-one, when he could be transferred to an adult prison. His sentence, nine years to life, made him eligible for parole when he turned twenty-two, but his parole could be denied. It is unusual for defendants to plead guilty without going to trial when they know they will not receive a reduced sentence or a plea-bargaining arrangement. Unless, of course, their lawyers suggest that they surrender their right to a trial, and they are too naive, dumb, mentally impaired, or young to understand what is happening to them. So why did Buddy plead guilty to the max?

"I don't know," he told me. "At the moment I didn't know what I was doing. I was so nervous . . . putting up with a bunch of people I didn't know, telling them about my entire life. My lawyer was telling me what to say. . . . He told me what was going on, something like we might be able to get into the judge's quarters, but it didn't wind up that way. He talked to me about six times."

It was not clear in the interview how much his lawyer had explained or how much he understood. He had, however, a nagging suspicion that his lawyer was working more for his father's interests than his own.

"This guy worked for my father. My father doesn't want me on the streets. Everybody else supposed to be on my side was working with my father. It was like every day I called my father, the lawyer was right there. I got the idea that my father was trying to get me the maximum. He wants to keep me in. Says I'm a threat to society. The lawyer said a jury trial would be a waste of time. He said, 'Um, if we can't plea-bargain for nothing else, might as well go ahead and plead to the maximum.'"

In the juvenile facility where Buddy was incarcerated, the staff after a year or so was impressed enough with his conduct to give him a job working on a building and maintenance crew. Buddy showed a gift of special hands. He could fix almost anything ever assembled by other human hands, including radios, TV sets, stereo components, automobile engines, and other mechanical contraptions. The staff often brought in things for Buddy to fix. He had picked up his gift from his father, though he shrugged it off as no big deal.

"I pick up most of it from watching people," he said. "I used to help some of my friends fix cars. So I guess I just learned that way."

Buddy was earning seventy-five cents an hour from his maintenance job, and working kept him satisfied and relaxed. He needed the money for personal things because he rarely got anything from his father. Buddy senior rarely called and had visited him only twice. On his first trip, he cursed Buddy junior loudly in the visiting room and told his son he was going to kill him. He also threatened the staff members if they ever let his son out. The threats were harsh enough for the facility to change its rules for allowing visitors to see Buddy. The staff did not like to talk about it, and the facility, by rule, was not even allowed to admit that Buddy was there. Buddy had just turned fifteen when he was interviewed. He did not like talking about the shooting.

"I don't like discussing it with anybody," he said. "I haven't met anyone to talk about it with. I talked to my lawyer about it briefly."

Though Buddy could not talk about why he had shot his mother,

he could talk about other circumstances of that day. He said he had
been on speed and cocaine.

"I took them as soon as I got up. I had a hangover from the last
night," he explained.

He had started taking drugs when he was about eleven or twelve,
he said, because they helped him to "slip into my own world and
have nothing bother me. My parents bothered me a lot and some of
my schoolteachers."

He got the drugs from older kids—sixteen, seventeen, eighteen—
whom he hung out with, and he took their word that he was using
opium, marijuana, cocaine, LSD, and more. He could not verify
what he had been taking, but he claimed it did the trick in getting
him away from the real world of home and school.

"Nothing was happening to me mentally and physically," he said,
describing his drug-induced reveries. "I was trying to get away."

His escapes did not go completely unnoticed.

"I would stay out three or four hours until the effect wore off then
hang out another two hours and then go home. My mother knew I
was taking drugs but she never got on my ass about it, you know.
She just said, 'You know what it does to you,' and I said 'Yeah,' and
she said, 'I want you to stop it this very minute,' and I said, 'Yeah,'
and then I just went about my business."

Some of the things he wanted to escape, he recalled, had started
when he was about five. It could have been earlier; he could not be
sure. But he remembered he had been about five when his father
was pounding on him.

"He loved throwing me into walls," he said. "He would push me
into the walls hard." His mother hit him too but not as hard or as
often as his father. Buddy senior, he said, struck him on the head,
body, legs, and arms.

What had he done to provoke his father? He had cursed his
mother. He was around eleven, maybe ten, when he cursed his
mother as much as she cursed him. So if he was cursing his mother
when he was older, what had he done to provoke his parents when
he was five, six, seven? There was a long pause before he answered.

"I knew I was doing something to provoke it, but what, I wasn't
sure," he said. "[Several years] later I wouldn't do my homework, go
out and stay out too late."

From the time he was young, they battled over food. His family ate
fish almost seven days a week at lunch and dinner and occasionally at

breakfast. On the weekends during the summer, his parents fished from their boat and later froze the fish at home. They made him sit at the table, when he was younger and less menacing, until he ate the food on his plate. After a few hours, they would take away the food but it would be there waiting on his plate later.

"That's why I started staying out later . . . to keep from eating dinner," he said.

The food conflicts, however, were only some of the factors that prompted him to stray from home and seek camaraderie with older kids.

"That's all I hung out with. I couldn't get along with kids who were the same age as me. I don't know why. Like they were the child and I was almost an adult. I've been hanging around adults all my life," he said.

He fought so many battles with the young kids in his upper-middle-class neighborhood and at school that he pretty much alienated himself from anyone his age. He never had friends over to his house, and rarely was allowed to visit the home of anyone else. Palling around was never part of his childhood. At home he was expected to be quiet. "Children should be seen and not heard," that figurative adage of some parents, was a real-life dictum of his home, his father frequently reminded neighbors. Buddy was expected to keep his mouth shut or else. None of the five psychiatrists who he says have examined him ever asked if he had been beaten. One, however, asked if his parents screamed at him a lot, Buddy said.

Buddy talked a little about why he appeared to be more angry at his mother, who beat and yelled at him less than his father. Peggy was the one who always told his father when he did something wrong. Peggy snitched, and his father disciplined. The week before she died, Buddy junior threatened to kill both of them. By then, Peggy could no longer tolerate the truancy and the drugs.

"And that's one of the reasons she took me to court and . . . started getting me to see a shrink," he said, "because of drugs."

It was also possible that she was afraid of him. Placing him under court supervision seemed the only answer.

"What started it all was that I tried to break into my own house," he said. "My mother opened the door but she wouldn't let me back in. She told me to go to school, and then she shut the door so I said the hell with it. We had a wooden front door with a stained glass window in it, and once you break through the stained glass you're home free. I just punched in the glass."

He also punched his mother about then, a week before the shooting. It was not the first time he had hit her. She had concealed the drug use from his father, but Buddy senior was becoming suspicious. It was all beginning to reach a critical mass that week when a neighbor on a brief visit thought she was witnessing convivial family warmth. She never heard his threats to kill his mother and father. A few days later Peggy was dead.

Buddy wanted me to be sure to tell people that cocaine and speed had affected his mind so much that he had killed his mother. He did not want anyone to think that he was a cold-blooded murderer. His father also told reporters that drugs were responsible for twisting his son's mind. Drugs might have been a factor, but they were not the reason Buddy got out his father's favorite gun and shot his mother. When I began researching this case, I visited the district attorney's office and talked with a prosecuting attorney who had not worked on the case but was familiar with it. When I asked about the motive for the killing and the cause of the conflict between Buddy and his mother, he suggested that I should not spend a great deal of time trying to discover the problem between them. The problem, he said, was with the father. When I asked what he meant, he said I would understand when I met the father.

When I eventually met the prosecuting attorney who had actually handled Buddy's case, he refused to discuss specifics with me but said he would not object if I talked to Kosinski. The veteran police officer got permission from his superiors to talk to me only because of the letter Buddy's father had sent to the police department, saying he would not appeal his son's conviction and please return his guns. Kosinski summed up the tragedy with two explanations. One, he said, was guns in the house. The other was Buddy's problem with his father. When I asked him to explain the latter point, he said I should talk with the father and then I would understand.

I sent Buddy senior a letter (which was never answered) and visited the family's neighborhood. A few neighbors offered varying accounts of what they had witnessed or heard over the twenty years or more they had known the family. Buddy junior's problem, they said, was with his father.

It was difficult for them to understand why Buddy had shot his mother and not his father. I thought it was possible that Buddy might have shot anyone who had walked into the kitchen that morning in 1982. For an abused kid, a simple threat or admonishment can trigger an uncontrollable rage that has been building up for years. Investigations of the root causes of parricides involving kids as young as Buddy invariably reveal a pattern of severe physical or psychological abuse or both. In another state there might have been an attempt to send Buddy someplace other than into a prison environment so that he might be helped along the road to rehabilitation. But in Buddy's state, when a kid as young as he is convicted of murder, rehabilitation is not the goal.

When the staff members of the juvenile facility learned that I was interviewing Buddy, their shock and panic reverberated all the way to youth-division headquarters in the state capital. Under the law, they could do nothing legally to stop him from talking with me, but they held urgent meetings with their superiors to discuss the unexpected intrusion. Because the facility had followed all procedures and regulations regarding Buddy's contacts with outsiders, no negligence was found and no one was blamed for any breach of division policy. So they had little choice but to tolerate my occasional contacts with Buddy. But they also decided not to notify his father. They did not want a repeat performance of his first visit to the facility.

After I told them what I had learned and suspected, particularly regarding the way his defense had been handled, a youth official tried to contact Buddy's lawyer. Buddy tried also. Under state law, appeals have to be filed within a year of the first trial, and Buddy was running out of time. When his lawyer could not be located, an appeal was filed by an attorney of the youth division just a day or so before the expiration date.

Of course, Buddy's legal status should have been reviewed when he was incarcerated, but it was overlooked by an overworked staff. And no one had expected to carry the ball for Buddy's attorney.

Sometime after the appeal was filed, the youth division ordered a psychiatric examination for Buddy and then tried to commit him to a psychiatric hospital. I was told that the action had been prompted by my contact with Buddy, but that the division was not acting vindictively. However, I was not reassured. I did not doubt that Buddy needed intense therapy, but I was suspicious because the division had waited almost a year before it suddenly decided to address his needs. It was not acting in his best interests but instead was trying to cover up its negligence in handling him, and because of that I was concerned about what was best for him.

It has to be mentioned that the staff of the juvenile facility opposed Buddy's commitment because it believed he was better off where he was. But I doubted that as well. While researching this book, I learned that abused kids like Buddy need intense therapy as soon as possible if there is to be any hope of their ever leading normal lives. Buddy was not receiving any therapy in the facility. He was not even meeting occasionally with the staff psychologist. While it might have appeared that hospitalization was best for him, the motivation behind the decision to commit him has to be questioned. Was hospitalization really in Buddy's best interests? Or would it somehow work out in his best interests? I could find no answers.

Just about the time commitment proceedings against Buddy were beginning, a higher court granted his request to appeal, and the youth division then suspended its actions.

Several attorneys whom I consulted about his case said they believed that he stood a good chance of receiving at least a reduced sentence because of the way his defense had been handled. In one sense that was good news, but on the other hand Buddy still needed the kind of therapy that unfortunately is available only in the best hospitals in the country for disturbed adolescents who are violent.

Buddy has a laconic manner. No one really bothered him at the facility, he said, and he did not bother anyone. He was cool, calm, he said. He would have liked to be able to go off the grounds of the facility, as some of the other kids did, for various outings. But he is a man-child convicted of a serious crime and he has to remain under tight security until he is twenty-one. Then the state can move him to an adult prison, where he will mix with some real criminals and maybe learn a few tricks that he can use when he gets outside.

On some days Buddy spent an inordinate amount of time sleeping, and the staff, I was told, was always watching out for signs of serious depression. He had been placed on a suicide watch after he was first arrested, and staff members a year later still kept an eye on him just in case. He once joked about killing himself, and their reaction startled him so much that he decided not to joke anymore about taking his life. And so far he has not talked with anyone about why he killed his mother.

# PART II

## Defending Battered Kids

# 9

# The Battered-Child Defense

Her parents had been separated for a few years, and since her mom was spending more time with her new live-in boyfriend, there were times when the girl needed to be with her father. One day she walked the mile or so to his house and decided to stay the night. Early the next morning she was jarred awake. Her father had crept into the room and climbed on top of her. When she opened her eyes, he was trying to stick his penis into her mouth. She shoved him off, grabbed her clothes, and fled. Unnerved and crying, she suddenly became angry and sprinted as fast as she could back to her home. Once inside, she found the gun her mom's boyfriend kept in the house. She grabbed the revolver and headed back to her father's home.

At fifteen, she had made one of the biggest decisions in her life: She was going to kill her father. On the way to her father's house she told herself over and over and over again how she was going to blow him away. But she spent much of her fury before she ever reached the house, and after a while killing him did not seem so important. In fact, shooting him just did not sound like it would be worth all of the problems his death would cause her. She turned around and headed back home, not knowing that her mother had called the police and told them her daughter had stolen her boyfriend's gun. A police officer spotted her walking down the road with the gun and arrested her. She was charged with criminal possession of stolen property. But she told her mother, a probation officer, and her lawyer what her father had tried to do to her. That was why she had taken the gun, but she changed her mind, she told them.

The attack by her father was never mentioned in court, and she was remanded to a correctional center. She sat there until a lawyer named Paul Mones showed up to try to get her out. She became one of the numerous anecdotes Mones would carry with him from his days as a juvenile advocate in West Virginia.

"When she told me no one ever said anything about what her father tried to do," Mones said in an interview, "I called up her probation officer and she said, 'Oh, yeah, it wasn't mentioned because the girl was loose anyway.' Which is my way of describing the juvenile justice system in the United States, which is also my way of explaining how I got interested in this area of abuse and delinquency, where we take kids who are victims of severe abuse and we make them the accused. It happens in the delinquency area, and it happens in the abused-child area. When I testified before the Senate's 1983 judiciary subcommittee on juvenile justice, there were people coming in from Montana saying that authorities were locking up kids in the county jails because they have to get the kids out of the house."

In the five years he worked in West Virginia, Mones estimated he had represented more than five hundred kids on a variety of offenses, from running away and skipping school, to burglary and felonious assault, to rape and murder. He started with a local legal-services office after he graduated from law school and then headed Juvenile Advocates, a federally funded agency. Mones's job was to keep kids from being locked in jail and to see that alternatives were developed for their treatment and rehabilitation. He had first become involved with kids as an undergraduate living in Buffalo, New York, where he worked with families who had been evicted from their apartments because of their kids' actions. When he arrived in West Virginia, he estimated that more than six hundred kids per year were going to jail. When he left Juvenile Advocates the number had dropped below forty. While also working to teach various agencies and authorities alternatives to sending kids to jail, he slowly became immersed in the area of children's rights, which includes providing legal support and advice to emotionally disturbed children in mental institutions and handicapped children who need special education. It was these involvements that guided him into the area of child abuse and neglect.

"There are two types of attorneys who work in the juvenile area: those who work in the child abuse, child protection area, and those who work in the delinquency area," he explained. "I've found that there are few attorneys in the country working on the relationship between both issues. There are several doctors and psychologists who have gotten involved in the relationship between abuse and delinquency but the area heretofore was not explored by the legal community. There are no law review articles on it. There is very, very little done in the area."

He had just started researching the relationship between child abuse and delinquency when he came across the Jerry Ball case. Jerry was a starting player on his Babe Ruth baseball team. At sixteen, he was quiet and reserved but had a lot of friends. He worked as a youth fellow at his local Baptist church and was a good student and played in his high school band. He was a nice kid. One day he was standing in his house and holding his baseball bat when his mother lit into him. She was eating pizza.

"I had my baseball bat, and I was standing around holding it," he told state police. "Then my mom started cussing me and stuff. I got mad and swung the bat at my mother and hit her in the head with it. Then I hit my dad with the bat. Then I hit my brothers [one eleven, the other six] in the head with the bat. Then after that they all started moaning and stuff. I then hit them all again. I hit all of them four or five times more than that. I didn't count. Then after that I dragged them all into my parents' bedroom."

He called a friend and told him what he had done, and while the friend was expressing his disbelief, Jerry heard his mother moaning. He told the friend to excuse him while he went to take care of some unfinished business. He took his father's .22-caliber rifle and shot his mother in the head and then went back to the telephone to talk to his buddy. His buddy still did not believe him, so Jerry took his father's truck and drove over to his friend's house. They rode around for a while, and then Jerry took him back to the house so that he could see for himself that Jerry was telling the truth. Jerry was charged with four counts of first-degree murder.

The neighbors and Jerry's coaches insisted to reporters that he was a nice kid. Jerry had never been in trouble with the law, and the police had ruled out drugs and alcohol as causes for his violent behavior. When they questioned him, he spoke lucidly and without hesitation. There was no apparent motive. Mones joined Lee Adler, Jerry's court-appointed attorney, in developing a defense.

"It was my responsibility to try to look into the relationship between the abuse and the act itself, for possible use as a self-defense strategy," Mones said. "One of the first things I did was call Jim Barrett, who defended Richie Jahnke in Wyoming."

That case, discussed earlier, is one of the most celebrated of a battered child striking out against an abusive, destructive parent. Jahnke, sixteen, and his sister, seventeen, after years and years of beatings and torment, ambushed their father outside his Cheyenne, Wyoming, home in November of 1982. Richie, charged with second-degree murder, was found guilty of first-degree manslaughter. He was sentenced to a five- to fifteen-year stretch in prison but the governor commuted his sentence after a public outcry.

In Jerry's case, Adler initially tried to introduce evidence of abuse as a means of keeping their case in juvenile court. The prosecuting attorney, whose investigation had revealed to him no evidence of any extenuating circumstances, wanted Jerry tried in adult court.

"The basic legal theory is that if the child is abused, if he commits murder, the abuse itself is something which can place the child in a category that is uniquely that of a juvenile. That is, the child who is abused and kills is basically a delinquent who can be treated as an abused child," Mones said. "We urge that they [delinquents] not be treated as an adult in criminal court . . . basically have them treated within a rehabilitative context of juvenile court. Juvenile court is supposed to be rehabilitative, whereas with adults it's pretty clear that punishment is at least the putative goal."

They were unsuccessful in convincing the court that Jerry should stay in juvenile court, and the West Virginia Supreme Court unanimously rejected an appeal. It was decided then that Adler would handle the litigation while Mones researched the parricide issue and tried to find expert witnesses—psychologists and psychiatrists—to testify for the defense. Mones noticed a dearth of written research, though several psychiatrists around the country were working in the area.

One of the best explanations for why some children kill parents was found in a 1962 article in *Social Research* by Dr. Douglas Sargent, a professor at Michigan State University, who was director of a child study clinic for Michigan juvenile court. His theory: ". . . sometimes the child who kills is acting as the unwitting lethal agent of an adult [usually a parent] who unconsciously prompts the child to kill so that he can vicariously enjoy the benefits of the act." He offered two corollaries: ". . . the adult plays upon the latent currents of hostility the child feels toward the victim—hostility which, without the adult's provocation and the child's special susceptibility to it, probably would remain inoperative and under the control of the child's ego; and second, that the child's susceptibility to, and readiness to act upon, the unconscious prompting of the adult rests upon the immaturity of the child's ego and the presence of a special emotional bond between the child and the adult."

Sargent cited several cases as examples. One involved Ernest, three and a half, who not only fractured his eight-year-old brother's skull with a bottle but torched another baby's crib and poisoned his milk as well. Ernest also hammered a neighbor's kid with a baseball bat, urinated in his sister's face, broke a puppy's leg, killed animals, and "left the house at dawn in his bare feet in midwinter and walked down to a nearby river, and so forth." Sometime after he was taken out of his house and hospitalized, Sargent wrote, a doctor reported that he was "probably less of a behavior problem during his stay in the hospital than any other patient we have ever had." The other cases involved a son who avenged his father by killing his mother's lover, and two parricides, both involving kids abused by their fathers. One especially stands out.

Art and his brother were frequently forced by their mother to stay with her ex-husband, who often threatened and beat them. He developed a delusion that he was Jesus Christ and believed he was going to die at the same age as Christ—thirty-three and a half. One day, after they had been threatened again with a beating, the two brothers were outside playing when they decided to amuse themselves by playing with their father's gun. Art, the older, decided they should load the gun and shoot their father. Standing thirty feet away, and as his father read the Bible, Art shot once, killing him. The father was thirty-three and a half when he died. Art was eight, his brother seven. Sargent's conclusion, because the father had not only taught his sons to shoot but said he believed he was going to die by their hands, was that "Art's father, in order to fulfill the requirement of his religious delusion, managed to commit suicide by provoking his children to kill him." The mother had also contributed, through her frequently expressed wish that her ex would die. Art's father's death was more than just an individual event. It was a family affair.

As he researched almost a dozen cases of matricide and patricide across the country, Mones found himself investigating cases of battered women who had killed their husbands and lovers, and claimed self-defense. There are strong similarities between battered women who are forced to kill abusive spouses and lovers, and battered kids who slay their parents. And Mones and Adler incorporated elements in their defense strategy based on the "battered-woman syndrome." Testimony by experts about the syndrome has been introduced into a number of trials to explain the behavior and actions of chronically abused women who killed their tormentors. Lower courts, according to a *New York Times* article, have increasingly upheld the use of such testimony. But Jerry never went to trial.

"What happened with Jerry was unique," Mones claimed. "He pled guilty to four counts of first-degree murder. The plea included a recommendation for mercy, which the judge accepted. First-degree murder without mercy in West Virginia is punishable by life in prison." Mones and Adler hoped that the testimony by their medical experts would persuade the court to give a sentence that stressed rehabilitation, such as a minimum of ten years but not in an adult prison.

One doctor was Shervert Frazier, an expert on parricide who was clinical director of McLean Hospital in Boston at the time of the trial. He was later appointed director of the National Institute of Mental Health. The second expert was Ronald Ebert, a psychiatrist at McLean. They both testified that Jerry was a kid who had suffered severe abuse, which triggered the murders.

"It is not clear how it was triggered by the abuse," Mones said. "It is a unique decision because after he pled guilty he was treated at McLean Hospital for several weeks."

Prior to being sent to the Boston hospital, Jerry was also seen by a psychologist whose research and study usually focused on women who had killed their spouses. She too said Jerry had been abused since his birth, and described him as a "nice kid" whose family life had been permeated with violence.

"His parents beat the shit out of him," she said. "After he pled guilty to murder, people started coming out of the woodwork with tales about how he had been mistreated by his parents."

One of the many things that they recalled was that Jerry had worn long-sleeved shirts in the summer to conceal bruises on his body. Despite the beatings, his easygoing manner endeared him to his friends, and he rarely expressed any real anger until that day in January 1983 when he started swinging the baseball bat and couldn't stop. He mowed down everyone in his way. However, he was later sorry that he had killed his six-year-old brother, who had never really done anything to him.

"He hit him to shut him up," the psychologist said. "His brother was screaming." After Jerry was treated in Boston, Dr. Frazier wrote a report to the court and described some of the inner workings of a family that neighbors considered a normal nuclear unit. Jerry's mother had been psychotic and frequently exploded in violent outbursts against her sons. She described herself to acquaintances as "out of control," alternating between deep depression and rage and abuse. Jerry's father was hooked on either drugs or alcohol and abused the entire family. Despite all this, Jerry believed he had had a normal upbringing and tended to minimize the abuse and his family's pathology. "He continues to refer to his family in the present and denies the murders and has great difficulty dealing with his actions," Frazier wrote. Jerry, he told the court, wanted to kill himself and would be suicidal for the next few years. He had olfactory hallucinations (he smelled burning bread), which stemmed from brain damage caused by the beatings from his parents. Frazier wrote that the lesions on Jerry's brain were "not of sufficient intensity to be connected to the murders. Rather, the murders are clearly connected to the rage built up over many years. His early humiliations, his long-standing mental illness, schizophrenia, and his immaturity in the context of a violent and abusing family lead naturally to his ultimate aggression. He needs to be in a closed hospital-like setting with treatment from three to five years of intense therapy." A final decision on Jerry's sentence was pending.

The popular perceptions of parricide have been shaped by spurious claims and depictions of bizarre youths and by fatuous opinions masquerading as empirical observations and facts. "Many of these are children who are not necessarily victims of child abuse, but sometimes just benign neglect," one doctor was quoted as saying in a 1982 *New York Daily News* article. "They are rebelling against the authority in their lives, for having been ignored, for being unimportant." In that article—"Blood Ties or Bad Blood: Kids Who Kill Parents"—the reporter cited about a half-dozen cases of teenage and adult sons and daughters who had killed parents. But benign neglect had little to do with many of these homicides. In one case, a twenty-one-year-old daughter who had been arrested for shooting her parents was remanded to a state mental hospital. A teenage girl mentioned in the article had killed a father who had raped and otherwise sexually abused her. A thirteen-year-old boy who had killed his mother had been physically and psychologically abused since he was an infant. A New Jersey man who had killed his father and severely injured his mother had a history of mental illness.

A 1983 *Newsweek* article, "When Kids Kill Their Parents," featured Richard Jahnke prominently and included several other tales of parricide. One account was about a seventeen-year-old youth who, after years and years of abuse, had killed his sleeping father with six shots from a .357 Magnum. Another told of a young man who had killed his father, but not of the psychological abuse he had endured from his father, nor the decision by the judge not to commit him to jail. A fourth anecdote involved a twenty-one-year-old man from a prominent west coast family who had raped and killed his mother. He was remanded to a mental institution pending trial, and the article never mentioned that he had a history of paranoid schizophrenia.

Of the six cases mentioned in the *Newsweek* article, three clearly involved abuse and battering and one indicated mental illness, specifically paranoid schizophrenia. Based on its research, however, the magazine observed, "According to some experts, the problem may grow worse." Why? It quoted a psychiatrist: "This generation seems to have more difficulty controlling its basic emotions. People used to internalize problems and get depressed. Now there's this frightening change; there's more extroversion, less inhibition."

This fear of a significant increase in the number of parents murdered by their children is not buttressed by facts—but a lot of adults would like to believe it. According to the FBI statistics, parricide accounted for 1.9 percent (405) of all homicides in the country in 1977. In 1983, it was 1.3 percent; in the intervening years, it fluctuated between 1.4 and 1.6 percent.

"We have always known the myths about children who kill their parents," Mones said. "They were always viewed as aberrant youth. People like to see these kids as these violent little bastards or kids who have gone crazy from drugs or who have been spoiled by a permissive environment. Most of these kids are cream puffs a lot of the time. Really violent kids, those acting out with violent behavior, would probably not kill somebody in their family. Kids who hurt somebody in their family would not think about hurting somebody outside their family. It was the Jahnke case that really showed us firsthand what is really happening. Family violence is not really appreciated in this country. I don't believe people appreciate the extent of it."

Of the over five hundred kids he had interviewed in correction facilities in West Virginia, he estimated that 80 percent were victims of child abuse.

"A lot of delinquency, I think, is clearly related to child abuse, yet the courts have by and large ignored the relationship in their treatment and handling of delinquent kids," he said. "Kids commit delinquent acts and incorporate violence as problem-solving mechanisms because that is the way they have been taught. If you look at some recent studies, ninety-five percent of the kids involved in hard-core delinquency were seriously abused. That's not to say that all abused kids will become delinquents but the number of delinquent kids who are abused is just unbelievable."

When Mones left West Virginia and moved to Boston, he expanded his research on the relationship between child abuse and delinquency, and child abuse and parricide. As he pursued both, he consulted on more cases of abused kids who had killed their parents in New York and Massachusetts, and again in West Virginia. In Boston he was trying to develop a paradigm for a battered-child defense.

"The theory is in an early stage of development at this point," he said. "We are really neophytes in this whole game. We're just a small group of psychiatrists and psychologists and a few attorneys."

He had not found much support for developing a solid self-defense strategy for abused kids who had killed their parents.

"There is very little support and interest among attorneys in the country," Mones explained. "Very few people see the need for research in the area or the need to even look at the subject. Most lawyers don't want assistance if it is a case they are appointed to. They approach it as a regular homicide. They don't want to push the issue of abuse. With wives, they will push the abuse issue. With kids it's rare. Kids rarely get off for temporary insanity. Most plead guilty to some form of murder, say manslaughter, if they are charged with a more serious charge that could end with life in prison. I think many times, based on my research anyway, that the lawyers induce their clients to accept a plea bargain when they would have been better off going to trial. Most don't see the seriousness of the abuse, or they see it and don't want to touch it. In fact, many attorneys I've spoken to never thought of exploring the issue, let alone using it as a defense. It is simply beyond their perception that a child could be so brutally abused that he or she would kill his or her parents."

In 1983, a *Life* magazine article reported that more than a million youngsters between the ages of eleven and seventeen run away each year. On the magazine's glossy pages, the black-and-white photos elegized the disconsolate tales of runaway kids. One was pictured concealing a Colt .45 in his jacket. In a squalid crashpad, a fourteen-year-old girl was injected with a drug. Many sell their bodies on the street for whatever cash they can get. "Without dealing in myth or exaggeration, there are 500,000 kids younger than seventeen involved in prostitution," the magazine quoted a Catholic priest who runs crisis centers in several cities as saying. "Nobody will dispute that. They have nothing to sell but themselves."

Most of these kids did not flee warm, loving families. "With abuse as prevalent as it is, then we should clearly understand why there are so many status offenders—runaways and truants," said Mones, who had worked with runaways in West Virginia. "The reason we have runaways is because we have a lot of abused kids who are trying to escape a violent environment."

Battered kids in violent homes find themselves trapped in an excruciating dilemma. They can run away to be street urchins and be preyed upon, or they learn to prey upon others. If they are picked up by the police, they can be charged with status offenses—running away and truancy—and be forced to return home to the violence they fled. Or they can just remain home and take the abuse. When some strike out in self-defense, they will be criticized for not running away from home.

"What you find in many of these cases is who is going to do it first, the father or the mother or the children," Mones said. "It's just a matter of time who does it first. Kids can't go to their teachers; they can't rely on friends. They have no place to go."

Equal treatment under the law frequently stumbles at the doorstep when it does not fall flat on its face. Feminists have fought to shove it into the home when it has lost its way. Their efforts persuaded courts in the 1970s to start recognizing the legal rights of women to protect themselves from brutal spouses. Who speaks for kids who strike back after years and years of chronic abuse? No one.

*     *     *

In their Long Island home without a telephone, radio, or television, newspapers and magazines littered the floor and unwashed dishes cluttered the sink. When the plumbing stopped working, they used pails for the toilet that would not flush. In the winters they huddled without heat. Once a week they left their home to shop for groceries. Eleanor would lead the way. Her daughter, Patricia, lagged behind by a few steps. In the brief moments when neighbors saw them on the street, Patricia always seemed to be scarred, and there were moments when she looked as if she had lost a big fight. Patricia rarely smiled. She had dropped out of high school after her freshman year, as best anyone could tell, and there was speculation that she was mildly retarded. Her parents had been separated for several years, and Patricia lived her life shackled to a mother who abused her at will. Eleanor, at sixty-one, had soured on life, and Patricia, at thirty-five, was paying for it.

One night Eleanor ordered her daughter to sleep on the front porch, where she had been forced to sleep so many times before. Patricia compliantly walked out but quickly returned. She was not going to spend the night outside. Her mother, on that August evening, grabbed a five-foot metal pole and bashed Patricia, severely bruising her arms. Patricia snatched the metal cudgel from her mother and struck back, cutting her mother's face and knocking out her lower teeth. In the heat of the battle, Eleanor suffered a heart attack and died. Patricia was handcuffed, arrested, and taken to jail.

"She's an unlikely person to be in court," attorney Edward McCarty told the judge at her arraignment. "She has no prior criminal history and she has significant roots in the community. She was devoted to her mother and yet she stands here before you, accused of killing her." Outside of the courtroom, McCarty told reporters that Patricia had been under pressure and acted in an impulsive moment. She was a loving and devoted daughter, and she and her mother had "lived for each other," he said. Rising to the occasion, he added, "it was like a Bette Davis movie." His comments were what one might have expected from a defense attorney but McCarty was a seasoned veteran of the Nassau County, New York, district attorney's office and responsible for handling major murders. A spokesman for the office was also quoted in the papers: "She was not out to kill her but to defend herself."

Patricia was not charged with second-degree murder, which carries a twenty-five-to-life sentence upon conviction, but with the lesser charge of first-degree manslaughter. When the grand jury convened a few weeks after her arrest in 1982, it refused to indict her. In a storybook ending, at least for the newspapers, her father returned and took her back to Texas to live with him and his present wife.

It had been an obvious case of self-defense from the beginning, and the police and prosecutor had proceeded with formal charges because, a spokesman for the district attorney's office said, "technically, there was a body." Under most state laws, the use of deadly force in self-defense requires a justifiable fear of bodily harm and the use of like force against like force. In Patricia's case she fought back after she was attacked, and the police, the prosecutor, and the grand jury believed she had had no intention of killing her mother. There were other factors: Patricia was not much bigger than her mother and there were conspicuous indications that her mother had mistreated her before. There also was the speculation that she was slightly retarded. And it was obvious that the district attorney's office did not want to go to trial.

It was a rare case. Violence erupted, an abused daughter struck back, a body hit the floor, and no one involved in the case screamed bloody murder. Newspapers, police, prosecuting and defense attorneys could slap each other on the back for a job well done. All interests were served, and Daddy, like the knight in shining armor, returned to the old homestead to whisk the princess to a new castle. And there were even kind words for the mother.

David was a member of the student council, played three varsity sports, performed in the school band, and was an honor student. The principal of the prestigious Texas prep school that he attended called him a "real good kid." His teachers described him as likable and attractive. He was the son of a prominent family, and his father was the president of an oil and gas company.

One Sunday after he returned home from church, David cut his parents down with six shots from a 12-gauge shotgun in the summer of 1981. He hopped on his bicycle and pedaled up to a passing police car and told an officer, "I just shot both my parents with a shotgun." His father was dead when the police rushed to David's home, and his mother died hours later in a hospital. The police told the press that the double murder had probably resulted from a long-standing family feud.

When the fourteen-year-old boy was arraigned in court, he was accompanied by three attorneys: one hired by his sister and two others from his father's corporation. The Lone Star State's criminal justice system did not sink its spurs into David's hide, but that was not because of an imposing show of force by an armada of high-powered attorneys. And it did not matter too much then whether he was a victim of child abuse or benign neglect, insane or emotionally disturbed, just plain mean or spiteful and contemptuous. In Texas, children under fifteen who are accused of serious crimes can only be charged with juvenile delinquency. They do not go to a penitentiary. David was fourteen. After a hearing he was sent to a psychiatric hospital to be held until he was eighteen.

Even more impressive than the law was the decision of the judge, who ruled that the boy should be allowed to receive a small part of his parents' estate, which was assessed at more than one million dollars. According to an Associated Press story, experts who had examined the boy said the father's strict ways "unleashed an uncontrollable rage in the son that had been building for years." The judge, according to the story, thought the "restrictions of the hospital and the boy's memory of his act were enough punishment." The judge was quoted as saying, "He also has to live with what he did for the rest of his life. That may be the worst punishment of all." The story also described the boy as a family pariah "whose relatives speak to him only through lawyers."

In 1982, a sixteen-year-old Wisconsin youth, who had once considered entering the priesthood, used a gun and knife to kill his mother, father, and younger brother. When he was charged, as mandated by the law, with juvenile delinquency, the sabers started rattling in the state capitol and some editorial newsrooms. Two state senators bellowed that they would press for new legislation to change the law so that murderous sixteen-year-old youths could be treated as adults. In a less obstreperous manner, newspaper editorials moaned that the youth could not be held past his nineteenth birthday unless he was committed to a mental hospital.

And of course there was the other David, described earlier, from Maryland, who in 1982 fatally stabbed his father but was sentenced only to eight hundred hours of teaching prisoners in the county jail to read and write.

There are times when a life is taken, and justice is not meted out with mace and chain, but the criminal justice system still responds in ways rooted in law and anchored in tradition. For Patricia, on Long Island, it was an obvious case of self-defense. She fought back to protect herself from harm, striking out with the very cudgel being used to strike her. In Texas, Wisconsin, and other states, kids under a certain statutory age can be prosecuted as juveniles for serious crimes with the hope, if not the promise, that they can be rehabilitated. Juvenile detention centers and facilities, Kenneth Wooden wrote in *Weeping in the Playtime of Others,* can mangle souls and bodies as thoroughly as any prison hellhole.

In Maryland, Judge Femia, who sentenced David, demonstrated how a judge can respond with extraordinary compassion and still have that judicial largess fit snugly within the law. Yet months later, he was harsher on Lisa, the fourteen-year-old girl who, with her thirteen-year-old boyfriend and their mutual buddy, twenty, was arrested on first-degree murder charges for her father's killing. Doctors who examined her said she was a victim of psychological abuse by her father, but Femia rejected that testimony. He said all they were able to show him was that the father doted excessively on his daughter.

"I really don't think that doctors can sit down and after the fact go back and find sufficient medical evidence to create a psychological path that leads to murder . . . and there could be no other outcome," Femia was quoted as saying in the *Washington Post* magazine. "I don't accept that. I think there could have been another outcome. There could have been another path, in fact."

He gave Lisa a sentence that could keep her in prison for fifteen years. In David's case, the mother corroborated her husband's abuse of their son. Not so in Lisa's case; her mother did not take the stand. The reason most young girls kill or involve themselves in their fathers' murders is incest. But that was never raised in her defense. An additional factor in the judge's calculations was that Lisa was accused of planning murder while David was said to have acted impulsively.

In the magazine article discussing his two parricide cases, Femia said the law does not recognize premeditated self-defense. "Under the law you must wait until the moment arises," he was quoted as saying. "You cannot anticipate." In cases where abuse is clear and recognizable, a judge could consider it as a mitigating factor in sentencing. "Facts such as those are things that judges have to consider," he said. "It will depend on whether or not I am convinced— the judgment of the judge."

However, the issue of abuse and parricide is much more complicated than just trying to convince a judge. Juries, prosecutors, the news media, and the community are all involved directly or indirectly. Even defense attorneys overlook or fail to appreciate how years of abuse can trigger violence in a child. Psychologists and psychiatrists make similar mistakes. Even with all the disclosures about the pervasiveness of abuse and sexual coercion and rape in families— in so-called good families—lawyers, judges, police, professionals, and the man and woman in the street still find it easier to believe that a young girl can plot a father's death because she is manipulative or contemptuous of her parents. Or that a son kills a mother because she forces him to go to school. Or that he kills his mother because she does not help him with his homework, as one New York City prosecutor convinced a grand jury before a judge threw out the indictment.

Kids are on the low end of the family totem pole when it comes to rights, protection under the law, and power. When law and order break down in the home, and a battered child strikes back, there has to be a better way to ensure the justice that eluded the child in the first place. When representing a juvenile who has killed a parent, many lawyers convince their client to plead to a lesser charge when they cannot get the case into juvenile or family court. And prosecutors frequently oppose having a parricide moved to a juvenile court if they can prosecute the defendant as an adult.

Many times lawyers have overlooked or disregarded abuse as a factor, or they did not realize its extent or significance. Surviving family members may not be cooperative, and many kids are not as articulate as Richard Jahnke, the Wyoming youth who ambushed his father after years and years of abuse. He shot his father because he thought his father was going to kill him. He had no reason to believe otherwise. One method that should be considered in defending abused clients in parricide cases is a battered-child defense. The following is a paradigm.

First, the nature of the abuse must be established. Was it physical? Psychological? Or both, as it is in many cases. Lawyers must recognize the signs. Was the kid pockmarked with scars and bruises?

Was there a history of broken bones? In many cases the abuse started when the child was as young as two, three, or four and continued well into the teens. There may have been sporadic beatings over several years. Despite the time lapse since the early years when the damage was inflicted or the on-again-off-again nature of the abuse, evidence may still be discovered.

"Physical abuse is much easier to document than psychological abuse," said Paul Mones, the attorney who had worked on more than a dozen cases of parricide. "Kids have a tremendous capacity for being beaten and abused. Their little bones [when they are toddlers] will just bend and twist and turn and sometimes fracture from constant beatings. From birth, kids are thrown into cribs and up against walls. When they are abused like that they develop cracks and fissures in their joints and long bones. And you can tell evidence of prior abuse like that by long-bone studies and full-body X rays of the child."

Lawyers may also have to hypnotize their clients if they have been so traumatized they cannot recall the specific nature of the abuse or refuse to discuss it. In some cases, another element that has to be considered is brain damage. Not the type that physically impairs or retards in an obvious manner, but a form that can be as insidious and elusive as the beatings and abuse that caused it.

"Lawyers should have some knowledge about organic brain syndrome," Mones said. "There can be temporal lobe lesions on the brain which the abuse triggers and causes the kid to become violent. In some cases the tip-off about the presence of lesions was olfactory hallucinations. The kids smelled burning bread or rubber. Sometimes they have said that while they were committing the crime and immediately after, their vision becomes cloudy and gray."

That gray cloud arises from an organic source that can be found with the use of an electroencephalogram. One study reported in a 1983 issue of the *American Journal of Psychiatry* said, ". . . extremely violent behaviors in adolescents were associated with psychotic symptoms and neurological impairment. Especially violent adolescents also had witnessed and been the victims of severe physical abuse." The report, prepared by a research team headed by Dr. Dorothy Lewis, of New York University, gave findings on fifty-five children. Twenty-one were homicidally aggressive. "Psychiatric symptoms and diagnoses did not distinguish these children from the non-homicidal children," the report said, "but the homicidally aggressive children were significantly more likely to: 1) have a father who behaved violently, often homicidally, 2) have had a seizure, 3) have attempted suicide, and 4) have a mother who had been hospitalized for a psychiatric disorder."

It should be noted that the report explained how a psychologically impaired mother could contribute to a child's violent behavior. It is one example of what happens when the burden of child care is carried by one parent. "Obviously, the fact that a mother has been hospitalized for a psychiatric disorder from time to time suggests that a child has experienced loss and inconsistent, erratic mothering," the report said. "Moreover, a seriously disturbed mother is likely to have been emotionally unavailable even when physically present."

Part of a defense effort should include a psychological autopsy of the abusive parent as well as a detailed history of the whole family, going back to the grandparents' treatment of the parents, if possible. That can be accomplished by interviewing friends, siblings, co-workers, relatives, and the surviving parent.

"Attorneys have to be willing and able to go out and do all the hoofing necessary . . . to speak to everybody about what kind of parent this was," Mones said. "And it is not an easy thing to accomplish because he or she may have been a bastard behind closed doors. They may have appeared as nice, upstanding members of the community but behind that door they came on like Attila the Hun."

Sometimes neighbors and friends have described a parent as too strict or too much of a disciplinarian. Abusive fathers in many cases also tend to isolate their families from the surrounding communities. David, who appeared before Judge Femia, was one example. Richard Jahnke was another. Vincent Whatley, in Oregon, was one as well. Though he lived in a rural community where families were already separated by miles of bush and bad roads, his father restricted the family even more, cutting out contact with the outside world except, perhaps, for school. Only Whatley family members witnessed the beatings as well as the flailing ax handles and gunshots winging in their direction.

In such cases, the fear of death or injury can be as palpable and convincing as any X ray, scar, or bruise. But the insidious nature of abuse in the family makes it extremely difficult to develop a defense for psychological abuse if there is no evidence of physical battering. Violence has been interwoven in the family fabric to the point that spankings, whippings, a slap across the head or face, or even an occasional punch are not considered abuse. It was only recently that a few states decided that it was a crime for a husband to rape his wife. So with a case of psychological abuse, care must be exercised. It must be demonstrated that a defendant suffered real torment from mental abuse and was not just the unfortunate victim of a tongue-lashing, severe scolding, or parental disciplining.

"To define psychological abuse or to measure it to give it a viable legal context, we have to define it in a certain way," Mones said. "A mother who periodically yells at her kids to do work around the house or a parent who just goes off once in a while can be said to be psychologically abusing a child from a certain perspective. But what I am talking about is a pattern, something that would form a recognizable pattern."

Some of symptoms of psychologically abused children are "very, very low self-images" compared to their peers. The kids might be suicidal. They also might be truant or chronic runaways, and get into constant fights with friends, classmates, and sisters and brothers.

"Interfamilial abuse between brothers and sisters is as high as that between parents and children," Mones said. "Children can't vent their hostility on their parents because the parents are authority figures. Some experts in the country have some hold on measuring psychological abuse, but it's very, very difficult to quantify and to really show people."

During the preparations for defense, the attorney has to be aware always of the welfare of the abused kid who has killed. It is not unusual for a kid to try to commit suicide.

"In one case I worked on, the kid committed the murders, then took all the guns in the house and traveled up to a 7-Eleven store where he was going to hole himself up and wait for the police so he could go down in a barrage of police bullets," Mones said. "Anyone who holes himself up in a 7-Eleven with a couple of rifles knows what is going to happen. He can't pull the trigger so he wants someone else to pull the trigger."

In another case he worked on, a psychiatrist said a youth who had killed his family after years and years of abuse should be kept on a suicide watch for several years. Robert M. Bloom, Jr., as recounted early in this book, to the distress of his lawyer convinced a judge to let him argue his own case. He had slain his father, stepmother, and stepsister. An abused young man from the time he was born, he convinced the jury to find him guilty of capital murder. In a separate hearing, he convinced the same jury to send him to the gas chamber. He was all of nineteen.

"This is part of the preparations strategy," Mones insisted. "You must be very, very concerned about the mental health of the kid."

And that is not just to protect the kids from killing themselves. It also serves to prepare them to participate in their own defense. After all of the fact gathering has been done on the kid and the family, then a decision has to be made on which course to pursue. There are two roads. One is self-defense, which means the kid killed to protect himself or herself. The second concerns the mental capacity of the kid. This would involve an insanity plea or an attempt to show temporary insanity or diminished capacity. Each has its strengths and weaknesses.

The insanity defense, despite the public perception, has been rarely used, and when it has been been introduced, it rarely has resulted in an acquittal. After John Hinckley, Jr., was acquitted by reason of insanity of shooting President Reagan in 1982, the seldom-used defense came under serious attack. Law-and-order types looking for an easy prey to exploit, and public ignorance with its general fear of mentally ill people, forged a pernicious force against the use of the defense. Courts and judges nowadays send psychotic people to jails where they spend their time in a kind of peripatetic limbo. They bounce from jail to a mental hospital back to jail again, over and over for years. A defense based on temporary insanity or diminished capacity, however, might stand a better chance when incorporated in a battered-child defense.

"A battered-child defense is very, very different from traditional self-defense because it is the perception that you have to overcome and educate people about," Mones said. "What is the perception of the child in these cases? It is not the traditional self-defense concept."

The law on self-defense evolved from early English common law, with the legal use of deadly force based on an adult-male perception. One man is fighting with another man, both are equally armed, and there is a justifiable fear of bodily harm. The laws, of course, as well as tradition, ignored the perceptions of women and children. In one sense the result has been justice for all with a little less for women and not too much for kids. (It wasn't until 1967 that the Supreme Court ruled that kids had rights to due process.) It has been rare for a battered child to strike back when he or she was being attacked. In most cases they were too afraid or too small. Also working against them, on a psychological level, have been the societal prohibitions against fighting a parent. When they did strike back, it came when the parent did not have the upper hand or when the rage was suddenly triggered after building up for years and years. If Jahnke or Whatley had been defending their families and themselves from menacing, gun-toting neighbors or intruders, they would not have been sentenced to jail.

"You have to educate the jury about the perceptions of kids," Mones said. "You talk to the jury about power equalization."

The kids' perceptions, when they were forced to kill, were that the parents, usually the father, could kill them anytime they wanted. The abuse was a constant reminder of how powerful the parents were and how they could act with impunity. The messages were that the kids were powerless to do anything, and the threats of death and bodily harm were constantly hammered into them.

"You argue that the combination of the repetitiveness of the abuse, along with the power that can be inflicted by the father, creates deadly force in the eyes of the child," Mones said. "It creates a justifiable fear of deadly force. The next blow could be the last blow. Or you argue that the abuse has acted in such a way as to diminish the child's ability to tell right from wrong, and because of that, the kid was acting under a pall of fear, such that they couldn't do anything but defend themselves."

What also has to be explained to the jury is the repetitive nature of abuse. The yelling occurs in a pattern and the beatings occur in a pattern. But at some point, the pattern becomes disrupted. The beatings become worse or the parent uses a different word, "and that clicks off something in the kid's mind.

"Jahnke's father told his son, more or less, 'Don't be home when I get back,'" Mones said. "Something had changed, and the kid noticed it."

Vincent Whatley and his mother and brothers noticed how bizarre Chuck Whatley had been acting for weeks before he died. He had always been abusive but the abuse took on a different tone. The day he hit Vincent in the head with an ax handle was the day that Vincent thought death was soon to follow.

Many women who killed their abusive spouses or lovers waited until they were asleep or off guard. The women argued at their trials that the years of physical and psychological abuse had created a setting in which they had to use deadly force. They killed when the men were asleep because it was the only time the men were not wielding the power.

The crucial step, however, in convincing a jury of a child's perception and getting ready for a battered-child defense starts well before a jury is ever impaneled. It begins with the *voir dire*—jury selection.

"Most attorneys will tell you that selecting a jury is ninety percent of the game because you educate the jury by your questions," Mones said. "In most cases you try to determine the best juror by doing individual *voir dire*. You say to the judge, 'This case represents such unique legal issues that I want to get each person in a room with you and the DA and I want to ask certain questions of this potential juror.' You want to know their attitudes on children, on self-defense, on abuse, whether or not they were abused. You ask, 'Do you believe a child has a right to defend himself? Do you believe this kid has the right to take up her hand and hit her father if her father has hit her?' It is a common tactic but it is where most attorneys fall totally on their face."

When he cannot convince the court to have the case referred to a family or juvenile court, an attorney may convince his client to plead to a lesser charge. Mones said that in most of these cases that he had researched, perhaps all, the clients would have been better off, or would have been no worse off, had they gone to trial.

"I think in many cases the problem is the inability of the attorneys to communicate to the juries, and the inability of the juries and judges to accept the arguments of the attorneys," Mones said. "I call it inability that they refuse to accept it. I think at this point, it's ignorance and also perception. They are unable to believe, to accept a proposition that a kid could be that abused. In most cases they don't believe the abuse because what happens again is that, as I said before, when you try to document the abuse, it's very difficult. Yet, we know that the amount of abuse is greatly underestimated."

More than a million abused kids is the conservative figure frequently mentioned. But there is another way to look at the numbers. According to FBI statistics, between five hundred and six hundred sons and daughters are killed annually by their parents. It is not clear what the ages are or how many of the "children" are adults. The National Association for the Prevention of Child Abuse, Mones

pointed out, estimates that five thousand kids are murdered annually
by their parents, but the deaths are concealed.

"Babies are brought into hospitals, and their parents say something
like he fell down the steps or suffocated in his pillow or he rolled out
of bed and hit the floor," Mones said. "These are things that doctors
shouldn't believe but they do too many times. Now, there are approx-
imately twenty thousand murders reported in the U.S. each year. If
we include the figures from the National Association for the Prevention of Child Abuse, it would increase the homicide rate by twenty-
five percent or so. When put in these terms, which nobody is doing,
we are underestimating the number of murders in the country by
more than twenty-five percent. It's the only area where police agencies admit that their numbers [on homicide] are wrong. If we know
that the number of kids killed is underestimated, clearly then we
know that the amount of abuse is greatly underestimated."

One day when she was thirteen, Clara walked out of school and
what she saw frightened her so much that she rushed to the nearest
Planned Parenthood office and begged for contraceptives because she
did not want to have babies. She was a big-city little girl and old
enough to be having sex with a boyfriend, but when the staff asked
her questions she gave them a response they had not expected. The
problem, she told them, was not about having sex with a boyfriend.
The problem was her stepfather. She had just left the school building, she told the staff, when she saw her stepfather walking past,
bearing a dead baby on a pillow. It was only then, as she described
this hallucination, that the Planned Parenthood staff realize how disturbed she was and contacted a hospital where she was placed under
psychiatric evaluation for five weeks.

The Planned Parenthood staff responded to this young girl in need
much faster than the city's child welfare agency, where she had complained numerous times about her stepfather. She had begged and
begged to be removed from her home and placed in a foster home or
anywhere else so long as she could be free of him. Her complaints
were scrupulously recorded. Two years later, after being raped and
sexually abused on and off since she was eight, Clara killed her stepfather with a handgun he kept in their home. The record at the child
welfare agency clearly showed that nothing had ever been done to
help her. Clara had also complained to her mother, but she had not
believed her daughter's story about the rapes. However, she had sent

Clara down to live with her relatives in South Carolina. But when Clara returned, the stepfather resumed the attacks. Tragedy followed.

Clara was charged with second-degree murder but the grand jury indicted her on a lesser charge of manslaughter. At that point an attorney might have agreed to a plea bargain to involuntary manslaughter, but it was not to be in this case. Her attorney in this case filed a motion before the court to have her indictment thrown out in the interest of justice. There was also a possibility, said Mones, a consulting attorney in the case, that either the judge would bounce the case back to juvenile court or the prosecutor would drop charges. Because the case had received little publicity and also because of the sensitive issues being considered, the girl was given a pseudonym and the city was not publicly identified. It was expected that Clara would not have to go to jail though serious legal issues still had to be resolved. Mones considered the case an example of the kind of paradigm he had been trying to develop for a battered-child defense. In Clara's case many of the tough issues were being worked out in pretrial motions and special considerations by the prosecutor.

The case can also serve as an example of the family dynamics and complexities in a parricide involving abuse. For example, the rapes were only part of the abuse. After her arrest and in preparation for a trial, a psychologist was assigned to work with Clara. The girl complained that her father had injected her in the neck with a hallucinogenic drug at night when she was asleep. Clara told the psychologist that she would awake the next morning with a stiff neck and would also find blood on her pillow. She also complained that when her mother was not home, her father would invite people over to her home, where they would set live animals on fire as part of black magic rituals. Her father, Clara complained, practiced voodoo. The visitors would leave before her mother arrived, and her mother never noticed that anything had happened in the house while she was gone.

At one point, the psychologist thought that Clara, because of her previous hospitalization and the bizarre descriptions of voodoo and injections of hallucinogenic drugs, was crazy. But Clara's mother, when the psychologist checked with her, corroborated the injections of drugs. Her husband would inject Clara, Clara's sisters, and herself when they were asleep, the mother told the psychologist. Though the mother insisted she did not know what kind of drug was being used, she claimed that it was strong enough to cause her to lose all of her teeth.

There were other problems. The mother and her daughters, who had been supportive in the early stages of the case, began to resent Clara. The father had held a good job and the family lived reasonably well; but months after he was killed, the family was forced onto the city's welfare rolls. They blamed Clara for their economic woes. Clara also began to deny that her father was dead, and a psychiatrist noticed what he thought were signs of neurological damage. She was a very disturbed girl and the doctors wanted her to stay in a psychiatric hospital, but she wanted to go home to her mother and sisters regardless of the growing acrimony. Despite all the indications for a solid defense, there were also signs of all the things that could go wrong to make the case a difficult one.

The battered-child defense, which borrows heavily from research developed on the battered-woman syndrome, is only an example of what might be done to help kids who kill their parents after years of abuse. It does not attempt to exonerate or condone what some kids have been forced to do. Instead, it is a way to suggest how justice and equal protection under the law can still be infused in a case where they were both tragically missing. It should be considered a stopgap measure until society recognizes the iniquities of abuse and mobilizes to eradicate it.

"I was on this airplane going from New York to Boston, and this guy next to me started talking," Mones said. "He told me he was in the furniture business in North Carolina, and when he asked what I did, I told him I worked with kids. 'Right now,' I told him, 'I work with kids who kill their parents.' This guy was a Horatio Alger story. He started out poor; now he's a millionaire. He started talking about how he has guns all over the house. And he has this gun in the bureau, and he was talking about the time he cocked it and put the gun to his wife's head. He had beaten up his wife a few times. Now, it's very, very common where they cock the gun and put it into a person's mouth. . . . If I have heard it once I have heard it a hundred times in wife abuse cases and child abuse cases. Cocking the gun is very common. Sometimes that is the thing that puts the kid right out. It's the sound of the click. It's a fear device.

"So then this guy said now his wife hits him until she gets so tired she goes to sleep. He claims he doesn't want to hit her anymore. So as he was talking about himself and his wife, he started talking about how he taught his boy how to use the gun when he was ten years old. And now he's noticed that his son has been acting strange lately. He said, 'Sometimes I get a little concerned, cause I know when I was young, my daddy said to me, "I'm giving you a knife. If anyone fucks with you, cut him." My daddy was raised like that and I raised my son like that. And I'm afraid one day he's going to come home and I'm going to piss him off and he's going to blow me away.'

"I think parents know the capacity of their children to do it. I believe that most of these people know what they are doing to their children. They are people who understand violence. They're people who taught their children about violence. And they know if they put a person to the task, what that person is going to do. I think they're asking for it. They might be in a minority but I still think they're asking for it. This is just my perception, not being a psychologist or a psychiatrist but just from the number of cases that I've looked at. It's a scary thing to talk about. . . . I think parents have a tacit understanding of what they are doing."

# 10

# The Miami
# Grand Jury

When Julie's mother, Gretchen, said she did not believe her, and the
detective accused her of lying about why she had killed her father,
Julie told them something they were ready to believe. She killed him,
she said, because he had grounded her one night when she wanted to
go out with some friends. Her father, Marty, died after he was
stabbed five times with a big kitchen knife. Julie, who had never
been in trouble with the police before, was charged with first-degree
murder. She was fourteen. Julie lived in Miami and, under Florida
law, kids fourteen and younger can be indicted, tried, and sentenced
as adults for crimes carrying life sentences, such as first-degree
murder.

Her case was the first parricide handled by Steven J. Levine, chief
assistant public defender for the Juvenile Division of Florida's Eleventh Judicial Circuit. Fortunately for her, however, he believed that
any kid as young as she was who killed a parent had to be seriously
disturbed or was having serious family problems. He wanted to know
as much as possible about Julie and her family in order to prepare for
an upcoming grand jury hearing. And the responsibility for developing that kind of background information was handled by the social
services department of his office. A psychologist and a social worker,
after jointly reviewing the results of that investigation, wrote in their
report that Julie's family was "disturbed to the point of chaos."
Levine also made his own observations: The tragedy was a worst-case
scenario of "your typical incestuous family." Julie, Marty, and
Gretchen are pseudonyms.

170

*    *    *

Before Julie was born, her mother, Gretchen, dropped out of high school and married a military serviceman. When the marriage failed, Gretchen, at nineteen, became involved with another man. But after a while she decided he was too possessive and took up with the thirty-two-year-old leader of a motorcycle gang. She stayed with him only to discourage her other obsessive suitor, but when the gang leader suggested that they get married, she agreed. After four other marriages and four children, her motorcycle sultan didn't want any more kids, but she wanted a child, and when she was pregnant with Julie they separated. They reunited when Julie was ten days old but separated six months later. During that half year, Gretchen sent Julie to stay with Gretchen's grandmother whenever her husband complained about having the baby around. Julie, who was frequently ill with various ailments, developed a nervous disorder that caused her to vomit whenever she was distressed. This continued throughout her early childhood. When she was two, her parents divorced and Gretchen decided to finish her education. While her mother worked on her high school diploma and later on a college degree in counseling, Julie lived with her great-grandmother and saw Gretchen only on weekends. Gretchen married again while pursuing her studies, and her latest husband formally adopted Julie, though the girl continued to live most of her life with her great-grandmother. After the marriage failed two years later, Julie continued to stay with her great-grandmother, who later took her from Kentucky to live in Miami.

Gretchen stayed in Kentucky and met her next husband, Marty. He proposed marriage about thirty minutes after they met, and two weeks later they married. Marty's parents, however, were upset with him for marrying a second time someone they hardly knew, and had him involuntarily committed to a psychiatric hospital. He was later released, and he and Gretchen eventually moved to Miami.

Julie was about nine or ten now and was a bright and attractive little girl, but she was also bearing a strong sense of abandonment. Gretchen seemed to lose interest in her daughter whenever she was involved with a man. When Julie started living regularly with Marty and Gretchen, her problems became more severe. Julie was unable to make a lot of friends because the family moved so many times that she bounced from one school to another. Gretchen and Marty expected her to embrace Christian fundamentalism as fervently as they did. And Marty was overbearing. He maintained high and unrealistic expectations for himself and anyone around him. He talked often about being a successful businessman, but his modest achievements were regularly offset by his big failures. Much of Julie's life was now controlled by Marty, who assumed all responsibility for disciplining her even though she had always been well behaved. He ordered her to address him as "sir."

By the time Julie entered junior high school, her B average had dropped to between D and F. That decline seemed to coincide with Marty's increasing sexual obsession with her. He decided the kind of clothes she wore and he preferred tight-fitting jeans and blouses. At twelve and thirteen, Julie looked more mature than most girls her age. She wore her hair in a frizzy, bleached-blond hairdo and was encouraged to wear a lot of makeup. Marty frequently embarrassed her when he commented aloud about her breasts, and he was almost ecstatic when she had her first period. He frequently said aloud that she would remain a virgin until she married. Sometimes he touched her breasts and buttocks, and when she complained to her mother, Gretchen would rationalize his actions. Marty punished Julie whenever she refused to kiss him on the mouth, and her mother did not interfere. Although Gretchen disliked the obsessive attention Marty forced upon Julie, she thought he was entitled to act that way because he was the man of the house. One night he sneaked up on Julie while she was sleeping and fondled her breasts. Three months after her fourteenth birthday, Julie had lost ten pounds and was sinking deep into depression.

One night Julie invited a boy, whom she had been secretly seeing, into her room without her parents knowing.

"Although she was not permitted to date," according to a report prepared by the social services department, "she allowed him into her room late one night . . . in what appeared to be a flouting of his [Marty's] authority, a test of Marty's interest and a desire to move sexuality into her peer group."

Julie's actions that night were not so unusual. She was trying to ward off her stepfather's unwanted sexual obsession by seeing a boy her own age. Marty flew into a rage when he caught them together and rushed her to the emergency room of a hospital for tests for venereal disease and pregnancy.

Two days later, as Gretchen prepared to go shopping, Julie was in her room and Marty was lying down on a couch in the living room.

The tension in the home was thick enough to cut with a knife. Marty had been acting more sexually aggressive toward his stepdaughter for several days, and this day he was just waiting for Gretchen to leave. After she left, Julie went into the kitchen and started washing dishes. Marty called her into the living room and started fondling her. She fled to the kitchen and picked up a knife when he followed her. He saw the knife, got angry, but still tried to embrace her. After she stabbed him the first time, she couldn't stop swinging her arm. When he fell she rushed to a phone and dialed the 911 emergency number and cried hysterically for help. When an ambulance and police cars arrived she was still sobbing uncontrollably. She told the police she had stabbed Marty because he was trying to molest her.

Julie was still at home when Gretchen returned from shopping. Without asking anyone what had provoked the stabbing, Gretchen told the police, "I bet Julie told you that her father was molesting her." Gretchen told them that nothing had ever happened between Julie and Marty. The police took them back to headquarters and asked Julie to tell them again what had happened. When she said her father had been molesting her for years, Gretchen slammed her fist on the table. "I'm not going to listen to this," she said, and stormed out of the room. The detective told Julie to stop lying and tell the truth. She repeated her story: Marty had been trying to molest her. When the detective told her he did not believe her, Julie gave in and said that she had stabbed him because he had grounded her the night before and would not let her see her friends.

"Part of the incestuous family dynamics is that the nonabusing spouse will [frequently] try to cover up or deny that anything happened," Levine said. "Our social services people were able to pick up a lot of it [the incestuous dynamics in Julie's family] and hired a psychologist who was an expert. He didn't really examine Julie but acted as a consultant."

The background information was gathered from interviews with Julie, Gretchen, an aunt, and a pastor who had known Marty well. Gretchen confided that she had witnessed incidents and knew that Marty had been very possessive about Julie, but she refused to admit that there had been anything sexual about his behavior. The background information, plus expert testimony on the nature and psychology of incest, was turned over to the state's attorney.

"We are fortunate here to have a state's attorney who will allow us to present our own evidence through [him] to the grand jury," Levine said. "It's not required that he do it as far as I can tell."

Julie's mother also testified before the grand jury.

"She at first wanted to help the kid and appeared before the grand jury and said, 'Please don't indict my child,'" Levine said. "But she never came around and accepted the incest."

The information and evidence prepared by Levine convinced the grand jury not to indict Julie for first-degree murder. Her case was then referred to juvenile court. She was still charged with first-degree murder but was no longer facing a life sentence.

"Our defense in juvenile court was essentially self-defense," Levine said. "We argued that in her mind she believed she was in danger and acted accordingly."

The prosecutor planned to call Julie's mother as a witness to testify that there had been nothing incestuous between her daughter and Marty.

"The state was also going to use as evidence a letter found in [Julie's] room that said that the stepfather was being cruel to her and she would have to do something to him," Levine said.

But a handwriting expert who examined the letter before the trial in juvenile court began concluded that the letter had been written by the mother.

"Her mother wrote the note as if it was the daughter writing," Levine said. "She was trying to take away the attention on the sexual molesting."

The letter was never presented by the prosecutor as evidence, but the judge found Julie guilty of the lesser crime of manslaughter.

"In juvenile court there is little difference in sentencing when found guilty of first-degree murder or manslaughter. We appealed the decision but the conviction was upheld. The judge's decision was based on the incriminating statement she gave to the detective. On one hand, 'I killed him because he was molesting me.' On the other hand, 'I killed him because he grounded me.' I still don't think they [the trial judge and appeals court] were right. I felt there was enough for the judge to acquit her because she was acting in self-defense. In Florida there is a doctrine of having to retreat if someone is coming after you and you feel you are in danger. Before you can use deadly force you've got to try and run away. The judge made a factual finding because she didn't run away. Our argument was that when we are talking about kids we're not talking about the same judgment that adults might have. Although the judge didn't come out and say it, it's possible that by finding her guilty he could make sure that she would get the treatment that she might not have gotten if she had been acquitted."

Although Julie acted petulant to adults, seductive to young boys, and unpredictably hostile to almost everyone in the juvenile facility where she was incarcerated, the social workers, psychologist, and doctors knew they were dealing with an "extremely vulnerable" and "badly damaged teenager." Julie, according to one report, "suffered from maternal deprivation from infancy." At fourteen, she felt betrayed by her stepfather and abandoned by her mother. And the life looming before her looked bleak and lonely.

"Behind her very brittle facade of denial and repression there is all manner of grief and rage which wells up even spontaneously very frequently," according to one report. "She has put herself in a most impossible situation as she has a functioning conscience which is far more strict than that seen in children her age and has rigid standards for herself that are almost impossible to achieve. On the one hand there is mountainous hatred toward her stepfather and her mother as well as herself for having been duped into participation in this cruel, outrageous lifestyle.

"Whether he committed incest overtly with Julie or not really begs the issue as the whole relationship between him and the girl was extremely sexually charged and certainly qualifies as incest," according to the report, prepared by a psychologist and a social worker.

Julie was alone in the world. She had killed her father and could not live with her mother anymore. Her great-grandmother had died one week after the homicide, and her friends, according to one doctor, "were not able to understand how she could have done something like this."

Everyone who examined her strongly recommended that she be placed in a residential psychiatric hospital for juveniles. One examiner insisted that the court "remove this girl from secure detention immediately where she is continuously being damaged by callous remarks." He also strongly recommended that Julie be excused from trial proceedings unless it was "absolutely mandatory" for her to appear.

"For her to be dragged through the hideous build-up to what has occurred would be . . . the worst kind of child abuse," the examiner wrote to the judge.

In late 1982 Julie was sent to an out-of-state residential hospital for girls.

"Our social services department is familiar with most of the private hospitals around the country," Levine said. "We get a lot of kids who are emotionally disturbed, who have severe problems, and there is a special fund set up so that when there is no state facility that can [help] a kid, and there rarely is [one], some special funds can be approved and the kid is sent out."

He said that almost everyone involved in Julie's case believed that "basically what Julie needed was long-term therapy for the years of guilt and abandonment and all the various other things."

What he did not say was that an acquittal might have also provided a psychological balm to assuage the guilt Julie felt for killing a man in self-defense. What happened to her, she needed to know, was not her fault. A woman facing that same threat might have done the same thing. A man threatened with rape by a more powerful opponent might have done the same thing. Levine, however, said the judge probably acted in her best interests. But it has to be considered an absurdity that the only way she could have received help was to be found guilty. Of course, Julie was fortunate. Some young girls who have killed sexually abusive or menacing fathers in self-defense have been incarcerated in state prisons.

Levine said that in cases like Julie's, he preferred to marshal his evidence in the initial stages of the defense to prepare for a grand jury. He did not believe that the Miami grand jury would ever indict a kid fourteen or fifteen years old in a parricide case if a history of abuse was adequately prepared and presented at a hearing.

"I try as much as possible in cases like this to flush out the nature of the family situation, the psychiatric or emotional problems the kids have . . . to get the momentum going in the early stages. Before I started working in the juvenile division, kids were routinely getting indicted all of the time. I don't think defense attorneys ever [took] the time to consider putting on some kind of evidence before the grand jury. No one ever did in Miami before I came to the juvenile division. I really don't think the grand jury really wants a kid tried in adult court." But he conceded that it was "more difficult to defend a kid sixteen or seventeen."

\*     \*     \*

Two years after handling Julie's case, Levine took on the defense of another youngster accused in a parricide. Julie had been sexually abused but this new case involved two murders committed by a kid who had never been touched by his parents.

"We just had a big birthday party for him in Youth Hall [a detention facility]," Levine said. "He's been there a year, and everybody in Youth Hall loves the kid. He's bright, witty, and personable. And nobody, I mean nobody, could believe he did what he did."

Zachary, Scott, Michelle, and Randolph are pseudonyms for members of an upper-middle-income Jewish family who lived in a posh Miami suburb.

Thursday was not a good day for Zachary. He got a failing grade in English and did poorly in math class. Besides those disappointments, he received two detentions and was thrown out of art class. Art was one of his favorite subjects. And in physical education class, he said later, "I got the teacher all mad at me again."

His mother too was angry when he phoned her about his bad day in school. Michelle was already upset about her own difficulties, and Zachary's problems only added to her rage. She scolded him and he knew he would be punished when she got home. This October day of burgeoning setbacks and disappointments seemed to confirm what his parents were always telling him: He was only as good as his worst grade. He felt like a failure—he could never recall a time when he had not felt like a failure—and it appeared that he would never measure up to his parents' expectations no matter how hard he tried. After he talked to his mother, he decided that today was a good day to resolve everything. He would kill himself. But first he would kill his mother.

He got out his father's .45-caliber Colt Python, which was concealed behind a dresser in his home. He loaded it and waited. He expected his mother to arrive shortly after 6 P.M., as she regularly did. This day, however, nothing worked the way Zachary wanted. His nine-year-old brother, Scott, came home unexpectedly. Zachary panicked. He did not want Scott there. He tried various ploys to get him to leave the house, and finally, when it was obvious that Scott wanted to stay home, Zachary lured him into the family room. He killed him with one shot to the head. Zachary left the body on the floor and waited for his mother. When she came home several minutes later, she inquired about Scott and Zachary told her he was in the family room. When she walked toward the room, Zachary killed her with a single shot to the head. He could not kill himself, however, so he went to a nearby lake and threw the gun into the water. Returning to the house, Zachary called his father and said that he had come home and found the front door open, but he could not find his mother or brother. His father called a neighbor, who came to the house and found the bodies. When Zachary was arrested that night on two counts of first-degree murder, he was twelve. He said later that he had planned to kill only himself and his mother, so that his brother and father could lead better lives.

For almost eight months after the murders, Zachary was the subject of almost a dozen psychiatric and psychological examinations and evaluations. He also had a neurological examination. The consensus was that he had killed his mother and brother after years of severe emotional abuse and neglect, plus a psychiatric disorder that had been untreated for years. Three years before he executed his mother and brother, a psychologist who examined Zachary had told his parents that he was so emotionally disturbed that it bordered on the "severely pathological." Michelle and Randolph told the psychologist that treatment would have to wait until they straightened out their careers and financial concerns.

When a load of psychological background information was presented before the grand jury, the jurors indicted Zachary as an adult but asked that he be treated as a minor. They did not want him to go to jail, but they didn't want him back on the streets at eighteen if he was so sick he could be dangerous.

Michelle had met Randolph when he was a career military officer with big ambitions. His father frequently said with pride that his son was born to be a general. When Michelle and Randolph married, she demanded that he leave the service. He did. Later, she demanded that he get rid of his gun collection. He gave away most of the weapons but kept some in their home. She also complained about his father. Randolph stopped seeing him for almost fourteen years, until the day he died, two years before Michelle did. Randolph loved Michelle for many reasons, one being the way she took charge of his life and gave it direction.

Both were ambitious and wanted to enjoy the luxuries that life could provide them. All they needed was more money than they had.

During the years they were together, they worked long hours and rarely took vacations. He worked in real estate and later taught night college courses. Michelle worked as a fashion consultant and held several different jobs. Unable to have children, they adopted Zachary when he was four months old, and Scott four years later.

Zachary was a healthy twelve-pound baby when he was adopted. He crawled, walked, and talked early and was toilet trained at two. It took Michelle about a month to train him. Zachary, however, remained enuretic until he was six or seven. His mother told a psychologist that her son's enuresis stemmed from his sleeping too deeply and not waking up to go the bathroom. Though he had been healthy when he arrived in the home, Zachary was later plagued with colds, croup, and repeated ear infections. No one knew why.

Zachary's IQ placed him in the upper 1 percent of the country's population, but dyslexia was a serious learning disability that stayed with him throughout school. He had problems reading, writing, and spelling, though no one, except his parents, ever accused him of not trying. He started out as an average to above-average student, slumped to average as he got older, and eventually started getting a few Ds and Fs. His parents always reminded him that he functioned well below his capacity. His attempts to do better only frustrated him and angered them. In first grade Zachary was described as "rambunctious" and a minor discipline problem; by seventh grade he had been expelled once and was constantly in trouble for being "aggressive" or unable to "keep his hands to himself." His parents tried special learning programs and even sent him to a private school, but he did not get any better. He just got into more trouble. Michelle and Randolph were adamant that he get above-average grades, and when he didn't, he was punished.

He could be grounded for periods ranging from several days to three months for getting grades lower than B. Zachary was not allowed to use the telephone or look at television when he was being punished, and was only allowed to leave his room for school, meals, and the bathroom. He was grounded so much during his school years that he was never allowed to attend birthday parties thrown for neighborhood youths, nor was he ever allowed to have one of his own. His parents at times ignored him for long periods of time as part of his punishment. His mother would suddenly scream at him or throw something if he crossed her. They rarely hit him but they also rarely hugged or kissed him.

When he was about ten and attending private school, his parents received so many complaints about his behavior and learning problems that they took him to a psychologist. The doctor thought that Zachary could not adequately distinguish between reality and fantasy. "His suspiciousness and paranoia borders on the severely pathological," the psychologist wrote in his report. Zachary's fantasies and thoughts pulsed with violence. The doctor believed that the hearing problems Zachary was experiencing were caused by "auditory hallucinations." Zachary heard nonexistent voices. "He cannot be allowed to go off by himself and he literally needs a teacher who is in arm's length of him most of the time," the doctor wrote.

Michelle and Randolph said they would get him help after they took care of their financial concerns.

Three years later, when Zachary was more disruptive in school and more in need of help, his parents finally decided to take action. But they ignored the doctor's opinion about Zachary's severe emotional problem. Instead, they told their son that he had an "attitude problem" and that they had decided to correct it by enrolling him in a military academy in Georgia. He would have to forgo his bar mitzvah, for which he had been diligently studying.

Zachary hated the academy the first day he arrived. He did not like cadet life and its hazing, and he was calling his parents every day and begging them to bring him back home. Ten days after he arrived, Randolph, despite Michelle's opposition, brought his son back. The home front now turned into a war zone.

Michelle was already deeply embroiled in a fierce squabble with her brothers and sisters over their mother's estate. Two of Michelle's business deals had also soured, and she was infuriated that she and Randolph had lost the large nonrefundable tuition payment they had made for Zachary to attend the military academy. When Randolph brought Zachary home, she threatened to divorce him. Randolph in turn blamed Zachary for causing the problems that now threatened his marriage. Zachary was punished by being prevented from having his bar mitzvah. The whole house was in an uproar that lasted a little more than a month. Then Zachary made his fatal decision, and the uproar was over.

"The psychiatrists were never able to identify exactly what kind of problem the kid had," Levine said. "It was a disorder that hadn't really manifested itself to be identified. All they can say is that the kid has a serious psychiatric problem. But you wouldn't know it if you met him."

There were mixed opinions about the disorder that everyone suspected affected Zachary.

"This young man is developing a schizophrenic illness," wrote one examiner. "He is in the earlier stages and there are strong indications that he has some paranoid delusional ideas in formation. If this is indeed the case, he is the youngest person I have ever seen with such delusional processes."

Another disagreed: "The continued cooperation of Zachary during the interview in itself provided convincing evidence that Zachary was not paranoid."

That examiner also wrote, "The subject's subsequent remarks clearly demonstrated that he has in fact experienced a great deal of sorrow and guilt for the killing of his brother and for the effect that this incident has had on his father."

But again another doctor offered his opinion: "Although he claims to regret his actions, I did not get the impression that he experienced much remorse and guilt. From the way he described his feelings it is evident that he believed his mother deserved her fate."

He also wrote, "Zachary has almost a chameleon-like capacity to adapt to his circumstances, as is evidenced by his present placement [Youth Hall]. He knows how to please people and to provide the responses that are desired and perhaps rewarded. He is the type of youngster who may appear to the treatment team as if he is making progress. That progress may prove ephemeral once he is returned to the community."

This psychiatrist recommended, as did several other examiners, that Zachary be placed in a residential psychiatric unit to receive intensive care. But he added that the boy's progress should be monitored by a doctor who was not affiliated with the hospital.

"The reason for this is that the treatment team may have developed a bias in the direction of becoming overly optimistic regarding Zachary's progress in their programs," he wrote. "An independent evaluator would be less likely to show that tendency."

Zachary's status, it was decided, would be reviewed after he had spent two years in an out-of-state facility.

Though the cause of Zachary's emotional disturbance was unknown, there was never any doubt about the source of the severe

emotional abuse and neglect that had been visited on him. Zachary's
mother was described as "paranoid, suspicious, guarded, untrusting
and hostile" by one examiner and "very greedy, eager for power and
control, aggressive and extremely suspicious" by another. His father,
it was decided, had held some feelings for his son but he had always
sided with Michelle when she criticized Zachary. Zachary had been
the scapegoat for anything that went wrong in the family.

Neither parent, according to the reports, actually knew how to
care for their children's emotional needs. "They treated them as min-
iature adults," wrote one doctor, and they neglected to provide the
kind of emotional development that all youngsters need in order to
mature as human beings. Levine said there was little indication of
any affection expressed to the boys. Neighbors said that they had
never witnessed Randolph and Michelle hugging and kissing their
kids. Zachary, after his arrest, said he believed that his mother had
hugged him on his last birthday. But he could not remember the last
time she had said she loved him. What he could recall was being
constantly rebuked.

"It was a lifetime of things like that," Levine said.

If that was so, then the emotional deprivation Zachary suffered
was many times more severe than that suffered by fourteen-year-old
Julie, who was frequently abandoned by her mother. Julie at least
had her great-grandmother to provide some nurturing as a youngster.
Zachary had no one.

Scott, Zachary's brother, suffered in his own way. Members of
one family who had known both boys described Zachary as respectful
and engaging, but remembered Scott as severely withdrawn. When
he visited their home, he had uttered only a few words. Scott coped
with his family life by extreme withdrawal.

Randolph and Michelle rarely associated with other families in the
neighborhood, and did not encourage their sons to be friendly with
anyone. There was a great deal of discord with their relatives—Randolph was not talking with his father and Michelle was fighting with
siblings—and no solid ties were ever developed in their community.
As a family, Randolph and Michelle and Scott and Zachary were
hermetically sealed off from the rest of the world. They were trapped
in their own nuclear unit.

*   *   *

Levine handled another parricide case involving a teenager who killed his father after years of abuse. But before Levine got far into the case, the boy's family decided to hire a private attorney. The youngster was indicted but the attorney was able to arrange a plea bargain. It allowed the boy to plead guilty to a lesser charge, and in turn, he would be enrolled in a military academy.

# PART III

## The
## Mentally Ill

There were few if any doubts that John was destined for success. A bright student with a facile mind, he graduated from college with honors in math, and he also spoke and wrote four languages. He served overseas in the Vietnam War, and when he came home he never fulfilled expectations. Success eluded him, and the erstwhile scholar passed through a succession of menial jobs. He was working as a dishwasher one summer in 1978 when he went berserk in his parents' New York City home and the police took him to a psychiatric hospital. He was later transferred to a veteran's hospital, and after a month he was released but continued receiving treatment as an outpatient. He was thirty-four years old.

Two years later on a summer day John got into a car and drove out of the city. He traveled several hours until he entered a small hamlet in upstate New York, where he parked on a neighborhood street. But he never got out of the car. For more than twelve hours he sat motionless, with the windows up on a hot, humid day. His enigmatic presence rattled the neighborhood residents enough to provoke some to call the police. When a patrol car arrived, the police found him distraught and begging for help. They took him to a local hospital, where he was later picked up by his parents, who brought him back home. When he sought readmittance to the veteran's hospital where he had been hospitalized, he was turned away. According to one newspaper, there were seventeen empty beds in the hospital, and its rules required that emergency cases always be admitted. But the doctor who examined John told him there weren't enough beds and that he wasn't sick enough to be admitted as an emergency patient. His parents had little choice but to take him back home. For the next few days he was seen walking around with a hammer in his hand, and early one morning he decided to use it.

He broke into his parents' bedroom, beat his seventy-two-year-old father unconscious, and chased his mother, sixty-five, out of their two-story home and into the driveway, where he knocked her to the ground and killed her. A neighbor who heard her dying screams called the police. John was charged with assault and murder, but later in court was found not guilty by reason of insanity and committed to a psychiatric hospital indefinitely.

Although this murder was reported in all of the New York City daily newspapers, it was not the type of anecdotal account that would normally be mentioned in a book on family violence. That's because mentally ill people rarely commit violent crimes. The authors of the definitive study *Behind Closed Doors: Violence in the American Family* write that mental illness is an insignificant factor in cases of family violence. "Granted, in some instances of physical abuse, the offender is so mentally disturbed that he or she cannot comprehend reality," they wrote. "But in the vast majority of cases of violence in the family, the participants possess none of the symptoms or problems which we normally associate with those who are mentally ill or suffering from personality disorders."

The Attorney General's Task Force on Family Violence also found mental illness an insignificant factor in their study. Task force members traveled to several cities and recorded testimony about beatings, rapes, murder, and general mayhem in the American family. Its final report, released in September 1984, included no references to any connection between mental illness and violence in the family. In *Behind Closed Doors,* it is estimated that mental illness occurs 10 percent of the time at most in family violence cases.

Only a small number of the country's estimated 30 million mentally ill people have committed violent acts, and most of the violence has been directed not at strangers but at authority figures (such as doctors and staff of mental hospitals), family members, and parents—the people most intimately involved with the deranged. But the chimera that mentally ill people are dangerous, unpredictable, vile, and evil and that they are regularly involved in violent crimes has been more persuasive than reality.

When John Hinckley shot President Ronald Reagan, his press

spokesman, a Secret Service man, and a police officer, the country was outraged. After a jury decided Hinckley was insane and acquitted him of all charges, he was committed to a psychiatric hospital, but the verdict sparked a resounding howl of indignation throughout the nation and seemed to confirm the worst suspicions about the mentally ill, the judicial system, and the insanity defense. In the ensuing uproar, there were charges that the insanity defense regularly allows dangerous criminals to escape punishment when they commit serious crimes, and that conflicting testimony by prosecution and defense lawyers confuses jurors and therefore results in an alarming number of acquittals. Other charges against the defense included the claim that many defendants acquitted on insanity grounds spend only brief periods in psychiatric hospitals, and after they are released they commit more crimes.

Those sentiments, however, have never been fully substantiated. According to testimony before the National Commission on the Insanity Defense, sponsored in 1983 by the National Mental Health Association, much of what the public perceives as the ills of the insanity defense is mired in stereotypes and myths. University of Virginia Professor Richard J. Bonnie, who testified for the commission, said preliminary research indicated that the "insanity plea is entered in less than one percent of felony cases and that acquittal by reason of insanity is an extremely rare event." Citing Virginia as an example, he said that the number of insanity acquittals there "does not appear to exceed 15 in any average year."

John Petrila, a counsel for the New York State Office of Mental Health, who also testified, said the defense is raised once in six hundred or seven hundred cases in New York and is successful about 25 percent of the time. Other data, also taken from *Myths and Realities: A Report of the National Commission on the Insanity Defense* and *Hearing Transcripts of the National Commission on the Insanity Defense* provide similar evidence. Of the thirty-two thousand defendants represented by the New Jersey public defender's office in 1981, fifty-two entered insanity pleas and only fifteen of those were successful. "All empirical analyses . . . have been consistent," Joseph H. Rodriguez, the public advocate of New Jersey, was quoted as saying in the commission's report. "The public, the legal profession and specifically legislators dramatically and grossly overestimate both the frequency and success rate of the insanity plea."

Another popular misconception addressed by the commission was that doctors testifying for the prosecution and defense often disagree, therefore confusing jurors and resulting in acquittals. "First of all, the experts do not usually disagree," Bonnie testified. "To the contrary, most psychiatric dispositions in the criminal process, including insanity acquittals, are arranged without fanfare, without disagreement among the experts, and indeed, without dissent by the prosecution." If the experts disagree and the case goes to trial, he said, "the defendant is usually convicted" because juries are very skeptical about psychiatric testimony and tend to side with the prosecution.

Most of those who have been acquitted for psychiatric reasons, according to John Petrila's preliminary research, have been people who committed misdemeanors. "When you look at the most recent data, in no jurisdiction does homicide comprise a majority of acquittees," he said. "The percentage of those charged with homicide range from seven and one half percent of acquittees in Missouri to about 47 percent in Michigan. In New York the percentage is decreasing. Initial studies revealed that in the mid-1970s in New York, homicide constituted about 53 percent of the acquittees. That figure has dropped in the most recent data to 37 percent." The percentage of homicides was dropping, he said, because more and more people charged with misdemeanors were being acquitted on grounds they were insane.

Other studies, according to testimony, have shown that defendants acquitted of misdemeanor charges on grounds of insanity were involuntarily hospitalized for longer periods of time than people convicted of similar crimes were incarcerated.

But it is the small number of violent and dangerous mentally ill people who have commanded the most attention and heightened public fears. And most of their victims have been people who were trying to help them.

A mother whose son was a veteran: "My son . . . he's the oldest of ten children. In 1964 he was 18. He was called to Vietnam, and he served three and a half years or maybe more. When he was discharged from Vietnam, he came back. I lost my husband in 1983. [My son] said, 'Mama, I'll take care of you because I'm the oldest now, and I'll take care of the family.' When he came back from Vietnam, he was a little unhappy. Well, he got married, started a family and had no problem. Then he was unhappy with his job. He re-enlisted again and went back in the Navy, and he went overseas again. One day we got a call that they were sending him back home. They sent him to Bethesda, Maryland, to the Navy hospital. He was there for a couple of months, and they released him. They never told me what was wrong or what to expect out of him.

"Well at that time, he and his wife were separated, and he came to live with me. He acted all right. I didn't see anything wrong with him. So one night we were talking, and I went to bed. He would walk up and down the steps. Like he would sleep in the day, and walk at night. I went down to ask him would he please stop walking up and down the steps so I could get some sleep because I had to go to work the next morning. He was always a good boy. He never talked back, anything. But he had a bat. For some reason he picked up the bat and he hit me up beside the head, a couple of times. I lost consciousness. He left, and they [police] picked him up. I didn't know what kind of help to get. My kids were scared. So one of them called the police. That's the only help we could get. We called them and they took me to the hospital. One of my daughters heard my crying and came down.

"I knew he didn't do this out of meanness because he was always a good boy, always seemed to listen to everything I tell him. And they picked him up. For some reason he wandered all the way to New York, and they picked him up in Jersey. They had him in a hospital there. So the authorities from Maryland went to Jersey, brought him back to Baltimore City Jail. We went down and had the hearing there at the town. At the courthouse they said they were sending him to Perkins [Hospital, in Maryland]. I couldn't afford a lawyer. So he had one of those lawyers from the state. He never contacted me, never talked with me. Anyway, they sent him out there, and I would go see him every weekend. I would go see him, and he seemed to be coming along fine. I really haven't had any problem out of him since. He's doing fine now.

"I pray to God each and every day that things will get better for him, and when he comes home—he has eight sisters, one brother, and the children—that they all get along just like nothing ever happened. I love him. We all still love him. We want him to come home because I'm sure that he didn't do anything out of meanness. It would have to be something wrong.

"But I really do think they let him out of the Navy hospital a little too soon. They didn't tell us what to expect."

A sister with a sick brother: "Two and a half years ago my brother
. . . was released from a penal institute in Hagerstown [Maryland]
where he had been for two years. He had been found guilty for having drugs, being involved with drugs. He was sent to Hagerstown.
While he was there that time they found out that he was sick, that
he was mentally ill. They knew this in the hospital. He would often
feel something coming on, something he couldn't control. He knew it
was a different feeling, that it was not normal. He would ask them to
put him in solitary confinement until he could control it himself.
Gradually he did, apparently. He learned to play the game with
them. As long as he didn't act crazy, he would be able to get out.

"One day came, without any notice, that he would be released that
day from Hagerstown. They gave him his $22 and put him on the
street. They gave him no counseling for his illness. They told no one
about the illness. They had a previous history that said something
else could happen to him. It had happened before in the same way,
people being released so suddenly, without any adjustment. They
cannot immediately adjust. They get confused, not knowing where to
go for help. They're just left to find their own way. He was out of
Hagerstown for five days, and the stress and confusion was tremendous. On the 19th day of May he killed my father. He stabbed him
so many times. [My brother] felt that he was hearing voices and he
felt that everything had come down on him.

"It's not his nature to be violent, but it happened. The state knew
he was ill, and they put him on the street. My mother saw the
beginning of this. She saw him attack my father and she ran out the
door and started screaming in the street until the neighbors came.
After [my brother] had done this, he went over to my mother and
just laid down on the ground, completely disoriented, blood on his
hands, not knowing where it came from. He said, 'Mother, I have
blood on my hands. I must have cut myself. I need to go to the
hospital.' He just laid there and waited for the police to come. A
pastor that had worked with him in Hagerstown knew [him], knew
he was basically a good person, but was disturbed, was sick. [The
pastor] came to my older brother, my mother, myself and suggested
we get a lawyer so that they would not put him in another penal
institution. He introduced us to a lawyer. My mother was too confused at this point. My brother was so angry he could not help anyone, and it was left to me to make decisions, to try to get [my

brother], desperately try to get him into Perkins where he would receive treatment for being ill. You must recognize the difference of someone being sane and doing something in a sane manner and someone who is insane and who does cry out for years, not knowing what is wrong with him, until the confusion builds and builds. He had only been out five days when this happened.

"Perkins has worked with [my brother] tremendously. I saw [him] about two weeks after this happened, when he was ill and when he was still very much in the state that he had done this. He was still telling me how it happened in a very matter-of-fact way. He broke out all the windows in the car, the car in the garage. He had thoughts of hearing voices. He thought motorcycles were coming after him. He had gone and taken his furniture out of the basement where it had been stored and thrown it outside. He had gone to my father and hit him, trying to wake somebody. Nobody could hear what he was trying to say. The voices kept coming back to him. He and my father had never had a fight in their lives. I saw him when he was very ill. He sat and told me exactly move for move, exactly what he had done. I went, sat there and listened. I went to my parents' house [later] and screamed for ten minutes. For one of the two years I was away in Utah after he had been found 'not guilty by reason of insanity.' My husband had, the same week my father was killed, found out we would have to leave in a few months. I was responsible for everything that [my brother] was associated with in straightening out his matters before I left.

"I saw him in the very beginning when he was very sick. I talked with his social workers, and they kept me informed at all times on his progress. While I was in Utah, he had a further setback. They described it from the hospital as being as sick as anyone could be. They didn't even give a term, a name to it. He's paranoid schizophrenic. He thought the bricks were coming down out of the wall and everyone was against him. He went down from that point.

"Now he has come up. He is on a very strong medication, a shot that he takes every week—I'm sorry—once every two weeks. His social workers and the therapist have worked tremendously. They have worked beyond and above anything that I could have ever expected people to do for someone. He's doing fairly well now. He's progressing, but you still have to live. I have to live with it. He has to live with it. He has to suffer with the thought of what he has done.

"He is not a hostile person. He is ill, and there is quite a bit of difference. For the rest of his life he will have to face this, which I do not think will be easy for him."

A father with a sick son: "My son, who is 23 years old now, was a scholarship student, a five-year scholarship at Cooper Union university, in New York City. It's the number one architectural college in the country. Our family: he's got two brothers, my wife and myself. If we had to take a vote, we would say that he was the most solid member of our family. That's just how we all felt.

"About 12 o'clock one evening, his roommate called and said that [my son] was taken to Bellevue by two policemen. What happened? [He] cried out in his room. The roommate knew nothing of it, slept through it, but the people in the next apartment heard him. They thought somebody was robbing the apartment or something. So they called the police, and when they came, [my son] didn't want to let them in. So they broke down the door, and seeing there was nothing wrong, they didn't know what, why, what happened that made [him] cry out in the night. They took him to Bellevue. Then his roommate called us and said that they had taken him to Bellevue.

"The doctor at Bellevue thought or the policeman thought perhaps he was on drugs or something. He has never been on drugs at any time. They took him there and the doctor kept him about an hour or so. In the meantime, [his mother] and I left to go up to New York. They had released him to a classmate of his, and he went to her apartment to stay until we got up there.

"They didn't keep him at Bellevue. They didn't check him. They didn't do a thing. Yet these two officers that brought him there had whatever you call it, a sense that something was wrong. The psychiatrist evidently failed to pick it up or to keep him for a day or two or some time and check him out some way or another.

"Well, when we got up there, we went to his roommate's apartment, where we got [him], and we brought him back to Baltimore. We had no trouble with him. We just felt [he] was tired out. He had been working on a project and hadn't slept much that week. We had never had any indication that [he] was ever sick. Never, until this call. Not through his whole life.

"Well, we came home. He and [his mother] went to her apartment. We were divorced, and I went back to my apartment, but I said, 'I'd liked to stay.' In the meantime I had made arrangements with a psychiatrist to see him in the morning. I said, 'Well, should we bring him in?' This was in the afternoon. 'No, I'll see him in the morning.'

"Well, that night he killed his mother, and he was taken to Perkins Hospital. He's been there for four years.

"Now, again, there was no way of telling that he was—how do you, like you said, how do you tell a madman? For every [one like my son], there's at least 300 out there that are fighting it solemnly. Instead of coming out and saying something, they figure they can beat it. So they keep it to themselves. In [him] it must have been growing for three, four, five weeks. No implication. No way of telling. Yet if the education was gotten out that, look, when you have these untoward thoughts, tell them to somebody. Get to somebody and something could be done. For every [one like my son], there's at least 300 on the verge, and they're fighting it, and with the grace of God, they may overcome it. Whether it's a chemical imbalance or whatever it is which is the trigger factor, we might as well hit that point.

"And the thing that I might as well get in here is that's why this work that this Commission is doing is so very, very important. You can do it, and let's not be too irrational like society is today. Right now because of the Hinckley case, we want a 'quickie' legislation to satisfy our unrest. So let's take time to get the right wording. It is so important. [The commission recommended the wording 'not responsible by reason of insanity' for such cases.]

"Well, to get back to [my son. He] is working now. He's been in the hospital for four years. He goes back and forth to the hospital every day, and he sleeps at the hospital. He stays with me on weekends. He has a job. He meets the public. He does very well, and each week or so he's graduating to the next step out in the community. He is just doing great. It's a tremendous blow to think here, like everybody should know, who's the next? That's the point. We're not just talking about one percent of the country. We're talking about 100 percent of the country because we don't know who that one percent out of 100 percent is. So everybody is involved. I guess it took me about a year or so to stop crying almost daily. I couldn't go anywhere there wasn't a reminder perhaps 30, 40, 50 times a day. My salvation has been to get in and work like heck to help [my son]. Perkins formed a parents' group for a couple of years. We have folks . . . and support groups throughout the country that are very important.

"It's just—I guess it gets to me. It just gets to me, and I'm not as precise as I could be."

*     *     *

An estimated 2 million people have schizophrenia, and several million loved ones, like the people who testified for the commission, suffer grief and anguish because of the disease. People afflicted with schizophrenia may see and hear things that don't exist, be plunged into terrifying worlds where disembodied voices constantly berate them or tell them what to do, have no sense of who they are, and believe that their bodies have merged with those of other people. They may also misinterpret actual events, and simple everyday sounds can be perceived as special messages being sent to them. Prior experiences and feelings may also become distorted or appear in bizarre forms once the disease strikes.

More than seventy years ago Swiss psychiatrist Eugen Bleuler used the word "schizophrenia" to describe a group of severe mental disorders that share some basic symptoms but also appear in a variety of forms. Some forms do not cause hallucinations and delusions. There are types of schizophrenia that appear suddenly without warning, while one form starts insidiously and does not reveal itself for months or even years. This type, once it has set in, progressively erodes a personality and there is no recovery.

The cause of schizophrenia has been the source of endless speculation. For a while, it was popular to blame the family or "schizophrenogenic mothers" for the disease, but such opinions have been roundly dismissed. Dr. E. Fuller Torrey, author of *Surviving Schizophrenia: A Family Manual*, writes that childhood trauma and domineering mothers and passive fathers do not cause the illness. He and many others now believe that the disease has a genetic predisposition and that a chemical imbalance causes schizophrenia. There is no known cure, but antipsychotic medications—such as Stelazine, Thorazine, and Prolixin—can decrease or eliminate hallucinations and delusions. One third of those with schizophrenia can completely recover, one third can improve enough to lead reasonably normal lives, and one third will deteriorate as their personalities disintegrate.

In many cases, parents have been the victims of attacks by members of that small group of mentally ill people who are dangerous and violent. These sons and daughters were invariably suffering from schizophrenia. Parents have also been active in various groups that have opposed the Reagan administration's position that would virtually eliminate the insanity defense. Many do not want their family tragedies compounded by having a sick daughter or son incarcerated in jail when the individual should be hospitalized.

One tragedy is enough.

In March 1983, a twenty-one-year-old man was arrested after his mother was found raped and murdered in the family home in Torrance, California. A court found him mentally incompetent to stand trial, and he was committed to a mental hospital until his condition improved. He had been diagnosed as paranoid schizophrenic. A little more than a year later, he was acquitted of the rape charge but found guilty of murdering his mother. In the same hearing, however, the judge ruled that he was not guilty by reason of insanity and ordered him committed to a mental hospital.

In a statement after the verdict, the man's father, according to the *Los Angeles Times,* told reporters he hoped the case would "encourage citizens and government to address themselves to ways of detecting mental illness and of treating it in ways that will be of comfort to those afflicted, to their families and to the public generally." The father did not want a family tragedy magnified by his son's going to jail. The father was the personal attorney to President Reagan.

# 11

# Anthony

Frank and Harriet installed a peephole in their front door so that they would not have to open it and expose themselves to sudden danger. They sometimes slept with a baseball bat near their bed, and there were nights when they did not sleep at all. Nothing in their lives had prepared them for the days when they would have to live in fear of their son. Anthony, their youngest, the promising craftsman and sensitive artist, regarded them with suspicion and treated them with contempt. He attacked them on the slightest provocation and taunted them with death threats. There were occasions when he menaced them with long-distance telephone calls from California, where he lived on and off, hustling as a street bum or foraging like a bag lady. In one harassing episode, he called them from a Rocky Mountain state to let them know that he was on his way to get them. His next call was from Nebraska. Just as their fear was about to swamp them, Anthony's third call came from California, where, for unknown reasons, he had returned after abandoning his trip.

Frank and Harriet shared years of endless fretting and worrying about his life and their lives. Anthony was hurting the only people he could depend on because no one else tolerated his bellicose and vituperative manner, or tried to understand that he was sick and getting sicker. People treated him like a leper and avoided him as if he had the plague. But Anthony's disease was schizophrenia and he aggravated it by taking drugs. His family also bore his problems, and it had all started so insidiously.

Frank, Harriet, and Anthony are pseudonyms for members of a

middle-class Italian family in Rochester, New York. Frank, a teacher, and Harriet, a housewife, had two older children. Anthony was their problem child.

He was born with an asthmatic condition that kept him from running and jumping with the other neighborhood kids, and he needed medication. The medicine, over the years, might have led to his drug addiction beginning as early as ten or eleven, according to a psychiatrist who later examined him. By the time he was twelve, Anthony was using LSD. By the time he was in high school, he was getting high regularly on drugs and slipping deep into the grip of a debilitating mental illness, as well as suffering from asthma. One day in his senior year, after repeated incidents of violence, Frank and Harriet called the police and Anthony was taken from their home in a straitjacket and committed to a local psychiatric hospital. A doctor diagnosed him as paranoid schizophrenic. Anthony was prescribed psychotropic drugs that would diminish his delusions and hallucinations, but when his condition improved he would stop taking his medicine and have a relapse. When he became uncontrollably violent, he was hospitalized again. This went on for three or four years.

When he graduated from high school, he moved out of his home but he did not stray too far from his parents. He had too much trouble supporting himself to completely cut his umbilical cord. Jobs lasted as long as a few days or as short as a few hours. He needed money to survive and to travel, because there were times when he flew back and forth between Rochester and California as if he were a suburban commuter.

By the time he was twenty, Anthony was using cocaine and morphine, and on a trip to India he started smoking opium. He had also beaten his parents several times and tried to strangle Harriet more than once. His parents had had him committed to hospitals, called the police when he was deranged, exercised patience during the bleakest of times, and prayed. Nothing made their lives any better, nor his. Things just got worse.

On a summer day a few weeks after his twentieth birthday in 1981, Anthony accused his father of "interfering with his thoughts" and attacked him with a knife. Harriet jumped into the fight to help her husband and the two of them drove their son off. Anthony fled into their home and locked them out. Later that night, they were desperate enough to call the police, but the last time he was taken away in a straitjacket had so upset them that they were not sure they

could bear the sight again. They waited until they believed he had
calmed down and then they slipped quietly into their home. But Anthony was waiting for them. While his mother was in another part of
the house, he attacked his father. He bashed Frank on the head,
cracking his skull, and cut his throat with a big knife. Harriet
rushed to help but it was too late. As she knelt next to her dying
husband, Anthony sneaked up on her and smashed her on the head
with a large statue, knocking her unconscious. He then tossed her
down the cellar steps. When she awoke he dragged her up the steps
and over Frank's bloody body. She started fighting for her life just as
a neighbor rushed to her aid.

After he was arrested and put in the county jail, Anthony told a
psychiatrist that the devil had ordered him to kill his father. But he
also told the doctor that Frank was still alive in his grave. Because
Anthony was incoherent and too sick to cooperate with his lawyer,
he was judged not competent to stand trial and sent to a maximum-
security hospital in upstate New York until his condition improved.
It was believed to be the first time in almost a decade that a defendant in the county, let alone in the city, had been found unfit to
stand trial, according to the morning newspaper.

For six months Anthony did not respond to the medication or any
other medical efforts to get him ready for trial. But after another four
months, his condition had improved enough for the doctors to certify
him competent to return to Rochester and be tried. But they also
noted, according to medical records, that he was still "somewhat of a
management problem due to his tendency to abuse medications, occasional outbursts of violence and occasional overt homosexual behavior
and frequent bronchial attacks."

Back in the county jail, Anthony, while his lawyer prepared to
argue that his client should be acquitted of murder charges because
he had been insane at the time of the murder and was still insane,
convinced the staff and inmates who were in contact with him that
he was crazy. He laughed and boasted about killing his father. Two
psychiatrists for the defense examined him and diagnosed him as
paranoid schizophrenic. He had been insane when he killed his father, they were ready to testify.

Dr. Russell Barton, who was hired by the prosecutor, however,
believed that Anthony had known what he was doing when he killed

his father and had planned it. He had also wanted to kill his mother, the psychiatrist believed, because he wanted to eliminate a witness.

Barton, an Englishman, had been the director of a psychiatric hospital in Essex before he settled in Rochester and opened a private practice. Barton, who had testified in previous cases for either the defense or the prosecution, examined Anthony about a year after he killed his father. Anthony was Barton's first patricide case.

During his examination, Anthony "was smiling all the time and kept saying that he was of the living dead and that he could communicate with his father telepathically," Barton recalled later. Anthony also told him that he was in telepathic communication with two friends who planned to dig up his father's body and cut out his "yellow esophagus" and give it to the lead singer in the rock band Genesis. He had killed his father, he told Barton, to get his yellow esophagus. Barton, however, thought Anthony was a "rogue" and a "cheat" and that he had killed his father "as a result of a long-standing row." Anthony also said that he had taken a hundred hits of LSD the night before the murder. Barton thought he was lying but he could not be sure.

"That amount can kill you," Barton said.

Barton thought Anthony was seriously disturbed but was suffering from a different form of schizophrenia.

"I believed," Barton said, reading from his report on his examination, "he was suffering from hebephrenic schizophrenia, a condition described in the American Psychiatric Association's *Third Diagnostic Statistical Manual of Psychiatric Disorders, DSM-3*, as schizophrenia, disorganized type. Hebephrenic schizophrenia begins during the early teenage years. It is earlier than paranoid schizophrenia and starts very insidiously. It relentlessly disintegrates and destroys the personality. An individual tends to laugh inanely and there doesn't tend to be any relationship between his emotions and what he is thinking or the situation he is in. Foolish giggling and preoccupation with trivial matters is another sign, but these matters tend to be very important to a patient having hebephrenic schizophrenia. He'll laugh at something that isn't funny or get angry over some minutiae while letting the most important things in his life sail past unintended."

Paranoid schizophrenia can start in the late teens or early twenties, "and there is usually more or less preservation of the personality," Barton said. "There is disintegration but it's not molecular.

It's not so splintered. Tiny bits of the personality, such as giggling without relation to the rest of the personality, the rest of the feelings, the rest of the thoughts—this doesn't occur so much in paranoid schizophrenia. In paranoid schizophrenia they have a basic idea, and from that, systematized delusions occur."

Hebephrenic schizophrenics have "unconnected delusions," Barton said. "They seem to be less tied up to one basic theme." Anthony had bizarre delusions but Barton was not convinced that every symptom Anthony exhibited was even schizophrenic.

"A man's voice inside his head said, 'Kill him, kill him,'" Barton said. "I'm not so sure that's so, because in schizophrenia the voice usually comes from outside the head or from the other side of the room, whereas in depression the voice comes from inside the head. In depression the voice speaks and denigrates the individual. In depression it's one or two words from inside the head, whereas in schizophrenia the voice continues and gives a running commentary, and [for example] it's coming from across the room."

Anthony had bizarre "ideations," Barton said, but there did not appear to be convincing evidence of the kind of auditory hallucinations expected in schizophrenia. Barton also thought that Anthony appeared "insouciant" about murdering his father.

"He just didn't give a shit that his father died or that he, the defendant, killed him," Barton said. "He acted as if he was clearly outside the situation, as though he was in the bleachers watching some sort of game going on in the ball park."

Despite what he believed, Barton told the prosecutor he also did not have "sufficient evidence at the time to make recommendations based on the diagnosis with reasonable medical certainty, and I didn't feel I had a mastery of the case." Barton would have preferred examining Anthony soon after he had been arrested instead of entering the case a year later. So he went along with the finding by the doctors for the defense that Anthony had been paranoid schizophrenic and insane at the time he killed his father.

Because of a state law, the prosecutor and Anthony's lawyer were able to agree not to hold a trial; instead they presented their findings to a judge, who ruled that Anthony had been insane at the time he killed his father. The judge committed Anthony to the same mental hospital that had worked to get him ready for trial.

About a year after he was committed, Anthony asked for a hearing to argue that he should be released from the hospital because he was no longer insane. All during his one-year stay in the hospital he had been pestering his mother for help. Harriet had been commuting between Rochester and the hospital to try to help her son, but she was also terrified of him.

"His mother continued to see him after the murder [and his hospital commitment], and he treated her even worse," Anthony's lawyer said.

Anthony died in the hospital before his hearing could be held. Rochester's afternoon newspaper wrote that he had died of cardiac arrest after a severe asthma attack. His lawyer said he "died under mysterious circumstances and I told his mother to get an attorney about his death."

But she was worn out already from the murder of her husband, and she did not want to be pulled into another investigation of a questionable death.

A mental health lawyer at the hospital said that Anthony had been entitled to a hearing under the law to argue that he should be released, but it was the opinion of the doctors that he would have spent the rest of his life in the hospital. They did not doubt that he would have tried to kill his mother if he had been released.

# 12

# Barry

"The first time I noticed that something was wrong," said Barry's mother later, "was one summer when some relatives came over. It was my husband's sister and her three kids. We had planned a camping trip. Both Matt [Barry's father] and Barry were enthusiastic about backpacking, and Barry was a pretty experienced camper. He was going to be like a big brother to his cousins, and we were all going on the trip. Well, at the last minute, Barry said he didn't feel well enough to go and went back to his room and closed the door. Backpacking was the kind of thing that he loved to do, and I knew something was wrong if he wasn't going on that trip. That was certainly one of the things that I recalled as the first sign that something was amiss." Barry and Matt are pseudonyms.

At Christmastime that same year, when his sister was home from California, hardly anyone in the family felt like celebrating because Barry was gripped by some strange malady. He complained of headaches and of an intense pressure in his head. He no longer cared how he looked or dressed. He neglected to change his clothes, and he continually ran his hands through his hair but would not use a comb.

"That was an unsettling Christmas because of the fact that Barry was definitely not feeling right. It's a terrible irony that this should happen to him because he was always somebody who valued family tradition and he loved the whole ritual of Christmas. When he was a little boy he used to get right under the Christmas tree and lie on his back and look up at the lights and just sort of bask in that whole Christmas spirit. Anyway, on this Christmas Eve when we were in the living room sitting around—I think I was getting some packages ready—Barry just started to shake. He shook all over uncontrollably, and he couldn't stop. He was extremely embarrassed by it, and his sister and I, when he was lying on the floor, put our hands on his arms and legs and tried to calm him. He appreciated that but he was just very embarrassed. And then later that evening—it's one of my most painful memories and I still choke up when I think about it today—I was standing across the way from him and he looked up at me with this anguished expression in his eyes, and he brought his fist down on the table, and he said, 'God, I think I'm going insane.' It was horrible to see that expression on his face as if he was saying, Here is something that is happening to me that I cannot do anything about. That's what I saw on his face, and I didn't know how to respond, and it was as if I too was helpless, seeing this realization coming down on him."

The next day Barry's mother and father contacted the first of almost a dozen doctors who would see her son during the next four years. The first doctor was a local psychiatrist and a family friend who prescribed some mild tranquilizers. The medication had no effect.

"This was at the beginning. Nobody knew what was going on at this point except something was happening that was pretty scary. We began going to see other doctors to see if anyone, first, could tell us what was wrong with him and, second, if there was anyone who could do something about it. We took Barry early to our family doctor. I spoke to him, wondering if there wasn't some biochemical connection. This was in that early period when I sensed that something might be biochemically wrong with him. I wanted him to be tested for low blood sugar because I knew that I was susceptible to this condition. Proper diet made a big difference to me but the doctor just pooh-poohed the blood sugar idea. I was grasping at straws, he told me. What I should do was face the issue and, obviously, my son was psychologically off and we should go get him psychotherapy, which we did. But that wasn't the problem. Barry just kept getting worse, not better. I'm not saying that psychotherapy is basically wrong but it's not the cure for schizophrenia."

Two years would pass before they learned that their son was schizophrenic, but they were never informed of how sick he really was by any of the doctors who examined him. Another two years passed before it was made known to the family that Barry was paranoid schizophrenic and was suffering from a brain disease that required psychotropic medicines or, as they are also called, antipsychotic drugs. By then it was too late.

"It was just incredible how those doctors covered their asses, if you'll pardon the expression, and disclaimed any responsibility. That was the biggest letdown of all: trying to find medical help, and everywhere we turned we came to a dead end. Either the doctors were incompetent or indifferent or totally unable to communicate with us as a family, or all three."

They took Barry to a doctor in Syracuse, New York, based on the recommendation of the local psychiatrist. The new doctor diagnosed Barry's problem as severe depression. It was the wrong diagnosis and, of course, he prescribed the wrong medication.

"It made [Barry] feel worse. It just about knocked him out. It wiped him out so that he could hardly do anything but lie down."

After three trips to Syracuse, just as it was becoming apparent that they had run into another dead end, Barry's sister contacted them with an idea. She was living in Berkeley, California, and had an acquaintance who supposedly had similar problems but had been successfully treated by two doctors involved in orthomolecular psychiatry. They treated their patients with massive doses of vitamins. Barry was not getting better, and the suggestion offered some hope, so he flew out to the west coast to stay near his sister while he underwent treatment.

"They did a glucose tolerance test on him, and he was indeed hypoglycemic [subject to low blood sugar] like me. He was switched over to a better diet, which of course was not a cure for schizophrenia either, but at least he was on the right track with that as a side issue. This one doctor tried to put Barry on some antipsychotic medication, on small doses along with the vitamins. Barry took them for a while but the doctor was very casual about it."

A friend described the medication as "tranquilizers" and chided Barry for taking them. The criticism, plus Barry's own lack of understanding, combined to convince him to rely solely on the vitamins.

"Antipsychotic medicine really isn't like tranquilizers, but they were called that by some people. When I went to Berkeley I called him [the doctor], and here's a point where I wish I had gone to see him instead of calling him on the phone. I called just to get a little information from him and introduce myself. I said, 'Barry doesn't seem to feel he wants to take this medication,' which at this time I

was calling drugs. Well, the doctor said that it was all right if he
didn't want to take them. It was a very loose-ended kind of response,
but I was ready to be educated. I would have appreciated being told
the importance of the medication. That was one point at which I
could have done better and he could have done better too. I should
have tried to find out more from that doctor. I don't know what
difference it would have made, but I believe that was the place
where I could have done better. I didn't realize how sick Barry was
or could become. At that time he seemed to be doing a little better,
and maybe it was because he had been taking some antipsychotic
medication for a brief period."

Almost two years had passed since that day his body had shaken
uncontrollably and he had told his mother he thought he was going
insane. Most diagnoses, when his family could get a doctor to talk to
them, were vague. The Berkeley doctor who was giving him vitamins
"used some vaguely related term for schizophrenia," but it was un-
enlightening. After two years of watching their son getting sicker,
the tension and frustration were beginning to mount.

"I was tired of these doctors' casual, put-off attitudes. One doctor
was sending me bills for psychotherapy, and I wrote him and asked
point-blank what was his diagnosis. He finally replied in this in-
verted sort of way . . . that Barry had one of the schizophrenias that
he would call a thinking disorder, and that the only correction for
this was long-term psychotherapy based on a psychoanalytic model.
That was a lot of hooey. 'Long term,' like he was going to be collecting fees for a long time. Any doctor nowadays who knows schizophrenia knows that psychoanalysis not only does not do any good but
it can do an awful lot of harm. That guy was incompetent. 'Thinking
disorder' is an euphemism for schizophrenia when people don't want
to use the word. He did make a diagnosis of schizophrenia but he
was trying to back away from it."

After ten sessions, Barry's confidence in the doctor withered, and
because he was no longer on the medication, his condition got worse.
Homesick and lonely, he returned to New York to be with his parents. When he arrived, they decided that he should try a mental
health clinic in Nassau County, New York.

"This was another orthomolecular place. We still did not know
that orthomolecular therapy wasn't going to solve the problem. We
paid the money in advance, and Barry was tested and seen in the

clinic for three days and then he came home with a bunch of vitamins. And that was all."

She and her husband tried repeatedly to contact the doctor treating Barry so that they would know what the tests indicated. They also wanted to review the recommendations. They were treated as if they did not exist.

"There was just no feedback. I think it might be a common occurrence because their answer was that they couldn't give out any information without the written request of my son."

Barry "scribbled out" a written consent that they mailed to the doctor. When they failed to receive a reply, they phoned him out of exasperation. The doctor told them at first he could not locate the paper, and when he eventually found it he told them that the consent was not written on regulation-size paper. They argued. Barry's parents told the doctor over the phone that Barry was standing right next to them and was willing to give a verbal consent. But before the doctor could reply, Barry told his parents to tell the doctor that he thought the vitamins were making him feel violent.

"It was one of the first indications that Barry might be experiencing some violent-type thoughts or delusions. He thought it was the high dosage of vitamins that was causing it. So I repeated this to the doctor. I said, 'My son's saying that these megavitamins are making him feel violent,' and he [the doctor] said, 'Oh, just cut down on the dosage. Skip the noon dosage and don't take quite as many.' That was his entire recommendation."

But he would not release any information on the results of the clinic's testing or its recommendations or prognosis. Barry wanted to try another hospital and voluntarily committed himself to one in Syracuse.

"He was there five days, and I called every day and said I would like to speak with the doctor. I was told the doctor was busy and that he would call back. I never got to speak to him."

Barry asked for medication after he signed in but he was told tests and evaluations would have to be completed before they could decide how to treat him. On the fifth day he called home.

"I could sense that he was getting discouraged about it. And I was afraid that he would leave there, that he would run away. And I wanted to communicate this to a doctor . . . but I was unable to get a hold of a doctor and he [Barry] did what I had feared he would do. He left. After five days he got a pass to come home over the July Fourth weekend and he would not go back. And after that he disappeared. When he came home from Syracuse . . . he was worse than when he went in. He was in awful shape. It was heartrending to see him walk in the door. His face was all flushed; his eyes were full of fear and kind of wild. And he started to cry. He was in bad, bad shape."

One morning they woke up and discovered that Barry was missing. He had fled to the west coast somehow hoping he might be able to survive on his own in a place where he had lived happily as a youngster. He found a doctor but no help and ended up living on the streets of Berkeley. His family never knew where he was living or how he was surviving. In the three months he was gone, Barry lost almost twenty pounds and soon looked like one of the emaciated street scavengers that can be seen in almost any city in the country.

In "bad, bad shape" when he fled, Barry was in worse shape when he returned unannounced. His mother discovered him one evening in 1981 as she was walking up the steps to the second floor. She was so happy to see him that she embraced him without noticing that he held a knife in his hand. While she was hugging him, he startled her by saying that he would not hurt her. Barry had never been violent so she was not quite sure what he meant until she saw the knife. Even then nothing made any sense until she realized that her husband had been stabbed. Without his parents knowing it, Barry had entered the house and had been waiting in their bedroom upstairs when his father entered the room. They had argued briefly, and Barry had stabbed him once in the chest. He died shortly after he told his wife to call an ambulance.

Barry did not harm his mother, but he forced her into the family car and refused to release her until they were far from home. He was arrested almost two weeks later in another state. He told the police there that he had killed his father and he was planning to kill himself. He was extradited to New York and placed in the county jail, but several weeks later the sheriff had him committed to a psychiatric hospital because he was so sick. The maelstrom in his head was matched only by the one that descended on his family. Barry's father was a prominent college professor slain by a son in a rural area where murder is as rare as gold. The family became grist for the local press, which ran with the subliminal theme of "weird son kills eccentric father." "The coverage . . . was abusive beyond belief," Barry's mother would say a few years later. The newspaper "worked the names of Son of Sam and Charles Manson into the text, and the drawings that their staff artist did of [Barry] and myself at the court trial could only be described as caricatures of freaks."

In the psychiatric hospital, Barry was given psychotropic medication.

"I think one of the ironies of the situation is that Barry is apparently one of those people who does respond to medication as far as controlling hallucinations and delusions. He has not had any of these symptoms since he has been on medication."

Before he was given the medicine, his lawyer had a psychiatrist examine Barry. Based on the doctor's findings, the lawyer prepared for an insanity defense. It was only about now, with Barry in jail (when he was not in the hospital) and his father dead, that the family learned what his previous doctors had known for months. A court order made the information available.

"The thing that really hurt, the thing that really hurt the most in all of this was that something terrible, a terrible tragedy had to occur before any of these doctors would reveal anything from their notes. The diagnosis of paranoid schizophrenia, the description of the terrible condition he was in, the adjectives they used to describe him. I could hardly believe that they were storing all this information and were not telling it to us."

Records from the mental health clinic in Nassau County said in part, "On intake he was disheveled, speaking in a whisper with fragmented thought and depression. His perceptions were described as changed. He reported anxiety around strange people. He felt tortured and hopeless. He had suicidal and homicidal thoughts but these were not prominent when he was seen. . . . indication of superior intelligence but he did not function at this level because of other factors . . . [Another test indicated] he was noted to have a tendency to withdraw, to view the world as hostile and threatening and possible denial of aggressive impulses projected on others. Depression, anxiety, inadequacy, insecurity and constriction were also noted . . . feelings of insecurity, hesitancy, anxiety, paranoia, hostility, aggression, negative self-concepts, poor reality contact, depression, poor interpersonal relationships and fear of the environment. His Rorschach test showed deep depression, pessimism, fearfulness, fright, suicidal trends, paranoia, repressed anger and hostility and sadistic trends. The diagnosis was schizophrenia of the chronic and undifferentiated type. He was advised to return to his home community for treatment."

The family never knew. Barry had never been threatening or menacing.

"None of that was told to us. It was never communicated to us over the telephone or in writing. It was as if it had never been until after the tragedy. Then it's a public record all of a sudden. This so-called recommendation to look for help back in his community [they had already tried six local doctors], if they did tell him that and he was as sick as they described him to be, how could they expect him to pick up on that vague kind of advice? It was the same story at the [Syracuse] hospital . . . with the notes we were not allowed to see at the time or after Barry had left the [Syracuse] hospital. It was only after Matt was dead and Barry was in jail and the courts demanded the notes and records that they produced them. The notes from the Syracuse hospital had been written by a psychology intern. I have no idea whether the doctor ever saw Barry. The doctor would not speak to me."

About six months after Barry was arrested, just a few days into his trial, Barry's mother and attorney were rudely shocked. The doctor scheduled to appear for the defense examined Barry just a few hours before he was to testify that Barry had been legally insane when he killed his father. His first determination months before had been that Barry was insane. On this day he found that Barry's condition had improved because of the medication he received from the hospital. The doctor felt that under New York State law, Barry could not be found innocent by reason of insanity. "When I first examined him in January, he was not competent to stand trial, and he was very much in need of treatment," he was quoted as saying in the local paper. "Communication with him was very difficult and the information which I received led me to believe he was in fact suffering from a delusion. Had he continued in the same way, I could have continued to support that premise."

Barry and his attorney suddenly found their defense crippled at the worst possible moment. The doctor's timing, as far as the prosecutor was concerned, could not have been better. Barry pleaded guilty to a reduced charge of first-degree manslaughter through a plea-bargain arrangement. When he was sent back to jail to await sentencing, he tried to hang himself. When his mother visited him he begged her to help him kill himself. On his sentencing date, partly because his attorney misunderstood the sentencing options available, Barry got the maximum: eight and a third to twenty-five years. Soon after he arrived at the state prison, he suffered another psychotic attack and was stripped naked and placed in solitary confinement within the prison's mental health unit. The prison eventually sent him to a psychiatric hospital where the average stay for prisoners was about sixty days. Barry stayed there more than eighteen months.

A few days after Barry was sentenced, the local paper printed a story featuring an interview with the doctor who had flip-flopped on his diagnosis. What stood out in the news article were the doctor's comments on Barry's imprisonment and the reporter's obvious slant in the story line. According to the article, the doctor said Barry would be better off in jail than if he had been acquitted because he was insane.

"He's likely to get more treatment this way," the doctor was quoted as saying. As head of the forensic service at a university, he should have known that a prison is the last place on earth for treating someone with a serious mental illness. "In many states, the law itself is so overprotective of the so-called freedoms of people that patients do not get the treatment they need," he said. "They can be discharged even if they are not cured. It is the nature of schizophrenia that people who suffer from it do not want to be treated. The majority of them do not want to recognize that they've got it. They'd rather stay in the world, so they go off their medication and do not see their doctors, and their condition worsens."

Barry had seen a dozen doctors who had treated his illness in a variety of ways, but the implication in this article was that he was in trouble because he had refused to see his doctors or take his medication. There was no indication or mention of the efforts of Barry and his parents to find a doctor who could help. The newspaper readers were left with a very different impression, and in case some of them still held lingering doubts despite everything the doctor had said, the article reiterated the point one more time. "With those conditions in mind," the paper reported, "[the doctor] said 'Barry is likely to get more treatment' as a convicted felon than he would if he had been found not guilty because of insanity."

Three years after Barry entered prison he was shuffling back and forth from his cell to a state hospital for the criminally insane.

Said Barry's mother, "He has not had any of the positive symptoms [hallucinations and delusions] since he has been on medication. He hasn't been actively psychotic, but he has negative symptoms of the illness. I think there has been some brain damage. He's rational. I can have a rational conversation with him, but it's obvious that it's difficult for him to carry on a communication. It has to go slowly, one thing at a time. There is some emotion there, even like the time he got sick in prison and was sent back to the hospital. At that time he was not in good shape. He was definitely anxiety ridden and depressed, but the fact that he could cry was, I thought, a good sign that not all of his emotions have left him. I think the saddest thing of all is to see someone you love who has lost the ability to express emotion. He is still able to express emotion under the proper conditions with somebody he trusts.

"What really disturbs me is that schizophrenia runs in thirds. Like one third will recover completely, one third will get a little bit better, and the other third will not get better at all. They'll get worse. Those who have the best chance of recovering completely are the ones who have a quick onset of the illness. Barry's didn't happen that way. He had a gradual onset and a delay in treatment.

"Something that the courts do not understand . . . is that by sending these people to prison and subjecting them to further psychotic attacks they are almost ensuring that this third group in the middle is going to go to the one third that doesn't improve. It will push them over from group number one or two into number three. The more often you have a psychotic attack . . . the less likely the person is going to be able to recover. The more often you have these psychotic attacks, the less well you are after you come out of it. Look what has happened to Barry. In the three years that he has been there he has been sent back to the hospital three times. That means he has gotten acute from being in prison, which is obviously the wrong environment for somebody with a brain disease. Not only are they not helping these people to get better but they're helping them to get worse. They're almost ensuring that when they get out of jail they will be the third that will have to be hospitalized and not be able to make it out in the world again. This is what I fear most for Barry, and why I want his sentence reduced and get out of that prison Ping-Pong game that they play with those people [sending them from jail to the hospital and back to jail]. If he's going to be in there seventeen years, forget it. We're both going to be dead."

Christmas, coming on the heels of Matt's death and Barry's arrest, only served to accentuate the depths of his mother's grief and loneliness. Expressions of sympathy from friends provided some relief but no protection from the howl of a press exhilarated by its first murder in years. And nothing prepared her for the frailties concealed beneath the amiable dispositions of people whom she thought she knew.

"So often, I think, you feel like a freak when something like this happens to you. You're made to feel outside of ordinary humanness. Some people, to protect themselves, cannot imagine that such a thing can happen to them or don't want to imagine it. So it makes it easier if they stay at a distance and pretend it has nothing to do with them or their lives and that it could never happen to them. On the other hand, there were some who helped, close friends who were wonderful and understanding in giving their time and love. They hung in there with me. Without them and the support of Matt's family, I don't think I could have survived the months and months of newspaper abuse or one of the worst nightmares a mother can experience, being forced to testify against your own child."

Sometimes friends or acquaintances or neighbors expressed condolences that embraced every member of the family except Barry. On other occasions the sympathy was nothing more than patronizing comments from people who pitied but could not empathize. And there were moments when people were self-serving, like the family doctor who blamed her and the family for what happened.

"After the tragedy occurred, he criticized me in a letter to Barry's lawyer, which he thought I would never see, for not taking his advice [to get her son a psychotherapist] and said he suspected schizophrenia all along. He had the gall to say that. If he suspected schizophrenia, why didn't he tell us that?"

It was not Christmas that year. It was a nightmare, shared not only by her, her son, and her daughter, but by Matt's parents as well. When she traveled to New York City to be with them during the holidays, she inadvertently took her first step toward addressing the chaos. Her mother-in-law told her about a woman in Seattle whose mentally ill son had killed someone, and that this family had been helped by an organization.

"She had gotten the name through a friend and suggested that I call this woman. And this woman put me in touch with another woman in Seattle whose son had killed somebody."

Both were paranoid schizophrenic.

"The second woman turned out to be very active in the [organization's] Seattle, Washington, group. Her son was able to obtain a not guilty by reason of insanity, and was in a forensic unit in a hospital. And she said I should call her sister who lived in New York State. Her sister also had a schizophrenic child, here again reinforcing what is usually being recognized nowadays, that there is a genetic component to the illness. That may not be the only factor but there is a definite connection. Anyway, this woman's sister lived in New York, near Poughkeepsie. Her daughter had not been involved in any criminal proceedings, but she was very seriously ill and was hospitalized.

"That's how I first established contact with people in NAMI [the National Alliance for the Mentally Ill]. It was tremendously helpful because I had no idea where to turn or what to do. It was like a network. People would mention other people and it sort of kept spreading out from there. And we would write or call and make contact, and people were very supportive. What I needed to hear from people was that they recognized the magnitude of what had happened. I didn't get that so much from the general public. It was more shock from them, and some other reactions, but not so much of 'We understand how you feel.' I could tell that they [NAMI members] really understood that in a way that other people couldn't. It made me feel more accepted and less dehumanized. What I think was the most important thing was to connect with people who didn't immediately blame Barry, who understood him as a victim as well."

In 1979, more than a hundred mothers, fathers, sisters, brothers, friends, and acquaintances of the mentally ill along with doctors, other professionals, and mentally ill people themselves, came together in Madison, Wisconsin. Representing eighty or so grass-roots organizations from around the country, they started off the weekend exploring ways to create a national coalition for the mentally ill. By Sunday night they had hammered out the bare bones of NAMI. The new organization opened its headquarters in Washington, D.C., and its membership and number of affiliates increased gradually. But after NAMI was prominently mentioned on a 1983 Phil Donahue TV show on schizophrenia, even NAMI officials were startled by its explosive growth. Within a year, more than three hundred new affiliates had joined.

The mentally ill and their families, who have been the primary providers of care, have been a constituency without clout. NAMI plans to change that. "In America, self-help groups flourish when the system is not working," a NAMI information letter states. "In

1950, the Association for Retarded Citizens was formed by families and friends of the retarded for whom the system was not working. Parents of autistic children and the learning disabled and people with cerebral palsy each formed an advocacy and mutual support group. Services and attitudes have been vastly improved for these groups. We believe the system is not working for the long-term mentally ill, and, hence, it is time for action." NAMI plans to exert some muscle in the near future. Said its Washington lobbyist, "We are on the threshold of a historic movement. We're going to be a tremendous political force in a matter of time."

"My introduction to this organization was very emotional," said Barry's mother. "It was as if I was trying to find what would be my place. I went to my first convention in 1982. It was very exciting and very painful. That convention came pretty close to the death of my husband. It also came on the heels of the Hinckley case. I was aware that there were some people even within the organization at that time who were a little leery of families of mentally ill involved in violence or homicide or, quote, 'crime.' It was an uncomfortable feeling for me to be not only in the minority of families of the severely mentally ill but another minority within that minority."

When another woman attending the conference spoke out about how difficult it had been to talk at a committal hearing for her son, Barry's mother was deeply affected.

"I started to weep. I was reliving that court scene where I had to testify against my son. My outcome was far worse because he was sent to prison."

Although she had planned to be only an observer at the conference, Barry's mother talked about how excruciating the whole experience had been for her, her family, and Matt's family too. After listening to her account, some NAMI officials approached her with the suggestion of starting a subgroup for people and families with similar experiences. That was how HELP was born. The letters stand for Help Exists for Loved Ones in Prison. The Donahue TV show on schizophrenia set off a deluge of phone calls and letters to NAMI's Washington office. And all requests for help and information involving schizophrenics in the criminal justice system were referred to HELP, which Barry's mother had helped start. Something else happened as well. John Hinckley's father attended NAMI's 1983 conference and talked about his family. The two events—Donahue on TV and Hinckley at the conference—brought about some attitude changes within NAMI itself.

"As a result of his being there and the talk he gave, not only because of that but it was a contributing factor, people's attitudes were becoming increasingly sympathetic toward persons like the Hinckleys and myself," said Barry's mother. "More and more people [in NAMI] began to understand that we had a unified cause and that the common denominator was mental illness. Whether a mentally ill person was in prison or the hospital or wandering the streets or in a halfway house, that was not the point. These are people suffering from a brain disease, and that's the message we have to get out.

"Let's talk about schizophrenia because that is very specific. Someone suffering from an illness as severe as schizophrenia and asking for help and not receiving it, that's really courting trouble. Because I think . . . I really think that in our case, and probably in most other cases, that violence and this kind of tragic ending could be avoided if the sick person were doctored properly. You just don't say shape up, kid, or get lost, or go take vitamins, or see a psychotherapist. Those aren't the answers. This is a brain disease, and unless you can find a doctor who will treat it as such, these [violent incidents] are some of the things that can happen.

"My son was sick for four years without having any of his doctors tell us or him that he needed antipsychotic medication. He just deteriorated. And we were trying to find him help in [New York] and in California where his sister was living. What he got into was orthomolecular psychiatry, which most physicians who deal in the field of schizophrenia and most research that had been done now demonstrate that very few individuals can be helped in this way. There may be a small subgroup that can be helped by this method, but in the vast majority of cases it has no bearing on the illness."

If NAMI had been in existence when her son was seeking help, she could have asked for assistance.

"Here is a good example of how this organization can help. I would have been able to call the affiliate in the San Francisco Bay area and say, 'Look, my kid is out there and he's in very bad shape. One doctor said that he has a thinking disorder, which is one of the schizophrenias, and he's trying to treat him with psychoanalysis. What do you think of this? Can you direct me to another doctor who can help him?' I would have been able to get some real practical advice from

NAMI. And this is another thing we're trying to do. Various affiliates are making up lists of doctors who are worth going to."

Besides being a founder and co-chairman of HELP, Barry's mother
also joined the NAMI affiliates in Syracuse and the Alliance for the
Mentally Ill of New York State. Because she was working on a college degree in the Boston area, she joined "a couple of affiliates" in
Massachusetts. She has also appeared on television.

"It was very difficult. I felt a great deal of emotion there [on the
stage]. Some of the women there were mothers of children who had
been killed by a mentally ill person. So I knew it would be very tough
being on the same panel. On the other hand I could feel for them. As I
pointed out to them, my husband also was a victim. I could feel for one
side as well as the other. But I don't think the rights of one and the
rights of the other are incompatible. You don't help one by coming
down with vengeance for the other. That's not the solution. The more
care we can get for the mentally ill, the less violent they will be. Most
of the violence is the result of neglect and mistreatment, and if people
can see it in that light I don't think they'll be so misled by this idea that
you have to put mentally ill people in prison to protect society. It is one
of the worst things you can do. If you put them in hospitals and or give
them appropriate treatment, then you might be helping to protect
society. So that was the kind of message I gave."

NAMI, which is based in Washington, D.C., has been forming
statewide organizations, and she, of course, will take an active role
in New York.

"By the fall of 1984, we expect every affiliate in the country to join
a statewide organization which will be overseen by the national
NAMI. We want to appoint a forensic chairperson for each state for
referrals from people who are in the kind of trouble I was in. We
want to start having those forensic resource people in every state.
We want someone who has useful information for people with a
problem involving the criminal justice system. I will be the forensic
research person for New York."

Her struggle to save Barry had not ended though he was incarcerated in a criminal justice system that could hold on to him for
twenty-five years if it wanted. An appeal after his conviction was
unanimously denied. An attempt to convince the trial judge to recon-
sider his sentence was also rejected. Barry, in a plea bargain abruptly
arranged after his doctor said he could not testify in Barry's defense,

pleaded guilty to first-degree manslaughter when his lawyer told him he had no choice. He was charged with second-degree murder, and because his primary defense witness was saying he had been sane when he killed his father, Barry could have been convicted of a crime that carried a sentence of twenty-five years to life. There were a number of sentencing options available to the judge, and some mitigating factors that he might have considered. Barry was a first-time offender and had had an unblemished record with no history of violence before his arrest. When he killed his father he had been sick from hunger and suffering from a brain disease. The judge, however, gave him the maximum under the law, eight and a third to twenty-five years. Barry, who could have been eligible for parole two years after he was convicted, was given a sentence that would require him to spend more than eight years in jail before he could be considered for parole. Because the state parole board usually requires convicted felons to spend two thirds of their sentence before they are paroled, Barry could be in jail more than sixteen years before he is released.

"One thing that is difficult for me is that even though I find a lot of support in NAMI, I am separated from the others because of Barry's conviction. Of the people I know in NAMI, where there has been a parricide, I'm still the only one who has a kid in prison. All the parricide cases where the defendants were suffering from schizophrenia, all the ones that have come to my attention through NAMI, were judged NGRI [not guilty by reason of insanity]."

One reason she asked for anonymity was that she was still pursuing other legal means of getting Barry out of prison and into a regular hospital. In the meantime, he languishes in prison until he becomes so sick that he must be moved to the Central New York Psychiatric Center at Marcy in upstate New York, an acute-care facility for mentally ill prisoners. Barry, so far, has been hospitalized there three times. His longest stay was more than a year.

"One of the times when I was visiting Barry at that facility, I was speaking with one of the doctors and he said to me that when he first saw Barry he asked himself, 'What's that kid doing there? He looks like the boy next door.' And my answer was 'He *is* the boy next door.'"

# 13

## William

One of their joys was to share lunchtime at home, so, just before noon, as on any other weekday, Gracie Griffin was in the kitchen preparing food. Sometime in the next thirty minutes, Amos Anderson would park his truck in the driveway, and she wanted everything to be ready when her husband walked inside. She did not want him sitting down to a table without food. This midday repast was one of their simple pleasures, and they rarely allowed any interruptions. But this week they had made an exception. When Gracie and Amos finally decided to remodel their two-and-a-half-story frame house, they hired Thomas Cariola, a self-employed subcontractor known for his skilled craftsmanship and reasonable rates. They wanted a special job for their home, a neighborhood gem with its white wood paneling and a boat occasionally moored in the dry dock of the front yard. Part of the remodeling plans called for new wallpaper and floral-patterned linoleum on the kitchen floor. Cariola had been working in the house for a few days, and despite the clutter in Gracie's kitchen, the two synchronized their efforts and managed to stay out of each other's way. On this Wednesday in June, as Gracie prepared Amos's lunch, Cariola hung wallpaper on the kitchen walls.

Upstairs in his attic bedroom, William Bradley Griffin, Gracie's son by her first marriage, was getting dressed. After putting on his clothes, he squeezed a pair of plastic earplugs into his ears. Over the plugs, he added a set of noise suppressors, which rested on his head like gawky earmuffs. The first set of plugs would have been sufficient to deaden the report of a blunderbuss. The bulky noise suppressors, known as Mickey Mouse ears, could have shut out the din of jet engines. Together the plugs and suppressors symbolized the depth of William's retreat from the world around him. Suicide and homicide—flip sides of the same coin—brayed in his mind and, with assiduous planning, he was going to embrace them both. He was dressed to kill and wanted to die. Inside his room, which had been off limits to Gracie and Amos, William had stored enough shotgun ammunition to kill everyone on his block. Into a satchel, stuffed with deer slugs and shells of bird shot, he tossed shells of military-type buckshot with devastating firepower for pulverizing flesh. William also fashioned a sophisticated sling that stretched like an umbilical cord from him to the shotgun. He could wield the gun with one hand or two. After he strapped on Amos's licensed .22-caliber handgun, which he had stolen, he opened the door of his room and went downstairs looking for Gracie. The reminiscences that William's family later told to reporters, the secret journal that William kept, and the accounts of police considered together allow some insight into that day in June.

William was the second child born in a hardworking black family living in Amsterdam, New York, about thirty miles northwest of Albany, the state capital. When he was still a toddler, the family packed up and moved to California, where his father served a stint in the Army. That first cross-country trip initiated the peregrinations that would be William's trademark. When his parents separated, Gracie returned to Amsterdam and William stayed with his father, who later moved to Detroit before settling down in Rochester. But Rochester was not to William's liking. It was a medium-size city in upstate New York with a racial and ethnic diversity queued in a pernicious pecking order. Frederick Douglass launched the black abolitionist newspaper *North Star* there in the mid-nineteenth century. A statue commemorating him overlooks one of the city parks, but Douglass would have found it difficult to be hired by Rochester's local newspapers during the 1950s. Too many problems in school and the city's strident ambience drove William back to Amsterdam to live with his mother at age twelve. But he continued to shuttle back and forth between parents, always seeking to find some elusive security that was not there.

When he graduated from high school at sixteen, William was a precocious, articulate, and self-assured young man who wanted to enter the U.S. Naval Academy at a time when high schools, colleges, and elite institutions throughout the country were still rigidly segregated. When he could not enter Annapolis, he shipped out to the Mediterranean as an enlisted man in the Navy. He finished his tour of duty in Philadelphia, where he met his first wife. And after three sons and his honorable discharge, they divorced. He lost custody of his children, but shook off the pain and returned to Rochester before heading to the west coast. There, he burned out in Los Angeles and then fled north to Berkeley and studied political science at a state college as the Free Speech Movement gathered momentum. The convulsive sixties laid bare America's social, political, and racial subterfuges, and his disappointments and disillusionments mounted. It was a decade when assassins picked off heroes with impunity, and the nation was wretched over the debacle in Vietnam. And it all weighed heavily on William Bradley Griffin.

William, who had once dreamed of being a naval commander, moonlighted as a cabbie and hustled odd jobs while he attended college. But his life was unraveling, and he intuitively knew it was time to go home to Gracie. He realized how important it was for him to get his head together, and Rochester was the best place for him to go and relax and reconnoiter. He married shortly before leaving the west coast, and he separated from his second wife shortly after they arrived in Rochester. But he was home at last.

"Bill loved my mother with a passion, that's why he came home to get his head together," a brother told reporters later. "But I can see things in Bill that would cause my mother to get in his way. I can hear it now. She would hear him moving through the closet or something. 'Bill what are you doing up there?' she would ask. That was the way she was."

Not that William didn't understand his mother. But his mind could not handle the tumult swirling within him, making him oblivious to the feelings of other people who also had desires, worked hard, and saw their dreams denied or their efforts fall short of expectations. William just struggled against burning out.

In 1976, after he had purchased a house as an investment and rented it out to a couple, their two-year-old boy, left unattended, picked up a book of matches and starting playing on the couch in the living room. An ensuing fire ravaged the house. When William later discovered he could not collect insurance, the shock of another defeat resounded through him. For four years thereafter, he hunkered down over lawbooks in the city library and pursued his case through local and state courts. He did not want an attorney. He wanted to fight and win this one himself. William lost each step of the way, with each setback reverberating against the previous loss. When the city demolition crew eventually destroyed the house in July 1980, they could have scooped up William along with the detritus.

During those four years of litigation, Gracie and Amos saw William retreating into a self-imposed exile of silence. He stayed in the attic for days without seeing anyone. He rarely spoke. Sometimes he would take a lawn chair to a nearby basketball court and sit and watch neighborhood kids playing ball. He never talked with them and he never played. In time, no one noticed him even as he sat there; no one noticed when he was gone. The self-assured dreamer slowly walled himself off from the world and anyone who cared for him. Gracie and Amos tried to help and understand, but in William's mind everything about his life was fraught with defeat and betrayal. Nothing seemed to be working for him: He was laid off from Eastman Kodak, denied veteran's benefits, and failed to get Social Security benefits. Defeats were piling up one after another.

He sought help from institutions and people who he believed would help him. He wrote to the United Nations. He appealed to the U.S. Supreme Court and sent letters to Queen Juliana of the Netherlands. All of these efforts to obtain "liberty and freedom" were recorded in a handwritten journal. When he filed a discrimination complaint against Kodak, he wrote in his journal that the company had "violated my rights by not employing me within some other division of the corporation." When the complaint was denied, he wrote, "This date liberty has been continually denied. And so it followed that all my other attempts within the forum of justice for my human rights were also conspired when I was consistently denied access and cases were dismissed. Society's position in the conspiracy was to deny me credit for several knowledgeable contributions to the commonwealth of which I have alluded to here in this manuscript."

William was seeking refuge in a labyrinth of inextricably woven facts and fantasies, transcending time, place, and temporal reality and imbued with his version of truth. His mind had not snapped but sought asylum in its disintegration. He often traveled outside Rochester to Syracuse, ninety minutes away, or Buffalo, about an hour away, to mail his pleas for redress and help to Queen Juliana or Emperor Hirohito of Japan or other national and international bodies and personages. On one trip, he watched the car's odometer run in reverse "and the maps I was using as references began to change their composition." In his mind he found a balm to salve his woes.

"I was consulted as how to help obtain the release of the hostages [in Iran]," he wrote. "I was approached by the Jecretary of Defense Harold Brown. Our plans were to use military helicopters." He recalled his meetings with King Hussein of Jordan and Queen Elizabeth of Great Britain, and crowed about winning Nobel Prizes.

"My first receiving of the prizes was during commencement graduations at Amsterdam high school. My second receiving was after a space flight and meeting with Queen Elizabeth."

It was about halfway through his three-hundred-page journal that William started describing his contempt for his "so-called" family.

"During my adolescence, entering high school one morning after an argument with my so-called brother, I was approached by an individual who offered me a solution to a problem that was repeating itself (namely my brother's contempt). The person suggested that I sell my soul to him and in exchange he would resolve the problem of my brother." With a mind warped by circumstance, and lost in a maze, he came to an irrevocable conclusion: "The family position in the conspiracy was also to deprive me credit for knowledge. Both society and family conspired to take my property, liberty and credit for contributions . . . for their own gain, creating a situation of crime which without question will lead to chaos."

After he bought his shotgun and concealed it and the hundreds of rounds of ammunition in his room, the man who had adroitly veiled his rage and confusion discontinued use of the post office box that he had rented so that no one would know about his correspondence. No mail that might have alerted Gracie or Amos, or aroused suspicion, ever arrived at their home. On that day in June 1982, when William, the second oldest of three brothers and two sisters, and the one closest to Gracie, walked downstairs, he could only recognize her as a conspirator in a crime against him and sentence her to die. But Cariola, a victim of circumstance, would die first: A deer slug burst into his heart, knocking him dead on his back. The next bullet killed Gracie, ripping off her finger as it barreled into her chest. Amos, who was getting out of his truck, never heard the shots. When he walked in looking for lunch, he saw a shadowy figure just as his stomach exploded in excruciating pain. It would be ten days before he knew that Gracie was dead and that the person who had shot him was no stranger.

William stepped over the bodies and walked out the door, moving on to his next destination with his gun at the ready.

"The circumstances," he had written earlier in his journal, "was entering a neighborhood bank and demanding the sheriff and state police take my life for not allowing me the position of liberty here in the dominion of earth. I do recall some so-called friends telling me that one person using my name participated in a act-situation just so described some years before." When he actually walked into the bank, William ordered the customers to leave and then herded the employees into a back room. He told the bank manager to telephone the sheriff's office, state police, and federal marshals in Virginia and give them his ultimatum: Kill him or he would kill the hostages. But the task of dealing with William would fall to city police who would not know for a long time that they were dealing with a deranged man who refused to hear anything they wanted to say. Blasting through a bank window, William shot the first police officer to arrive at the bank. The wounded policeman scurried around his squad car and hid behind a wheel while William unleashed a fusillade. He kept trying to kill the policeman by skipping deer slugs and ricocheting shotgun pellets off the pavement and under the car. The second police officer to arrive was hit before he even got out of his car. In the bank, William paced from one end to the other, shooting at anyone and anything that provoked him. He fired more than ninety rounds.

"His main goal was to get killed," said Lieutenant Robert Mayer later.

William fired repeatedly in the direction of the Megiddo Church to provoke the police snipers he thought were inside to shoot him. He shot at the wrong windows, but the marksmen in the right windows could not get a bead on him.

"We had our negotiation team at the bank within fifteen minutes, phone lines linked up with our hostage command post within another ten or fifteen minutes," Mayer said.

They vainly tried to communicate with a man who could not hear them and did not want to talk. They wanted to avoid more bloodshed.

After almost two hours in the bank, William sent out his last message: Unless the police executed him, he was going to start shooting bank employees. From the bank he had already shot two police officers and wounded two bystanders watching the bank siege. When time ran out in William's mind, he selected a young black woman

who was a teller and walked her to the front door of the bank as she
pleaded with him not to hurt her.

"No, no, please don't shoot me. I have a son," she said.

When he shot her, the blast blew her through the bank's glass
door. Moments after he killed her, William stepped into the sights of
a high-powered rifle and died himself.

If the police had captured him alive and he had been brought to
trial, the deranged man in all likelihood would not have been found
innocent by reason of insanity. Being emotionally disturbed, mentally
ill, paranoid—all signs of a person in need of help—would not have
stopped William from going to jail. In the eyes of the law, William's
delusions of grandeur and persecution, murdering his mother because he believed she was a conspirator, and his wish to die because
"liberty and freedom" had been denied him were not solid grounds
for an acquittal based on an insanity plea. There were few prosecuting attorneys who would have had problems putting William in jail
for the rest of his life. The methodical way that William went about
purchasing a shotgun and concealing it from Gracie and Amos would
have been just one of the many signs that William was responsible
for his actions. He would have been judged competent to stand trial
and to understand his rights, and found guilty of murdering three
people. But how sane is a man who commits mayhem as grisly as that
perpetrated by William Bradley Griffin?

# PART IV

## Matricides, Patricides, and Mass Murders

Israel was talking on the phone to his mother when his son pointed a stolen .38-caliber Smith and Wesson handgun at him and shot him once in the back of the head. When Israel's mother heard the gunshot, she suffered a heart attack. Israel in New York City and his mother in Puerto Rico were both rushed to hospitals. When the police walked into Israel's apartment that day in March 1984, they found his son hiding under a bed. He was three years old. Israel had taught him how to pull the trigger and allowed him to play with the loaded gun, according to police. After Israel died, the death was ruled an accidental homicide.

This is not the type of case that one would normally expect to be included in a book on parricide. Israel's son was too young to understand what he was doing, and the fatal shooting was an accident. When I first read about this account I decided not to include it, but later changed my mind.

It was a needless tragedy that resulted from the inexcusable negligence and callousness of a father who showed no regard for his son's life. But this case cannot be categorized under child abuse, and though some people might pause to think that Israel was out of his mind when he gave his three-year-old son a loaded gun for a toy, mental illness was not a factor either. I hesitated to treat this as just an unfortunate accident because of the unmitigated cruelty shown the young boy. However, it seems appropriate as an introduction to a series of accounts that, for a variety of reasons, cannot be categorized under child abuse or mental illness. While some actually belong in their own discrete categories, others are still tied up in litigation and the exact cause of the killings is unknown, but the information available is too compelling to be ignored. The elements of the following cases in many ways overlap each other, even though the tragedies were miles apart or separated by time.

# 14

## Vic

New York's tabloids trumpet themselves as champions of the people, protecting their readers from insensitive bureaucrats, the insouciance of public officials, and the harsh vagaries of day-to-day life. They regale their readers with regular feats of journalistic swashbuckling as they expose crime in the streets, crime on the sidewalks, crime throughout the city, state, and country. They are vigilant watchdogs, sniffing out muggers and murderers alike, and when Vic was arrested they ate him alive.

In a September 1982 story of less than three hundred words, crowned with a gargantuan headline worth thousands more, the *New York Post* limned Vic as a neighborhood weirdo, an urban psychopath. He was just what the editor ordered. Facts and details attributed to unnamed police officers, and quotes and descriptions ascribed to anonymous youths and unidentified neighbors, summoned images of an anomic youth whom only a mother could love.

"A 14-year-old boy," the *Post* story started, "described as a loner was charged last night with stabbing his mother to death with a knife he bought to impress neighborhood youths." The "loner" was also an arrant coward: "Police said he locked himself in his room as his dying mother, _____, 38, was being taken to the hospital." The *Post* also said that his mother, "a widow, was stabbed once in the back." Recreating the fatal scene, the tabloid added, "She was found bleeding by her father—who said he had heard shouts and a violent argument between his daughter and his grandson at the two-family home."

Near the end of the story, the *Post* reiterated its message:

"Neighbors and youngsters in the community painted a picture of a shy, lonely boy with no friends—who had a very bad temper and would throw tantrums." One youth was quoted as saying, "The kids used to tease him and tell him to get lost. He was a lonely person." And in case any reader missed the message, there were additional quotes: "He was always alone—he would roam the neighborhood or sit on the porch by himself at 4 a.m." and "He would throw a temper tantrum if he didn't get what he wanted."

With fewer words, a petite headline, and two reporters instead of one, the *Daily News* offered a similar story but with variations. Vic had been arrested and charged with murder "after detectives found him huddled in a corner of the apartment he shared with his mother,———, 39." The *News* account paralleled the *Post* reporting that Vic's grandfather had heard screams during a dispute. "The father," the *News* said, "who was in a bedroom, found his daughter, who was divorced, bleeding in the living room." Further into the story, the *News* reported that the police said the mother had not only been stabbed once in the back, but "slashed several times with the knife." In the *News,* Vic the "lonely person" was also Vic the "slow learner who sometimes sat alone in front of his home in the middle of the night." The *News,* ferreting out a possible motive, something stronger than the *Post*'s in-the-heat-of-an-argument stabbing, cited accounts from neighbors that "relations between the mother and son were strained."

Except for minor discrepancies—such as the age of Vic's mother, whether she was widowed or divorced, Vic's cowering in a locked room or huddling in a corner—the newspaper accounts were almost interchangeable. The *Post* editors might have inquired why their reporter did not have the slash wounds in their account of the slaying, but minor discrepancies can be expected in reporting by competing news organizations. More than one million people read one or both news stories about the macabre fourteen-year-old boy who had slain his mother, and they would have relished the follow-up stories about his indictment, trial, and conviction. They also would have appreciated reading that this ferine child of a parent's worst nightmare would be sent away for a long, long time, getting just what he deserved for slaying his mother.

Printing follow-up stories, however, would have been self-incriminating for the tabloids and would have confirmed the suspicions of a skeptical public that newspapers mangle truth to create news.

The papers would have been hard put to explain the sharp differences between their reporters' claims of police confidences and the subsequent police testimony and evidence presented before a grand jury.

One can speculate on what the opinions of the millions of readers might have been if, through some necromantic spell, they had been made aware of the conflicting accounts as they read the newspaper stories. Readers might have thought that one paper had rewritten the story of its competitor, which had been deceived by police who distorted the results of their investigation in order to sway public opinion and strenthen their case. Others might have assumed that the tabloids had fabricated their stories to sell more newspapers. The discrepancies would have been strong enough to provoke derisive howls of laughter, except for the gruesome fact that one person was dead and a young boy now found himself orphaned and fighting for his life.

Follow-up stories would also have exposed the district attorney's office to the public scorn that it richly deserved. Why, a reporter could have asked, did you strive for a second-degree murder indictment against Vic and portray him as a heinous criminal in the face of evidence that strongly suggested something else?

His real name is not Vic, as in "Victor." Vic is an anonym, standing for "victim." Vic was mugged one day in New York City, and the "vicious thugs," to borrow a tag frequently used by New York tabloids, skipped free with impunity, got away with their crime without so much as a slap on the wrist. Vic was mugged by the press and mugged by the district attorney's office, and what happened to him could have easily happened to anyone else.

His mother died the night he was arrested, and when he learned of her death, Vic sank deep into depression and despair. An already-shy young boy, he became painfully withdrawn. Like many mugging victims, he found himself wary of people. A paranoia that set in seeped deep into his bones, and when he was released on bail, he learned that a friend was someone who did not know who he really was. Whenever his friends discovered who he was, they also discovered that they did not want to be around him anymore.

Vic was too distraught to appear before a grand jury, and so the district attorney's office agreed to a temporary postponement. But weeks later, Vic was still unable to appear. His attorney asked that Vic's statement, which had been videotaped by the district attorney's office the night he was arrested, be shown to the grand jury. The assistant district attorney prosecuting the case, who had discretion in determining what evidence he would present to the grand jury, refused. Instead, on the hearing day, he swore in another assistant district attorney who summarized Vic's statement about the fatal stabbing. Two police officers, an associate medical examiner, and Vic's maternal grandfather also testified. After hearing all of the testimony, the grand jury indicted Vic for second-degree murder.

Vic's attorney appealed the indictment, asking that it be dismissed for several reasons, principally on grounds of insufficient evidence and defective grand jury proceedings. Almost three and a half months later, Justice Jerome L. Reinstein issued a decision.

"Viewed in the light most favorable to the People," Reinstein wrote in his seven-page decision, "the evidence established that the defendant stabbed his mother in the back, causing her death, shortly after they concluded an argument over defendant's homework." He wrote that there were no grounds to support the contention "that the evidence presented to the Grand Jury was legally insufficient to indict." But he threw out the indictment "because of defects in the grand jury proceedings which may have impaired the integrity thereof and resulted in prejudice to the defendant.

"The *Daily News* and the *New York Post* each carried a highly inflammatory, distorted and prejudicial account of the incident," he wrote. "Whether or not any of the grand jurors had read either one of these newspaper accounts, is unknown. They were never asked." They should have been. "There is generally no Grand Jury voir dire to determine bias resulting from publicity attendant upon an investigation," wrote the judge. "Nor, it would appear, is there any such requirement. Nevertheless, the cases which have considered the issue have pointed to either proper judicial instructions to the jurors to disregard media accounts of the incident or to an affidavit from the foreman that the grand jury considered only the evidence submitted to it.

"In this case," he wrote, there was only the assistant district attorney's "unsupported assurance . . . that each impaneled grand jury is instructed to consider only the evidence presented to it and 'that instruction was likely to have been still present in the minds of the grand jury.'" The prosecutor's assurance was not enough.

A second flaw in the proceedings concerned the testimony of the associate medical examiner. Vic had told the police and the district attorney that he had accidentally stabbed his mother when she stopped abruptly and turned toward him as he was reaching toward her with the knife in his hand. When the medical examiner, who had performed the autopsy, was asked at the hearing if she could determine "whether or not [the fatal] wound would be consistent with someone who stops abruptly on the knife, [she] responded, 'No, I can't say.' When asked in three separate questions if she could express an opinion as to whether or not the deceased could have (a) 'been swaying back' or (b) 'backed into' or (c) 'been turning' when the knife entered the body, the associate medical examiner responded, 'No,' in each instance." Each answer, when read literally, indicated that the medical examiner could not determine whether the victim had been accidentally or deliberately stabbed. "But when compared with her answer to the first question," Reinstein wrote, ". . . the grand jurors could have believed that the injury" could not have been inflicted accidentally. "This apparent ambiguity," according to the judge, "should have been clarified."

He also concluded that the prosecutor should have allowed the grand jury to see Vic's videotaped statement. Reinstein found that at one point during the jury hearing, when a juror asked about part of Vic's videotaped statement, the prosecutor "failed to recall" Vic's specific response. "And at another point," Reinstein wrote, "he testified to contradictions made by the defendant. Whether or not there were such contradictions, and the weight to be given them, should have been resolved by the grand jurors after viewing the entire statement.

"A right sense of justice," the judge decided, "would dictate that [the] defendant's entire videotaped statement be shown to the grand jurors." It has been extremely rare for a supreme court justice in New York to throw out an indictment for second-degree murder. "While perhaps no one factor alone would be sufficient to require dismissal of the instant indictment," Reinstein wrote, ". . . the cumulative effect of all three [defects] does." After the decision, the district attorney had to decide whether to drop the case or seek another indictment. But it was now apparent that Vic had told the truth when he said he had accidentally stabbed his mother as she "swayed" into the knife in his hand.

Before he was appointed to the state supreme court, Reinstein presided over juvenile cases where the defendants "were so short you were putting telephone books on their seats so you could see them," he recalled much later. "Not that they didn't commit vicious crimes because they were small."

Reinstein said that when Vic's appeal had come before him, it was apparent that the boy's grandparents supported their grandson's statement that the death had been an accident. The judge indicated but did not say that he too thought it had been an accident.

"The grandfather was supportive of the child and an uncle who was a clergyman also was supportive of the child," he said.

Reinstein was very critical of the news accounts, showing just the hint of a disparaging sneer.

"I thought it was fair to ask the grand jury if they had read about the case," he said. "You would ask trial jurors. Most jurors in the [New York City borough] read the *News* and the *Post*. If you asked them, I'm sure they would say they read the *Times*, but I'm not so sure."

If they had read *The New York Times* that day, they might have seen a three-paragraph story under a pint-size headline—BOY, 14, CHARGED IN MOTHER'S SLAYING. "A 14-year-old boy," the story started, "was charged with murder last night for allegedly stabbing his mother to death when she refused to help him with his homework. According to [the district attorney], the 39-year-old widow was slain in her home. Her son [Vic] will be treated as an adult."

Vic had lived in California with his mother and father until the day his father died of a drug overdose. His mother, after a dispute with her in-laws in California, cut off contact with her husband's parents and moved home to New York City and her own parents. She and Vic lived with her parents while she tried to put her life back together and her son attended school. They shared a room in the small, two-bedroom home and they became close friends. When Vic came home one day with a 007 gravity knife that he had purchased—it was just like the knives the other boys in the neighborhood were carrying—she wished he had never purchased it but was not too distressed. Vic was mild-mannered and even-tempered and had never been in a lick of trouble, so there was not much reason to believe that carrying the knife would cause any problems.

When Vic's mother walked into their room one evening, she told him to put the knife away and do his homework. He started acting childish and refused. When she reached for the knife he was playing with, he quickly drew his arm back to keep her from grabbing it. She turned and started to walk out of the room in exasperation when he reached toward her with the knife in his hand, and she suddenly turned and "swayed" into the blade. Vic's mother turned and walked out of the room, passing her father as she headed toward a couch in the living room. He asked her if she was okay. She told him she had a headache. When he asked Vic what had happened, his grandson, in a moment of panic, told him he was not sure. When Vic's grandfather saw his daughter bleeding, he told Vic to dial 911.

After he called for medical assistance, Vic sat on the couch and comforted his mother as best he could, and after she was rushed to the hospital he remained on the couch and cooperated with the police. When they asked him what had happened, he at first told them he did not know, but eventually said he had accidentally stabbed his mother when she "swayed" into his knife. When they asked him what hand the knife had been in, he contradicted himself. Flustered by the questions and their obvious insinuations, worried and confused about how seriously injured his mother was, he told them all they had to do was ask his mom, and she would say that he was telling the truth, that he had accidentally stabbed her.

When they took Vic back to the precinct, he reiterated his account of what had happened and agreed to be videotaped. As the police and an assistant district attorney taped his explanation, his grandmother several times moved into camera range to say that her grandson was a good boy who had never been in trouble and that he would never deliberately hurt his mother.

Vic's world collapsed when they told him his mother was dead and that they were charging him with second-degree murder. A day or two later, he was released on bail put up by his grandparents. Longtime residents of the neighborhood where they lived, they were forced to move because of all the publicity. Their claims that the death had been an accident were mere whispers amid the clamor fanned by the news reports and nurtured by the ensuing gossip.

At his new school, Vic found breathing room until a student remembered reading a story about a weird fourteen-year-old boy who had murdered his mother. Though he and his family had left New York City proper, they had to remain in the vicinity because he was still out on bail. His grandparents, also suffering because they had lost their daughter and their home, were too old and too tired to pick up stakes and move again. Vic was going to have to suffer through school.

Some brief, infinitesimal respite was provided when Reinstein threw out the indictment. That ended when Vic was reindicted for criminally negligent homicide. This time the case was remanded to family court, which conducts its proceedings out of earshot of the news media and the general community. There judges are supposed to take into consideration the interests of the juveniles and the community as they adjudicate cases. If Vic's case had been handled in family court from the beginning, he and his family would have been spared the notoriety that comes with a second-degree murder charge. Vic, at worst, would have had to wrestle only with his own deep sense of guilt and shame and not with the consequences of being a pariah. In that sense family court was too late, but it still offered a chance for faster proceedings in a less grueling environment.

In Vic's case, however, family court did not deliver what it promised. The case was postponed at least twenty times and passed from one judge to another and dragged on for almost a year. "It was an exceptionally long time for a case of this nature to go on in family court," said Vic's lawyer, one of three who handled the case at different stages. "He got caught up in a system that didn't care about kids per se but had other priorities, which weren't him." According to a family court memorandum, cases are to be adjudicated within ninety days.

This lawyer, who agreed to talk but asked not to be identified, once handled a case in which a boy had killed his brother. "One brother was trying to throw the younger brother over the banister, and the younger one struck him in the eye with a ballpoint pen, which broke through the supraorbital ridge [over the eye] and caused brain swelling and death," the lawyer said. The younger brother was charged with criminally negligent homicide and the judge, in a nonjury trial, decided that a "reasonable person could not have perceived such a risk" of death from a ballpoint pen. The boy was acquitted.

"The gist behind murder statutes is that you don't punish people for the act, but you punish them for the state of mind," said the lawyer. "For example, I shoot you in the head and you die. You can presume I was trying to kill you. If I shoot you in the leg, and complications arise in the leg and you die, no one would have presumed by that kind of wound that I meant you to die; again, it's state of mind. Criminal negligence is the lowest culpability in law because there is no willful doing. It is almost a civil statute. When the grand jury indicted Vic again on criminally negligent homicide, it decided that he did not perceive the risks. . . . If he had perceived the risks he would have been guilty of some degree of manslaughter. The grand jury in its decision said that the evidence could establish at most that he was unaware of the risks but the risk was such that a reasonable person could perceive it. The risk that he could cut her is not criminally negligent homicide. There had to be a risk that he would kill her."

It was a freakish accident. Two pathologists examined the mother's body. "One pathologist said it [the knife] didn't require a significant amount of force to penetrate, and the other said it was hard to determine the amount of force," the lawyer said. The 007 knife had an extremely sharp blade and Vic's mother was thin and anemic. When she was stabbed, the knife did not plunge all the way into her body, nor did it strike a vital organ. Right after she received her injury, she sat down on the couch and her father asked what was wrong because she looked so pale; she told him she had "a headache."

When this lawyer first met him, Vic had been "nearly catatonic, very withdrawn, and was talking incessantly about his mother, how much he wanted to see her, how much he missed her." That had been almost a year earlier. "It was not the greatest thing for the kid that this case has gone on this long," the lawyer said. "I wanted to negotiate but I was reluctant to try the case right away because of all the heat" on the district attorney's office, presumably to take a tough position. "The assistant district attorney had his own reluctance in regard to this case. Between the two of us there were blocks in getting the case out of the way and done with. When there was a chance of negotiation, then he [the prosecutor] would put it off. And at other times, I had to."

The lawyer's personal problems also made it painful for him to work with the case.

"I had psychological problems too. My mother has had cancer for the last year and a half, so that, for whatever unconscious reasons, I also avoided the case a lot. The difficult psychological problems that he was going through, and that would have been brought to the surface in a trial, I didn't want to deal with either."

After having his case drag on for almost eighteen months, emotionally and mentally ravaged to the point where anyone near him was affected, Vic, at sixteen, pleaded guilty to a misdemeanor in a plea-bargain arrangement worked out between his lawyer and the prosecutor.

"He did not want to go through a trial and hear all of the testimony," his lawyer said. "It was a difficult decision to advise him to take the misdemeanor or to advise him to go to trial. We had a good chance of winning a suppression hearing, but if we had lost the suppression hearing we could have lost the trial. He could have been found guilty of causing the death of his mother."

The suppression hearing would have involved Vic's attorney asking the court to throw out the statements Vic had made to the police. There are specific legal procedures that police and the district attorney's office must follow when juveniles, such as Vic, are arrested or taken into custody. The lawyer said he had noticed several breaches of Vic's rights. Reinstein, in an interview several months before Vic pleaded guilty, said without elaborating that he would have thrown the statement out if the case had appeared before him.

In June of 1984 Vic was awaiting sentencing for the misdemeanor he had pleaded to. He was just wrapping up the final days in an excruciating school year during which his schoolmates knew him as the kid who had murdered his mother by stabbing and slashing her or, if they read *The New York Times*, had killed her because she would not help him with his homework. Because the case was in family court, Vic's records and the misdemeanor conviction will be permanently sealed. As this story was being written, his attorney and a social worker were fretting over what would happen to Vic after the sentence. They wanted to place him in a treatment facility because of his serious depression.

"Because he is sixteen years old, no one wants to take him," the lawyer said. "He falls above the age of adolescence for institutions and agencies that could take him; and the nature of the charges against him, once they find out the nature of the charges, prejudices agencies against him. He is very depressed and the family situation is not healthy."

His maternal grandparents, despoiled of their home, daughter, and good name, could no longer shoulder Vic's burdens or let him lean on them. His uncle and other relatives on the west coast, though supportive in the beginning, were not prepared to help someone in need of as much help as Vic.

If he had not bought the knife, or had bought one with a duller blade, or had done his homework instead of playing with it; if his mother had not turned as he reached, or had not been thin and anemic; if she could have said, "It was an accident," instead of "headache"; if the police and prosecutor had been thorough in their investigation and less sanguinary; if the tabloids . . . if, if, if.

# 15

## Adam

He lived in a blue-collar neighborhood in St. Paul, Minnesota, and I was waiting for him in a parking lot outside of an office where we were supposed to talk. He was ninety minutes late. It was his way of saying that he was having second thoughts about being interviewed. Before I flew into the Twin Cities, I had talked to him by phone more than once to make certain that he really wanted to meet with me. Each time he seemed enthusiastic, almost gung ho. I had been told that he was very sensitive, but on the phone he sounded like an up-and-coming actor expecting to be interviewed about some new murder mystery in which he played a major role. When we finalized the arrangements over the phone, I assured him I would not use his real name or identify his family.

I had been told he was about twenty, but when he finally drove up and got out of his car that day in the parking lot, I thought he could have passed for a high school freshman or sophomore. He was short and solid and moved like a young boy, not like a poised young man. He wanted to look composed and confident but his stride betrayed him. He walked as if he had sucked in all his confidence in one breath, and it dissipated with each step away from the car. Someone was sitting in the passenger seat, and the young man who looked like a young boy left the engine running when he got out of the car. As we shook hands, he said he had shown up to say that he could not be interviewed because he had made last-minute plans with a friend. He was sorry that it had happened so suddenly, but maybe we could get together some other time. I suggested that we go inside the office and talk for a few minutes. He agreed reluctantly. As we walked into the office he reminded me that someone was waiting for him outside in his car and that he had left the engine running.

I call him Adam. He was sixteen when he killed his father. He had not been abused and was not deranged, and he never went to jail though he spent time in a psychiatric facility before being transferred to a juvenile facility. He was kept in custody for two years. When I interviewed him, he had been living at home about two years with his mother and sister while he attended school. He had just started his first job a few weeks before I flew in to interview him. Adam came from a hardworking Irish family where everyone was expected to pull his or her own weight. For them, the family that worked and prayed together stayed together.

He was visibly uncomfortable when we sat down in the office. We talked briefly about school and his job but there was little time for any polite talk or warm-up for some of the serious questions I needed to ask. The first question: Do many of your friends know about the slaying?

"Oh, hey, I live right over there," he said, smiling nervously and talking about the neighborhood where he had few friends.

How did they treat you when you came back?

"Being away a couple of years, you come back, kind of wonder what they're going to say, how they'll act," he said. "At first I came back, I just sort of didn't go around too much, you know. Kind of just hanging low, kind of meeting them all over again. They didn't treat me any different. Kind of amazing. They treated me like [Adam]. A couple of ones I really knew asked me why. I gave them a pretty frank but not thorough answer, you know."

Did they make you feel like you were ostracized or unwanted?

"I never heard anything like that, never felt anything like that," he said. "I knew this guy down the street. Ever since we knew this guy, he likes to give people a hard time. He's retired. He doesn't think any different. He sees me and says hi in the morning when I go to school. My cousins and stuff . . . they don't really ask too much about it."

Adam lived in a big-city neighborhood where, unlike some urban areas, generations were stacked up one after another. Sons and daughters who moved out of their homes as young adults did not move out of the neighborhood. They set up their own homes nearby, and when their kids move out of the house they too will stay in the area. It was a neighborhood where everyone knew each other, and a kid who killed his father could not be cloaked in the kind of urban anonymity of a New York City, a Chicago, or even a middle-size city like Rochester, New York.

What about publicity? Was there much?

"When I first got in, they took me to a juvenile detention thing downtown," Adam said. "They told me in the morning after the arrest, 'You're going to be in a lounge, a secured lounge. There might be a radio or TV going, so if you hear anything, don't say much [to the other kids].' I didn't hear anything. Five months later I learned about a newspaper article about it. There wasn't much about it."

It was about this time in the interview that he reminded me that he had to go, that someone was waiting for him.

As he was about to get up, I told him that I just wanted to ask a few more questions and that it would not take too long. When he settled back down in the chair, I asked him what had happened between him and his mother and sisters.

"I got a lot of support and stuff, you know, when they locked me up," Adam said, as his voice got softer. "They always came out to visit me. I left sorry, you know, well, uh . . . after I thought about it [the shooting], remembered it, well, you know, one of my oldest sisters, a stepsister . . . I was feeling . . ." He was about to talk about the shooting and how bad he felt when he suddenly changed his mind. "Never mind that! They don't treat me any different. They give me a lot of support."

It was about then that he started jingling some keys in his pocket. He wanted to talk about how bad he felt about killing his father but it was stirring up too much remorse and guilt and confusion inside him. So I asked him what his life had been like when he was away from home for two years.

"Well, I was in a psychiatric unit," he said. "You wear robes. . . You can't have sharp objects. You can only eat with spoons."

Did they make you feel weird?

"Oh, yeah," he said with a burst of nervous laughter, "they really make you feel weird. They talk really soft to you, and almost [avoid] you. First part of the time, you can almost feel the nervousness around them. There were other people up there who were really terrible wacko. There were people to be paranoid about. I can see why they were there."

Adam was placed in the adult section of a psychiatric hospital, and for a while he thought the doctors were only trying to dig into his mind. But after some months, he thought they were trying to help him.

"After I got more comfortable, I started talking, and they put me down in the juvenile part," he said, informing me that it "was not like a psychiatric ward. The staff use to joke about it, that they called it [the juvenile section] a psychiatric ward for insurance purposes."

We did not talk much about the adult psychiatric unit, and in case I had missed the point that he was trying to emphasize, without coming out and saying it he reiterated that he was normal. He did not have to. I did not think he was crazy, but he obviously wanted me to be sure.

"Almost anybody was sent there," he said, "no matter what your problems. It was, uh . . . people [kids] were sent there for having problems at home, not for doing anything criminal. It was all right there, but it was still a lockup but more open."

After a year, he was transferred to a juvenile residential unit outside the psychiatric facility. He was allowed to make weekend visits home. When hospitalized, he had missed attending a real school, and the halfway house where he was staying allowed him a real classroom life.

When we had been talking for a bit, and I thought he was going to relax, Adam started making moves toward the door. He reminded me that someone was waiting for him in a car with a motor running. I told him that I had only a few more questions, and then I asked him what he had done after he shot his father.

"After it happened, never mind how it happened, I can't talk about it . . . it's hard to explain," he said. "After it happened, my mind was totally blank. I just ran. It was wintertime, and I just slipped on my boots and ran. First, I went towards the flats; it's open fields. Things started going through my mind. . . . I just, I just said I couldn't get away. I couldn't. I knew it. I came down to the busiest street, on West Seventh, and a cop came. He was pretty mellow about it. They didn't handcuff me. The cop said, 'Hey, are you [Adam]?' I said, 'Yeah.' He frisked me down and told me to get into his car. First time I'd ever been picked up."

At this point, he was a jumble of nerves and conflicting strategies. He affected bravado in one moment and in the next he was near tears. All the time he was jingling the keys in his pocket.

Did you ever talk about the shooting much with anyone?

"Oh, yeah, the doctors, staff members. Up in the juvenile psychiatric center they were really concerned about me, 'cause you can go back there months later. . . . They treated you like a human being. They remember you. They ask how you are. They don't treat you like somebody you aren't. They treat you just like you are. If that's the way you want to be, you know, then that's how they treated you. That's why it was so nice up there. They gave you so much support," Adam said.

He again said he had to leave because someone was waiting for him in the car, but I persisted and told him just a few more questions.

If you had to do it over again, I asked, what would you do to change things to keep from shooting your father?

"I would go back and stop it," he said, after a long silence.

How?

"I don't know how you could do that either. If I had to do it over . . ." But his voice trailed off.

He was visibly shaken, so, to make it easier on him, I asked what would he do if he were his father and he wanted to avoid the tragedy.

"The best thing for him would be to be around more," he said, in a pained pianissimo voice. "It was like I wanted to be something and he wanted me to be someone else. I was being dragged apart."

At this point, Adam wasn't just talking to me. He was talking to himself. And he was talking to his father.

"You wouldn't talk about it too much," he said. "I was being dragged apart. You wouldn't talk about it too much. I was being dragged apart, and no one would talk about it too much. It was like I wanted to grow up to be someone, but I never really told him and never really gave any hints, and I never even gave any hints. It was like I was the worse of the two."

He was not jingling his keys, and he was barely moving. I could just make out that he was breathing.

"Just be more open," he said. "So that's what I would say. Don't close up."

How does it feel now to be without him?

"Just sometimes it can get really bad, you know—you wish he was there for something," he said. "Like, wow, you [his father] could have really showed me something. God, then you [meaning himself] just go right down. Right down. Once in a while I'll mention his name and such and it won't bother me. Then you [himself again] think, God, and then go down, just right down. When it really comes down to it, and I think how much [he misses his father], yeah, then I get down."

When he was young, about five or six, his father took him to baseball games and spent more time with him and the family. But then there was a change.

"A definite change," Adam said. "It was almost like when I was little, then there was more time for us and stuff. He started working full time at a factory. I remembered when he used to work [part time] at a gas station and that was close to home. Yeah, there was a definite change. Mostly he just went towards himself more."

Why was that?

"Yeah, well, he had a thing about alcohol for a while," Adam said. "I remember Mom and I'd go with him [to buy liquor]. It got really bad when he started telling me not to tell Mom, and then Mom would ask me [if his father had been drinking]. And then I would think, What am I going to say? Who am I going to protect? Like, how can you lie to your mom? And then, of course, if you don't and you're putting down your dad and you're going against him, and what's he going do and then . . . I was scared. It was scary. That's why when he started going to the store, he could go by himself. He would get mean. But even when he wasn't even trying to be mean, he was so blasted he'd manhandle you."

His father did not beat anyone, Adam said, but he was so clumsy when he was drunk that it was best to stay out of his way.

"Sometimes he would get so drunk, you would just laugh at him," he said, adding that he had noticed the change in his father when he was about ten or eleven.

I never got the chance to ask him if his father had been frequently depressed or any other questions, because Adam had made up his mind to leave. The pitch and tempo of the jingling keys escalated into an incessant racket, which was joined by repeated thumps of his leg begging into the table where we were sitting. Adam reminded me that he had a friend waiting for him, and though he was sorry, he had to leave. He made motions to get up but he did not move until I signaled that it was okay for him to leave. As we walked to the parking lot I told him I wanted to try and talk to him again. He, of course, thought it was a good idea.

I believe Adam said everything to me in that short interview that he would ever have said, no matter how many times we met. He had not yet made peace with himself about what he had done, and was probably as honest with me, a stranger, as he was with himself. I wanted to talk with his mother, but she was not happy about Adam's talking to me, though she had not tried to stop him. In any case, she was not talking to me.

Answers to many questions I would have liked to ask both of them I got from Paul Anderson, a probation officer who had been assigned to Adam's case and was frequently in touch with him, although Adam's probation had ended about a year before I met him. Anderson summarized for me some of the findings of the judge, prosecuting attorney, a psychiatrist, and several others who at one time or another had been involved in Adam's case. They all seemed to feel that he was a good kid who could be rehabilitated and should not be sent to jail. Anderson made that clear before he gave me much of the background information on Adam and his family. Of course, what he said about Adam—a good kid who had never been in trouble with the law, intelligent, never a problem in school—applied to many of the cases I researched and many of those I read about of kids who had killed a parent or were charged in a parent's death.

As a youngster, Adam had been a good student in school, but he had had few friends and was always shy and a little withdrawn. He spent most of his free time around his home and in his room. He was a voracious reader, worked on several hobbies, and enjoyed doing a lot of things by himself. Because he was never in trouble or hanging around with the wrong bunch of kids, his parents did not think that there was anything wrong with his staying in his room so much. He had his own television and sometimes ate his meals in his room by himself.

After Adam entered high school, his grades began to slip. It was about this time that his father was drinking heavily, and his parents fought over the way his father wasted money getting drunk. His mother worked on a factory assembly line, and his father also worked but he was spending the family's hard-earned money on booze, and they were struggling to keep from losing their home. The tension in the home escalated, and Adam's three sisters, his mother, and other family members who did not live at home frequently denounced the father. During all of this, Adam's grades were getting worse, and though he never argued or fought with his parents, the increasingly bitter family imbroglio began to wear on him. But no one noticed.

In Adam's sophomore year, it looked as if the family was going to lose its home. His father had squandered much of the family savings. Everyone was angry, and Adam, who rarely said anything in anger, began to fantasize about killing his father. The rest of the family was wishing aloud that his father would leave or die.

One day Adam walked into the house with another bad report card. His father and his mother screamed at him, and then they starting arguing with each other. One word led to another, and Adam's mother finally screamed that she was leaving, told her husband he could take care of the kids and the house, and stormed out of the house. The father screamed and then he fled as well. Adam, who had heard every word, panicked. The world as he knew it was about to end; the choice was between his father and his mother, and he was closer to his mom. He loaded a gun kept in the house and waited for his father to return. When his dad walked in, Adam shot him once in the chest and fled.

"After he shot his father, he left the house and went to his old school where he went to kindergarten," Anderson said. "Then he turned himself in. Within a few days, he was charged with second-degree murder."

In Minnesota, as in several other states, sixteen-year-old youths and kids much younger can be treated as adults for serious crimes like murder. But everyone involved in Adam's case believed that he should not go to jail. His mother, sisters, and other relatives rallied behind him. A psychiatrist who examined him said Adam had suffered "an extreme psychotic episode" and recommended that he be placed in a hospital setting and on medication. The doctor also said that the youth was a latent schizophrenic.

A point has to be made here about latent schizophrenia. According to the book *Major Psychiatric Disorders,* edited by Frederick G. Guggenheim and Carol Nadelson, the term "latent schizophrenia" was "sanctioned by [Eugen] Bleuler in 1911 to classify persons whose conventional social behavior he felt concealed underlying schizophrenia." Simply put, it was a label for "normal-looking" people who held jobs, attended school, and were considered socially acceptable, but unexpectedly exhibited psychotic symptoms or signs of schizophrenia. Other terms to describe the same observations were "ambulatory schizophrenia," "subclinical schizophrenia," and "schizophrenic character." The popular term today is "borderline personality" or "borderline schizophrenic."

According to *Major Psychiatric Disorders,* these are the features of the disorder: lack of connection between feelings and events; depression or hostility; a history of impulsive behavior; social adaptiveness—the person seems socially acceptable and performs normally; brief psychotic experiences; loose thinking in unstructured situations; and relationships that vacillate between transient superficiality and intense dependency. According to the book, one or all of the symptoms may be present during an initial interview by a psychiatrist.

"The kid had brittle psychological defenses," Anderson said. "That, coupled with the abandonment by his mother" and the two years of household strife, "set off a psychotic episode."

After his year in the hospital, Adam was transferred to a residential center where the staff "tried to get him more involved with others of his own age," Anderson said. "Socially, he made a lot of improvements."

When he was first examined, the assessment of Adam also noted that he showed "marked social immaturity"—he had no friends and was withdrawn. He also showed a "shallow emotional response to the tragedy." In other words, he displayed a negative affect, and some, such as a reporter or a recalcitrant prosecutor, could have easily misread this sign of severe emotional and psychiatric trauma as indicative of no remorse.

However, it did not happen that way. One tragedy, which could have been avoided, had resulted in a death, and all sides—medical, legal, and familial—joined to avert another. And among all of the factors that lobbied to keep Adam from doing hard time as a criminal, or being swallowed up in the labyrinth of a psychiatric hospital, perhaps the most important was Adam's family. Appearing before the court was a hardworking family with a God-fearing mother who attended services regularly, had a full-time job as a factory worker, and raised a family at the same time; relatives who wanted to help; and a meek and mild but seriously disturbed sixteen-year-old defendant who had never been a problem at home, at school, or with the law.

Also appearing by proxy—through records, testimony, and other accounts—was a man who had failed as a father, husband, and breadwinner. I would have liked to know what drove him to the bottle, and if, as I was told, it all fell apart in a two-year binge. I also would have liked to know what Adam meant when he said his father "would get mean" when he was drunk. Adam said there had been no beatings or battering going on in his home, but I wondered if there had been threats, and just how heated the arguments and tiffs really were. What happened in Adam's family could have happened, under the right circumstances, in other families in that neighborhood, city, or state.

In his article mentioned above, Dr. Douglas Sargent writes that a child who kills can be acting as the "unwitting agent" of others who unconsciously prompt the child to act out their hostility toward the victim. In other words, a family member killed by a child was not the victim of an isolated act. The fragile psychological inhibitions of the child were swamped by the covert or overt wishes of other members of the family for the victim to die. Adam might have been thinking and fantasizing about killing his father for more than a year but perhaps others were too. However, their psychological defenses against something that we all think about doing at one point or another were much stronger.

Sargent also strongly suggested that in such cases real tragedies might be averted. In another article, he wrote that "diligent attention to the many distress signals sent up by these troubled families would have been the first and most essential step in the preventive chain, alerting the environment to the existence of a lethal situation. Only then could prompt effective action be taken to head off catastrophe." Some of the signs: escalating acrimony over months or years, violence in the home, a withdrawn child, guns in the house—just to name a few.

When Adam was released, the psychiatrist recommended that he "be more independent" and not return home, Anderson said. The doctor thought that Adam was too close to his mother, and by returning home he would be "assuming the father's role" in the family.

"But the kid wanted to go home, so he did," Anderson said. "He finished school, he's working, and he's no longer on probation."

Adam was doing everything expected of him.

Anderson had been a probation officer for about fifteen years, with his first eighteen months spent working with adults before he switched to juveniles. Adam was the only kid he had been assigned who had killed a parent.

"More often than not, kids with serious family conflicts, or who think [their lives] aren't worth living, run away, attempt suicide, or commit it," he said.

# 16

# For the Love
# of Money

For almost ten years, Nancy lived in a trim, two-story brownstone with her husband and two sons. After her divorce, she took over the house, keeping it as attractive as any on the block. She did that through earnest, hard work and a spunkiness that pulled her through the most difficult times. In the neighborhood, residents spoke affectionately of her as a loyal, unflappable friend, someone you could trust with your life, a woman you could always depend on, no matter what the situation. At the plumbing company where she headed the payroll department, her fellow employees considered her a joy to have around. She was someone whom the people she met could not easily forget. One cold night in January, she became grist for the New York City tabloids that extol the glitter of Big Apple Chic on one page and shriek bloody murder on another.

Nancy's story was an all too familiar shriek. Someone had broken into her home and stolen her valuables. But before he left, he strangled her with his hands and, to be sure that she would never awaken, cut a length of telephone wire and knotted it tightly around her throat. She was found lying face down in her pajamas with the cord still around her neck. It was cold-blooded murder at its best in New York City, and her death reminded her neighbors that no neighborhood was spared the ravages of crime and that you were not safe even in the confines of your own home. When the news broke, her friends could hardly stop crying.

No one grieved louder than her son, Larry, who told the police how he had found his mother's body. Larry, who lived in the basement apartment in the brownstone, told the police he and a friend had returned home and noticed the door unlocked. When they walked in, they found the house ransacked and immediately noticed that the television was missing. He cried out for his mother, and when he got no response, he started to worry. A prescient awareness warned him not to enter his mother's bedroom, so he asked the friend to go instead. Later, as he explained what had happened to the investigating officers, Larry could not control his screaming and grieving over his mother's death. Visibly shocked, he managed to give the police a tentative inventory of missing items that included furs, jewelry, a television, cash, and Nancy's 1978 Buick Regal. He appeared as if he were almost ready to collapse from grief when the police left the house.

At the funeral, Larry, thirty-two, wailed uncontrollably, draping himself over Nancy's coffin. After the services, he drove several of his friends to an all-night disco where they tried to boogie their cares away. On the way home, one of them noticed that they were riding in a 1978 Regal and asked Larry how he had recovered his mother's car so fast. Larry said the police had found it and returned it to him. When they arrived at Larry's brownstone, the police were waiting for him but he refused to talk, exclaiming that he was trying to recover from his mother's death and that they should stop harassing him. He ordered them to leave. On the way out, one of the police officers looked into the garage and discovered the 1978 Regal that had been reported missing. When they returned to the house and asked Larry about his mother's car in the garage, and why he had not notified them about its return, Larry exploded in anger, excoriating them for being insensitive and cruel while he was still in mourning. He again ordered them to leave. But when they left, they took the car with them, impounding it as evidence in the murder investigation.

The detectives who visited Larry's friend Barry, however, received a different response. He wanted to cooperate and help with their investigation, though he said he did not know anything that would be of use to them. They asked him if he would come back to the police station with them, and as he grabbed his coat, Barry told them that he had been expecting them to question him because he knew they were questioning other friends of Nancy's and Larry's. When they arrived at the station house, the detectives, who knew more than they had indicated, and Barry, who knew more than he was saying, played a game of cat and mouse. After a short while, the mouse lost and sang like a canary. In a clear, audible voice that night, three days after Nancy's murder, Barry spoke into a police tape recorder: "I was approached by Larry and told to burglarize his home . . . and murder his mother."

In 1969, shortly after Nancy divorced his father, Larry moved into the basement apartment. After a string of bad luck, he needed a place to stay. His marriage had soured quickly, though he was still friends with his ex-wife, Joan. He could not hold a job, and his mother, lonely, living in the big house by herself, gratefully let him move in. Larry supported himself by working at odd jobs and doing an occasional stint as a carpenter. He refurbished the basement apartment and performed chores around the house in exchange for living rent free.

The arrangement worked well when they did not fight. And they fought most of the time. When he procrastinated or failed to complete a task that Nancy wanted him to do or he had promised to finish, she would burn him in vitriol. He was not worth the pain she had suffered bringing him into this world. He parried with forearm blows and body punches that knocked her to the ground. At 110 pounds, Nancy and her vituperative salvos were no match for Larry's physical poundings. Squat but built like a World War II pillbox, Larry outweighed her by forty-five pounds. Pitched battles erupted over her drinking, his inability to hold a job, or his frequent homosexual trysts in her brownstone. And while she imbibed heavily, he soared on amphetamines or landed with Valium. Each fight grew more percussive than the previous one. Two years before Barry wrung her neck, Larry hurled his mother down a flight of stairs.

Somehow they always found the path to rapprochement, no matter how flimsy the excuse, so that she did not have to live by herself and he did not have to move out of his rent-free apartment. In 1978, he segued from open wishful thinking that she would die to vivid descriptions of killing her. And he ranted and raved about it to anyone who would listen.

A few weeks after New Year's Day 1979, Larry and his mother argued bitterly about his damaging her car and procrastinating about having it repaired. It was a 1 A.M. fight, and Larry complained bitterly to a friend, Joe, who was just dropping by for a quick visit later on, that his mother was "a drunk and no good," and that he was having problems with her and wished she would die. He then moaned loudly that his life would be so much better if he could only find someone who would kill her for him. He was still complaining later in the day when another friend, Barbara, dropped in with her new lover, Barry. The two lovers had been using Larry's apartment for their occasional assignations, and with Larry's help Barbara was able to meet clandestinely without tipping off her husband or slinking away to some seedy hotel. The pair sat passively while Larry unleashed a stream of recriminations that had been building up for years.

"She has so much money, she would be better off dead," he bellowed.

He turned to Barry and, in a fit of pique, dared him to help, not expecting any real reply.

"You could be rich if my mother was to die, because she owns a brownstone," Larry said.

"If I could get the brownstone, I would do it," Barry eagerly replied.

Larry promptly told him that he could not have the brownstone because he wanted it himself. However, she also had thousands of dollars worth of jewelry, furs, and cash that he could have if he wanted. Barry's desperation flared like a Roman candle.

Like Larry, he worked at odd jobs when he could find them, and he hustled drugs on the side for the quick hunk of extra cash he could not make any other way. But now his suppliers were threatening him because he had lost several thousands of dollars in cocaine and marijuana in a robbery. He could not go to the police, and he needed the money fast, and he did not care how he got it.

Larry took him, Barbara, and two other friends who had come over upstairs to his mother's living quarters, where he and Barry conducted an inventory of Nancy's possessions and rehearsed her murder. It was a dress rehearsal before a live audience. Larry said he wanted Nancy shot, and then grimaced because he thought shooting her would be "too messy." Barry quickly added that a gun would also be too loud. He preferred chloroform but thought he needed a prescription to buy some.

"Maybe we should strangle her," Larry finally said.

"Yeah," Barry said, "that would be better."

Larry, however, did not want to participate in the actual killing. He hated his mother but he did not want to see her die. And he also did not want her to see him watching her die. Barry would have to run this lap by himself.

With their friends still present, the two conspirators selected the jewelry and furs Barry would take after he killed Nancy. Larry, in a grand display of largess, tossed in Nancy's television to sweeten up the pot for Barry. He then sketched a scenario.

Barry would kill Nancy that same night, which was her bowling night. When Nancy left home to go bowling, Larry explained, Barry would sneak in through the back door that Larry would leave unlocked, take as much as he could carry, kill Nancy when she returned, and drive away in her car, which would be parked in the garage. Larry would pick up the car several days later. After they finished making their plans, Larry drove everyone home in Nancy's car and returned just in time to start arguing with his mother again. The argument was not part of the plan, but it helped him to storm out of the house in a rage. He left the back door unlocked as he fled.

"I entered the home at nine-thirty or quarter to ten," Barry said into the tape recorder at the station house. "He left the door open for me. I went in through a garage door which was left open for me, through his room directly up to the second bedroom on the upper floor."

Nancy had not gone bowling that night. She was in the bathroom putting her hair up in curlers, and then she came out and discovered Barry rummaging through her drawers.

"And in my panic," Barry said, "I did the only thing I thought I could do. In my panic, when I saw the woman, I did the only thing I thought I could do to protect myself, and, losing my mind, killed the lady."

"I told her to get on the bed, to lay down. I was going to tie her up and at that point she went to grab me and put up a struggle and I killed her. I was in a complete panic at that point, at which point I grabbed the telephone cord—I cut the wire and I tied it around her neck. I tied it and made a knot. I then went into the bathroom and finished what I was there to do and left."

He did not panic enough to forget his take: a color television, a mink coat, a mink cape, a mink stole, jewelry, cash, and the car.

For Larry's and Barry's trials, which were held separately, the Queens district attorney's office rounded up a network of friends, lovers, former lovers, acquaintances, and Larry's ex-wife, who all, at one point or another, had witnessed the choreographing of Nancy's death. Some of them had known her for years, yet not one of them had warned her or hinted about the death plot against her. They all dissociated themselves from her killing as easily and crudely as Barry had when he told the police how he had panicked and "losing my mind, killed the lady."

No one was more loquacious about his incredulity at her murder than the man who had been wishing and hoping she would die before he started planning her death: her son.

After the juries deliberated less than an hour all together to find first Barry guilty and then Larry, Nancy's son faced the judge who was about to pronounce sentence.

"Before the sentence, you have a right to make a statement to the court," the clerk told Larry. "Do you have anything to say?"

"Yes, I do," he said. "I have a few things I'd like to say. Please excuse me if I stumble because I'm very nervous. But I'd like . . . I'd like to stand here and tell you I am perfectly and totally innocent and didn't know anything was going to happen, and certainly never intended for it to happen. I feel that the case that was brought against me was based on Barry's twisted self-serving lies and Barbara's lies to protect herself. And the People [the prosecutor] took that, and based upon that, manufactured a case against me. And strengthened all the weak points in it. I believe [the] People dictated, virtually dictated some of their testimony, and other remarks were taken out of context and therefore misinterpreted. . . . I feel the witnesses were either coerced or twisted, or whatever, to strengthen the weak points in the case. I could go on and on with how I feel."

He staggered on for almost five minutes.

"But what you have got to believe is that I in no way conspired with this [Barry] in any way, never promised him anything. I never thought this was going to happen. But I didn't take any extraordinary measures to prevent it from happening because I didn't think it was going to happen. My mind was clogged. I was stupid. I was so stupid that I can't believe it, to even conduct a conversation such as I admitted to. And never denied. But at the same time, I was totally convinced that it was dropped and dismissed and that nothing was going to happen. My irrational behavior, I can't excuse after the fact.

I can't excuse it. I can account for it but—out of being terrified and acting, you know, totally irrationally afterwards, and just not thinking straight. My pill-clogged mind was just distorted . . . and I'm not looking for mercy, I'm just looking for understanding."

The judge finally interrupted and gave a sentence that would keep him in jail with Barry for fifty years before he could be paroled.

# 17

# Aaron

Aaron hoped the thoughts would go away if he did not pay any attention to them. But he could hardly ignore them. He took a job at a fast-food restaurant, with the idea that he would be so preoccupied with work that he would not know they were there. But at night he tossed and turned, and before long he thought he was losing weight. He could not shake them by pretending they were not there, and he could not lose them by burying himself in work, and he could not even dodge them in play. But he tried. His friends still saw him as mild-mannered, affable Aaron with the winsome smile. The teenage angst that sullied their lives never appeared to touch him, and he seemed immune to the melancholy that weighed on them. But it was unreal. The thoughts persisted, and after five months he found them irresistible. Aaron was obsessed with death. "I don't have to watch TV or look at a book to know when death is going to go because it just happens," he would say later. "I can tell. I really don't have to think about it. I just have to turn my head, or, you know, nod, or just think about something." And death was in his mind, he would tell the authorities, "most of the time." But no one ever knew until one evening in November. A sheriff's dispatcher was the first to find out.

"I just shot my mother," Aaron told the dispatcher when he telephoned for help. Aaron, his socks covered with a gelatinous red goo that stained his hands and soiled his shirt, shivered in the basement of his home. He was afraid to stay and afraid to run. He begged the dispatcher to send the police right away, and if they didn't hurry,

Aaron planned to rush over to a neighbor's home. The dispatcher, working fast to patch in the village police on a phone line that would not connect, told him to stay put. But Aaron ached with terror that his father would walk into the home at any moment. "He'll be home at nine, and I don't want to him to see me," Aaron said. "I'm gonna go outside if they don't get hurrying."

During that twenty-seven-minute conversation with a man he had never met, Aaron gradually eased out his story. "I'm cut too," he whined.

"You're cut up?" the dispatcher asked.

"I don't know if it's my . . . my finger's broke," the boy said.

"Your fingers, how did your fingers get broke?" the dispatcher asked.

"My little sister," Aaron said. "I didn't have enough shells to kill her so I had to strangle her . . . put a knife through her. She was trying to take the knife at me and everything. . . . I'm so afraid."

There had been no fear earlier that night when he was upstairs in his bedroom reading a driver education manual. It was about then that some inexplicable mechanism tripped, and he casually walked down to the basement and took his .308-caliber automatic rifle, the one he used to hunt deer, from the cabinet where his father kept the guns stored. He put four bullets in the chamber and one in his pocket. Then he walked upstairs.

Pam, his sister, was watching television when the first shot whizzed passed her and blasted a quarter-size hole in the front door. The second shot shattered her face, mangling her features into a hideous mask before she slumped to the floor. He whirled, and before his mother, sitting in the next room, could ask why or tell him to put the gun down before he hurt someone else, he shot her in the head. He turned quickly and fired a just-in-case shot into Pam's body.

Aaron put the rifle down because it was out of bullets and, forgetting about the last shell in his pocket, walked into his sister Jenny's room near the kitchen. "I didn't do it," she said, cowering in her bed. "You didn't do it, I did it," he said, as he grabbed her and wrapped his hands around her neck. She passed out just as the doorbell rang. He left her on the floor and walked to the front door. It was his next-door neighbor. She wanted to know what was causing all the noise that sounded like gunshots. And why, she asked, was broken glass on the front porch? Was there something wrong? Could she help? "I threw a rock at the window," Aaron told her unconvincingly. And while the woman hesitated at the door, Jenny rushed into the living room and screamed. Aaron hurriedly told the woman that he would have to "go calm Jenny down" and quickly shut the door.

After grabbing Jenny, he pulled her to the basement door, where he was planning to throw her down the steps. But then another idea popped into his head. He dragged her down the basement steps to the sink, where he tried to drown her by forcing her head under the faucet and turning on the hot water. But she fought him fiercely and he was not strong enough to immobilize her. He gave up and was dragging her back upstairs when she slipped from his grip and hit the floor, cracking her skull. But she was still conscious. He snatched her back up the steps and into the kitchen. Grabbing a knife, he slashed her, cutting her arms and hands as she tried to ward off the blows. He almost severed the tip of her finger with one slash, but Jenny fought back. She grabbed the knife he held and slashed back at him. He slashed back more. And they fought there on the kitchen floor.

Then the phone rang. It was the next-door neighbor again. She told him she knew something was wrong. But Aaron, who had Jenny "cuffed up" with one arm so that she could not escape, assured the woman that everything was okay and hung up. This time he grabbed a big kitchen knife and plunged it into his sister's neck. The blade bent. He grabbed a knife with a bigger blade and stabbed her again in the neck. This time, a pathologist would testify, he cut her carotid artery "clean off."

Aaron left Jenny's body in the kitchen and walked into the basement, where he started a fire, but his rage was spent. As the small fire flickered out, he called the sheriff's office. And well before the village police arrived, Aaron set about making their job as easy as possible. He told the dispatcher he would do anything they asked as long as he could escape from the home he had transformed into an abattoir. He turned on all the lights in the first floor and basement, as the dispatcher had asked, and walked out of his home with his hands on top of his head like a prisoner of war. But unlike many POWs, who offer only their name, rank, and serial number, Aaron tried to explain how a mild-mannered sixteen-year-old boy goes about killing his mother and sisters.

He told them he had wrestled with thoughts of "death and killing people" for about five months. It had started sometime in late May

1983. It was about the time when, fifty miles south of his town, a tiny hamlet was roiling in the spasm of its first mass murder in memory. News accounts of the murders of Hans and Sally Zimmer and their son Perry, ten, inundated the community and spread far beyond the village boundaries. The accounts did not mention the identity of the killer. He was a fourteen-year-old boy, and Wisconsin laws prohibit the identification of juvenile offenders under seventeen. Outside Wisconsin, however, it was another story. The name was not released or mentioned but the suspect was identified. It was the Zimmers' fourteen-year-old son, a choirboy and "really nice kid."

The Zimmers had lived in a small town tucked away in northern Illinois for six years before moving to Wisconsin in April 1983. Hans, an airplane mechanic who had been laid off before the move, and his wife and two sons were devout Catholics. They were a "very fine and respectable family" and the two boys were good students who never got in trouble at their parish grammar school in Illinois. In 1982, the parents sent their oldest son to Holy Name Seminary, a high school for young men considering the priesthood. But after ten weeks, the boy dropped out. "I think he found the program a bit more academic than he could handle," the school's rector was quoted as saying.

When Hans decided to accept his brother-in-law's offer to work for him in Wisconsin, the move was just another element of frustration. Both boys disliked leaving Illinois but the older one took it harder. He told his friends he was planning to run away, but there was something more smoldering in the Zimmer family. In late May he repeated his threat to a friend and this time he added an ominous hint. He said he was going to kill his mother and father and brother before he fled. The threat worked its way through the local grapevine but no one made an effort to warn the family until a counselor at the boy's old high school in Illinois alerted the sheriff's office in Iowa County, Wisconsin, where the Zimmers were living.

When deputies checked the home, they discovered that they were too late. A few days earlier the Zimmers' oldest boy had attacked without warning. He shot his father five times with a high-powered rifle, hitting him twice in the head and once in the heart at close range. He left the body where it fell. On the wood-and-cement patio at the rear of the family's home, he attacked his mother with a large knife, cutting and stabbing her more than a dozen times in the face, head, and body. He dragged her body out of sight from the backyard and hid it in the toolshed. He went inside the house and caught his brother upstairs near his bedroom and stabbed him more than twenty times. With six handguns from his father's collection of weapons placed in the trunk of the family car, the boy sought freedom and headed south with credit cards and cash he had taken from his parents. As he wound his way toward Kansas City, he picked up a hitchhiking eighteen-year-old and told him his parents had given him permission to drive cross-country. They set off for a good time.

When they stopped at a Kansas City motel, an employee became suspicious because of their ages. Police had warned local merchants to beware of two youths with stolen credit cards. When the Zimmers' son walked in, the night desk clerk pegged him and the hitchhiker as the culprits. But she was wrong. One was a murderer and the other was just a hitchhiker. She called the police, who detained the two youths while they checked the younger boy's story about his parents allowing him to take the car, cards, and guns on a cross-country trip. They called the Iowa County sheriff's office in Wisconsin, which had already discovered the bodies of Hans, Sally, and Perry at their home.

The discovery hit like a carefully concealed time bomb in a community where homicide was a virtual stranger. Its last obstreperous visit in the early 1970s briefly shattered the bucolic charm of the area with the death of two men. The victims had been brutally slain and their bodies set afire. But the community's alarm over those slayings faded away in the realization that they were outsiders from another state who had been bumped off in a drug-related caper that went astray. It was easy to dismiss people like that involved in things like that. They had chosen the way they lived, and their death was no loss to the community.

It was not easy to sweep aside the murder of the Zimmers, however, or even try to forget them. They were considered to be like many of the other families: hardworking, churchgoing, God-fearing people. Their death struck close to home. Each new tidbit of news and every recounting of the story fueled a sense of helplessness and outrage.

When the county authorities started extradition procedures to bring the Zimmer boy back, the newspapers played up the fact that because he was fourteen he could not be charged as an adult. Wisconsin has a progressive piece of legislation called the Children's Code. Any kid under sixteen who is arrested for a crime cannot be treated as an adult, not even for the most serious of crimes, like mass murder. Youths found guilty can only be held in a juvenile facility until they are nineteen. If they are found to be insane, a judge can send them to a mental institution where they can be held indefinitely, but there must be yearly review of their cases and treatment.

A tempest stoked by news accounts, editorials, and proclamations by some state senators began to build up. When the Zimmer boy's lawyer was quoted in the newspapers it appeared for a while that the storm was about to explode. "Why is he getting only the maximum of three years?" the court-appointed attorney was quoted as asking. "Because a skillful and competent judge and district attorney are hampered by the law." Two state senators jumped into the fray by introducing a bill that could lower the age at which a youth could be waived into adult court from sixteen to fourteen.

In one newspaper editorial, the writer noted, "A 15-year-old Mineral Point boy pled no contest to delinquency in the slayings of three members of a family. He was committed to Ethan Allen School at Wales for a year of psychiatric review. The case calls attention to the handling of grave offenses allegedly committed by juveniles. A pending bill would permit the waiver into adult court of youths of 14 when the offense has resulted in death. No single case should dictate the legislature's decision. But lawmakers surely must heed cases such as the one in Mineral Point in setting policy on juvenile offenders." Like several other articles about the murders, the editorial did not explain a motive or identify the youth, but it insinuated that the public was not safe from marauding youths who stormed houses and wiped out entire families. They could get away with murder. The Zimmer tragedy was no less serious because a son had committed the murders. But the violence was in the family.

Two officials involved with juveniles and criminal justice tried to temper some of the criticism of the state juvenile laws. Criticizing two proposed laws to change the age at which juveniles could be brought into adult court, the executive director of the Wisconsin Council on Criminal Justice was quoted as saying, "In almost every case, the question is what would happen if the juvenile was waived. The reaction of people in the field is generally that most of those youths would have been found not guilty by reason of insanity" if tried in adult court. The head of the Youth Policy and Law Center in Madison told a reporter that changing the law would "Satisfy the public's desire for revenge but it would do nothing to protect the public." He said that few juveniles sent to juvenile facilities ever reappeared in the adult criminal system.

The two bills were defeated and the tragedy faded into the background of everyday living, if not from the public conscience, until Aaron was arrested that fall. There was no doubt that he was going to be treated as an adult. Aaron was charged with three counts of first-degree murder. His attorney argued to have the case handled in juvenile court but the court was not persuaded by his arguments. And even though Aaron's father said he would be willing to have him home and would accept responsibility for him, and neighbors offered their support as well, the bail was so high that he could not be released. The prosecuting attorney said one of the reasons he had demanded a high bail was because of some statements Aaron had made after he was arrested. It was so easy to kill, he said, that he was afraid that he might do it again.

Under the masthead of the *Daily Herald* ran a big headline: WE'RE ALL-AMERICA. In a big picture, the mayor stood with downtown Wausau in the background. "Wausau is blushing with pride today," the story started. "Its citizens have been recognized nationally for bettering their community. They have made Wausau an All-American city. Wausau is one of the nine cities in the nation to receive the All-America honor. In the 35 years The Citizens Forum on Self Government National Municipal League, New York, has bestowed the awards, only two other Wisconsin cities—Madison and La Crosse—have won it." The big story was WE'RE ALL-AMERICA but the lead story was BOY, 15, HELD IN MURDER OF 3 FROM FAMILY. The boy was described as nice, quiet, and no problem in his neighborhood or school. He came from a good family. He had shot his mother and father and brother, eighteen, while they were watching television one evening. According to the newspaper account, the boy then walked into the den with the shotgun he was using, smiled at his sister, and shot her once. He also hit her in the head with the butt of the weapon. He then hopped into the family's pickup truck and drove to a friend's house.

The shooting took place in a small burg just outside Wausau, which is a few hours north of Aaron's hometown. It occurred about five months after Aaron's sisters and mother were killed. Aaron's case was awaiting an appeals court decision before proceeding to trial when this third Wisconsin parricide and mass murder in less than a year happened.

The newspaper, reporting its first "multiple killing in the county since 1955," covered all the angles in depth but in a low-key manner. It described the family and the kid in interviews with neighbors teachers, schoolmates, and friends. It also explained what could possibly happen to the youth under Wisconsin law. And in one story it succinctly explained how a "nice" kid could one day slay his family. Quoting a clinical psychologist from a local health-care center, the paper, under a modest headline—ISOLATION, RAGE CAN LEAD TO VIOLENCE AGAINST FAMILY—declared, "Violent or tragic acts like murders by a family member usually do not spring up out of the blue, local mental health officials say. It's not uncommon for neighbors or those close to the family to report, 'I can't understand it . . . he was the nicest person or the nicest boy.'" The psychologist said later in the story, "Families almost always are 'closed systems,' operating quite differently than what is conveyed on the outside to neighbors and friends. They [families] can present a good face to the community, but on the inside it can be quite different."

# PART V

## Garry—
## A Special Case

*Still Life with a Tormented Lover* hangs in a makeshift gallery in one of the sepulchral corridors of a maximum-security prison. Depicting a world frozen in perpetual silence, it juxtaposes an interminable moment from the past with a moment of anguished longing in a present that has no future. On an askew chessboard, two goblets stare into each other's souls across a checkered no-man's-land of vibrant black and red squares. In the background a shattered goblet rests on a blood-red square littered with glistening shards of glass. The painting was another bit of arcanum by a man the staff and inmates call The Artist. While in jail he has won several awards in statewide competitions, and the deputy warden has praised him as a "model prisoner" whose art enlivens the brooding ambience of the institution. In order to protect the few people who matter to him from another round of embarrassment, The Artist requested anonymity in this book and was given the pseudonym Garry.

Garry inherited his talent from his parents, German artists who immigrated to the United States in the early 1950s ostensibly so that his mother could complete her college studies. But they never really planned to return to Germany. Except for an occasional letter or telephone call at Christmas, or a rare visit by someone from their homeland, they cut off contact with their relatives and friends. His parents seldom talked about their past and families, and his father objected when Garry's maternal grandmother, during a visit stateside, wanted to teach her grandson German.

His brother visited Germany after Garry's imprisonment and met some of their relatives, but he refused to tell Garry anything about the visit other than that he had been there. He had not forgiven Garry for making him an orphan by killing their mother a few days after their father died suddenly of cancer. But Garry managed to cull bits and pieces about his parents and his German roots. With his mother and father dead, Garry clung to his family with time-worn images, anecdotes, and fleeting contacts with an elusive brother who both hated and loved him.

Garry said that his mother's family in Europe had raised horses for the czar. His father, who grew up in Berlin, was the son of an aide to the German ambassador to London. The war savaged both families. As the Third Reich disintegrated, Garry's father was drafted into a Hitler youth camp. Shortly before he and the other high school boys were to be shipped off to the front lines, the Russians stormed Berlin. One day a detachment showed up at his family's doorstep, asked for Garry's grandfather by name, and took him away. He was never seen again.

Garry eventually met an uncle, and for a while, after he was imprisoned, he exchanged letters with his maternal grandmother. She wrote to him in German, and he used an English-German dictionary to translate her letters and write to her. He could not speak or write fluent German but he could "make out words and phrases" and communicate, if not as lucidly as he would have liked.

It was shortly after his grandmother died that he painted his still life with the goblets. It was the only one of his works that embodied both him and his mother as subjects. He had been scared off by the images that emerged when he tried to render her with oil and canvas. The still life would have to do for now. Its symbolism encompassed several meanings. On a simple level, he hinted, the shattered goblet represented his mother. The other two goblets represented him and a nurse with whom he had been infatuated when she was working in the prison. Except for a woman who was a friend of his family, and his old girlfriend on the outside, he felt uncomfortable around women.

"I can't relate to women. It scares me to think that they might know what I did to my mother and imagine themselves in those circumstances and they might be afraid of me. Any woman who knows what I did would be repulsed by me. Working with the nurse was a real challenge. I had always wanted to talk to her. I wrote letters to her [eighty-six pages of which he was too shy to deliver]. I really wrestled with the problem. I would break out in a cold sweat and start to stutter every time I talked to her. I assumed that she knew about me."

It appeared that everyone in the prison knew about him his first day inside. The inmates spit on him and threatened to kill him.

"They heard about my crime on the radio. There's a lot of superficial mother love here. They talk about swearing on their mother's grave and on their mother's name but it's only superficial. I just stayed in my cell and away from everyone else and eventually they forgot me."

While Garry was avoiding them he cut his wrists with the shards of a busted light bulb. But he was shaking so much he could not hold still long enough to sever an artery. He bled just enough to "soak a sheet," and the next day he was placed under psychiatric observation in a special cell. In there he resorted to his "bugout role," a reassuring skit from his high school days, when he liked to put people on. This put-on was brief, unlike the previous ones.

"I took a broom, water pail, some coloring, and a paper clip and put a sock on my hand and played Captain Ahab fishing in a water bucket. I was acting it up and having a good time. But I found there was no advantage to it here when I saw some guys walking around on Thorazine. After seeing those guys all doped up and with glazed eyes, I decided not to play the bugout role anymore."

Instead, he went looking for glue and found toluene, an aromatic liquid solvent used as a thinner in paint, varnish, and lacquers. He used other solvents, which were more powerful than his first love, rubber cement. He had been sniffing glues and thinners for almost two years already but a friend and others rode him until he stopped using it regularly in jail. However, it took a few years. Now he used it intermittently, depending on the depth of his depression, which could be bottomless and engulf him if he was not careful.

"I work myself to death. I paint all night and work all day. It leaves me no time for thought. Thought only depresses me."

When his angst became too much, he smoked marijuana. But if he smoked too much it only aggravated his despair. Then he just sat and wallowed in it. And if he wallowed too long, he "instinctively" reached for his glue or thinner. Christmas, his birthday, was one of those days when he "instinctively" had to have one or the other.

Garry had been in prison for seven years. He came in shortly after

his nineteenth birthday and would not be eligible to leave until he
was over forty.

"I'm guilty. I'm not going to argue about it. I can't justify it. On
some days I feel no price is big enough to fulfill justice. There are
other times I mumble and grumble. I've spent years trying to block it
out of my mind. It has been hard to live with. It was an awful
experience and everything that has been connected with it too. I'm
so ashamed that unless someone knows about it ahead of time I can't
talk about it. It's like dropping an H-bomb on people."

When the police picked him up in 1976, they questioned him for
about an hour. His signed statement read as if it were a straightfor-
ward account, but it was essentially the sum of his answers to specific
questions. It read, "I slugged her once when her back was to me. I
thought that would knock her out. It didn't. I grabbed her arm and
started hitting her with the bar. I probably hit her 10 or 12 times. She
cried out '[Garry]' and then she fell to the floor. She laid on the floor
bleeding and breathing and this thought about hitting a deer entered
my mind. One time we [he and his father] hit a deer with a car and the
only way we could put the deer out [of its misery] was to hit it once on
the head and then cut its throat. So, when I saw my mother lying over
there bleeding and in pain I decided to cut her throat. I left the room
to get a utility knife and when I got back she was still bleeding and
breathing. I knelt down and cut her throat. [After he was certain she
was dead, he got some wet towels to "clean up the mess on the floor"
and also grabbed a rope and some rugs.] I came back to the room and
wrapped my mother into the old rugs and started to tie her in it, and I
felt this urge to have sex with her. I took off her shorts and pants and
she had this body suit that snapped. I unsnapped the body suit and had
sex with my mother. Then I cleaned up the mess with the wet towels
and I grabbed the rope and dragged my mother into the cellar and
placed her behind the furnace." When he told the police everything
they wanted to know, he thought they would let him go. He did not
expect them to arrest him. After he was arrested he did not believe he
was going to prison for a long, long time.

For the last two years that they were together, Garry and his family lived in a "gorgeous" twenty-five-room house with a three-car
garage, two and a half acres of fruit trees, and stables for horses. It
was about one hundred years old. Inside there were thick beige car-

pets, white Danish-modern furniture, high ceilings, and huge and exquisitely done paintings on the wall. Sometimes visitors would see Garry working on his motorcycle, which was propped up on the winding staircase of his home. But those who knew the family had learned to anticipate the unexpected. One day Garry's father picked up the new car that he had purchased for his wife and wrapped a "gigantic" ribbon around it. He drove it home in deep snow and surprised her with his idea of a gift-wrapped present. On another occasion, when he knew that a neighbor was due back in town from a trip to Germany, he rounded up Garry and his brother, and the trio commandeered an unused billboard on a heavily traveled road that led to their neighborhood. When the neighbor rode past on her way home she was greeted by a big welcome-home sign.

"They were outlandish, nutty, and creative, and they always did fun things like that," said an old family friend. "They were interesting people and wonderful artists. Charlotte [a pseudonym for Garry's mother] had a heavy-sounding accent. She reminded you of Zsa Zsa Gabor and she was very charming. Carl [a pseudonym for Garry's father] had a heavy accent too and he was tall and very handsome. Charlotte could get very excited and exuberant over the littlest things. Garry is just like her. He can get excited about a pretty postage stamp."

They were eccentrics with verve, and this friend became part of their lives when she enrolled in an art class and met Charlotte. She knew the family for thirteen years, visited them in their home, and had them over to her home. Yet, they were virtual strangers to her when Carl died and Charlotte was killed. What she could tell me was the sum of the little knowledge she had acquired from years of friendship and what Garry had learned and told her. She was one of Garry's few friends and she did not want her name mentioned. So here she is called Rachel.

"Charlotte and I were good friends, yet she was a private person. When she told someone I was one of her best friends it blew my mind. She was so private. I didn't know for years that her parents raised horses for the czar."

The war exacted a heavy toll on both families, and it has not been made clear how Garry's parents managed to survive. Carl's father was just sixteen when the Allies invaded as he was about to be shipped up to the front lines with a Nazi youth group. He and his brother fled and walked back to Berlin. The day after they arrived the Russians took their father away and shot him. Garry's parents rarely talked about the war or their experiences but Garry learned that they had grown up "with real difficult emotional problems." Rachel was unable to explain how those problems manifested themselves since around her the couple had always maintained an air of exuberance and wit. When she first met the family Garry had been a dazzling ball of creativity.

"He was a real pleasant kid. He always enjoyed himself and had a lot going for him. He was gifted creatively. It was obvious from the time he was five. . . . He was doing really nice things in kindergarten."

But he did not get along with the kids in school. There were plenty of fights, yet she did not believe he was a bully and that he started fights. But Rachel was not sure why he was always fighting. Maybe, she surmised, it was because Garry was so eccentric and gifted and came from an exceptionally creative family.

"I remember being in their house for coffee one day. He had come home for lunch, and I remember him coming in a door. He shut the door and folded his arms and went, 'Whew,' like it was all behind him and he was safe for the time being."

Garry was the oldest son and the most creative but Charlotte favored her younger son, Larry [a pseudonym]. Carl did not appear to have a favorite one way or the other, though Garry spent a lot of time with him working on the family's sailboat, doing odd jobs for him such as painting signs or graphic work, or just playing chess.

"Carl did fantastic pen-and-ink drawings. Charlotte was a very good painter. Garry picked up both. Charlotte was always trying to help 'poor Larry' because he had no talent. Larry was her little 'Fifi.' Her husband thought it was strange. He would go up the wall when she called him 'my little Fifi.'"

She could not recall Garry having any real childhood problems other than fights, which were not too serious, and a rivalry with his brother for his mother's attention. But that did not appear serious either. He was a gifted kid with an ingratiating personality, a vivid imagination, and a sense of humor that bordered on the absurd. Even after his problems started when he was about sixteen, she said, he was still wacky and fun to know. At home, however, it was a different story. After his family moved into their spacious new home, he started hanging around with an older, rougher crowd of guys. He came home late and argued frequently with his parents about curfew. With his new cadre of friends he roamed the nearby counties burglarizing homes and businesses. His arrest at school created a minor flap, but because he was a juvenile and it was only his first offense that the court was aware of, he did not have to serve time. Of course no one but Garry and his friends knew about the plethora of places that had been pillaged on their nocturnal raids. Drinking liquor and smoking marijuana were among his favorite pastimes. LSD also gave him a big kick, but glue showed him the road to Nirvana. His mother was seriously concerned, but his father, in the early stages, chalked it all up to kid stuff.

"Charlotte was trying to deal with it. She hassled [Carl] to deal with it. His father's thing was that kids will be kids. That one time Garry was arrested at school, his father's attitude was that he didn't think it was a big deal. With the burglaries, the father's reaction was that 'you ruined my day with all of this commotion.' He saw it as an inconvenience. There was no discipline. You can look back and see what made this happen. It was a combination of drugs and alcohol. The combination of any of those two things could throw his brain out. It's phenomenal that he didn't kill himself."

Garry's mother and brother were at the hospital the night that his father died. Garry passed up the visit to go out with his buddies and get high. At the funeral he was so strung out that he could not grieve. He would not grieve for his father or his mother until he was in state prison. He had to learn how to mourn.

From a letter written by Garry, who delineated significant periods in his life by age and topic:

> Age 5: One of my earliest memories is from when I was 5 years old. We lived on [a street] just below [a college] and at night I looked out over [the city], the lake, and beyond to the farthest stars. At that time I had an inkling of INFINITY. School Age 10: In elementary school I was doing poorly. It was discovered that I needed glasses. I also had the luxury of being ganged-up on by my parents and teachers. I was pressured into learning. I soon became a proficient student and took much pride in being the best at whatever I did. I sat in the first row, raised my hand to answer every question and got very good grades. I enjoied racing through reading comprehension tests while others dodled [sic]. There began my sense of pride and competition. 5th Grade.

Home Age 10: At home I was the eldest child on the block and often had the responsibility of playing shepherd to the younger ones. Among the few older boys I played with I felt better than they at my task, and made friends mad at me for being bossy and telling them always *how I wanted* things done. Fighting at Junior High School [city]: At Junior High School I was the small fry. Only had a couple of friends (the majority were bussed in from rural areas while I walked in). I was often required to fight my way home through a gauntlet of city bullies. I had a lot of spirit and fought my challengers. At one point I gained the recognition of [name of boy] who was the top honcho and thereafter had a bit of respect around the school. I spent many a day in the principal's office for fighting. X-Best Friend: Then my best friend took the love of a girl whom I physically rescued from an attack by several of the bullies. I beat the shit out of him several times for that. She was a whore anyway, but I still feel for her. She hated me for turning on my best friend.

When he was sixteen, Garry's parents decided they needed more room and moved the family into its spacious new home outside of town. That move brought him to the beginning of the end, he said. He attended a new school where the two most imposing student cliques, he decided, were the rural red-necks—local farm boys—and the grubby blue-jeaned crowd of kids who wore long hair. He launched his new school debut by getting into fights with the rural kids he considered red-necks.

"At [school] I was the small fry again—this time among literally giant farmers. The Hatfields were all at least six-four and two hundred–odd pounds of badness. They each took turns pounding the shit out of me for being a 'long hair.' There was no use in fighting back, and as I was eventually left alone I ended my fighting career."

He never really explained the fisticuffs in high school, but when he was in grade school he was fighting because he antagonized the other kids with his arrogant and bossy ways. In high school he eventually linked up with people of his ilk, the "long hairs." They were kids like him who perceived themselves as different.

"I was always weird. I wanted to be different. Not necessarily weird, or in a sense a grotesque weirdness, but something like a knight in shining armor riding down the streets of [his hometown]. That kind of weirdness."

Or going to school dressed like Alice Cooper, as a friend of his did one morning. Or wearing long frizzy hair that branched out from his head like a strange species of strawberry-blond bush spreading in all directions.

"I wanted to be different from the run-of-the-mill people. My parents went along with it."

He cited his old bedroom as an example of his differentness. On one wall he had painted a pop-art mural. He converted his bed into a coffee table and used an old car seat as a couch. For a bed he slept on an old mattress that he had tossed on the floor. When he found the skeleton of a mouse underneath the floorboards of his room, he glued the bones back together and tacked his creation on a wall. He did not want to be included in the run-of-the-mill people, and his talent definitely set him apart, but he needed them to recognize that he was "different." Being different made him special, and he needed that to hold off feelings that he just might be worse than the people—rednecks and bullies—that he scorned. There is no visceral thrill, no sense of being special, gained from being a knight in shining armor walking down the street or an Alice Cooper clone strolling down school halls if no one notices. Garry was a junkie for attention, and people's attention gave him his fix.

"Jeffrey was my one and only really friend. In the four years that we were together our relationship deepened to the point where we often knew each other's thoughts. We used this 'talent' to play pranks upon people we hung out with. We had some stage acting abilities and used these also to perform for our unsuspecting friends. Theatrical games we played, always with the intention to shock or amaze those who watched. We had one routine 'The Nirt War' that we played: Two best friends (Jeff and I) break into a terrible argument of wholly fabricated design. Spontaneously we would know exactly where, when, and how to do this for the best effect. We would make up anything to carry out the act. One time we had a fight with fists (all a act, no harm done) that made a mutual female friend break out in tears."

When Garry linked up with the "long hairs," he narrowed his contacts to a handful of older guys whom he tried to emulate. With them he "started doing the things that older guys do and not what children do." He went to bars and tried to pick up girls and get laid. His girlfriend, JoBeth (a pseudonym), thirteen, was the sister of an older girl he had dated. But there was no sex for him, only frustration. He wanted to have sex, Garry claimed, but there were other concerns that signaled moderation.

"I had looked forward to having sex with her but it was something she didn't want to get into. She had older sisters who had a lot of problems. One got pregnant. Others were loose and wild. Her parents were very protective. I didn't want to jeopardize the relationship or anger her parents. I didn't expect her to put out with me or whatever. We were going to get married. I could wait."

In the ensuing year, he recalled, significant changes took place. While he continued to get good grades, he also was getting drunk on liquor and high on marijuana. He also was roaming around the country burglarizing homes and businesses with his new friends. The good times frequently caused him to come home late and that angered his parents, especially his mother.

"If I came home late Mother was more angry than Father. She would scream and arouse Dad. It's a common thing, a mother yelling at a kid and getting Dad aroused. I talked back to both of them. I argued over their judgments. I told them, 'I'm not going to do this' or 'I'm not going to do that.'"

His girlfriend tried to steer him into meditation and chanting but he tired of it quickly. He and Jeff, however, because of their mutual interest in myths and legends, and because of the influence of some friends who were reading J.R.R. Tolkien's novels, drifted into black magic and occultism.

"I cannot say how Jeff truely [sic] felt about the occult. For me, it was more of a hodge-podge and that together with wild rock and roll music all went together in experimenting trying to find something."

One brew of black magic called for a "concoction of raven's brains," but they could not find a raven so they used the brains of a blackbird.

His dabbling in the occult left him as empty as his attempt at chanting and meditation. During the lull before he started his next quest for the elusive "something" that was missing from his life, his girlfriend's brother turned him on to LSD. But his experiences with glue were more profound. He started with rubber cement during the summer vacation just before his senior year.

"I enjoyed being confused. It was so different. It was better than school, mowing the lawn, and riding my motorcycle and anything else back then. Glue was everything I needed. It was a 'true' religious experience as opposed to the occult, which left me feeling

there was more to it. Glue was mine alone to enjoy. Glue was my best friend."

His best friend sent him careening into telephone poles, parking meters, and support beams. He used glue about a half-dozen times that summer before his mother discovered him getting high. For days she had been smelling it throughout the house, and then she caught him using it in his room. But that did not stop him from using more. Garry became more cautious, and though he sniffed glue once in a while at school or at parties, it was his room that he preferred. That fall he started smoking, drinking, tripping, and sniffing more.

"I liked glue the best. I was almost unconscious. I was in that never-never land between awake and sleep when all things seem possible, all things are within your province."

His hypnagogic hallucinations became vivid, almost real. One night when he was in his room with his black-light bulb burning in a lamp socket overhead, he saw a girl from school with whom he was infatuated standing at the foot of his bed.

"Luna [a pseudonym] was really beautiful. She also was a snob. But after seeing her at the foot of my bed I had the hots for her."

At school, every time he caught her attention or approached her he immediately shied away. After repeatedly failing to overcome his fear of rejection, he surreptitiously got her locker combination number and when no one was around drew pictures of "occult stuff" on her notebook. But he wanted more, and because he wasn't getting sex from his girlfriend, he decided he wanted sex with Luna. On some nights, with thoughts of Luna making him almost feverish, he drove within a few blocks of her home and parked the car so that he could trek to her house. He always carried his glue. He hopped fences, dashed through backyards, fled from dogs, hid behind trees, and made his way as close to her home as he could. There he sniffed his glue.

"I always expected her to have the window opened and would invite me into her house. She was like a fantasy to me. I had real love with JoBeth but Luna was a fantasy very connected to glue. When I masturbated [outside her home or in his bed] I would think of her. That was about as far as I got with her. See, I had loyalty with JoBeth and fantasy of Luna. One satisfied one need and the other was like money in the bank."

He eventually lost interest in Luna when he discovered the little people living in his room. Some lived in his stereo system and came

out when he played music. Others pushed pieces of colored chalk across the ceiling grooves of his room. They were assisted by another bunch who ran a railroad especially for supplying the ceiling dwellers with more chalk. A scorekeeper kept a tally of the number of "beasts" that Garry slew in the nightly battles fought in his room. Another group of mystical characters were life-size, and they took him on magical tours of other worlds. When the glue people started revealing themselves regularly to Garry, he eventually decided he no longer needed to go to bars or hang out with the friends who had introduced him to drugs and burglaries.

"I felt like a king with a kingdom. I had a whole bunch of people who were loyal to me and depended on me."

· For eight months he sniffed glue, increasing the amount as he needed more and more to enter the mystical world populated by his little people. To enter his kingdom he believed he had to follow a ritual. He had to be in his room, where he played rock music by Black Sabbath just before he sniffed his glue. Though sniffing became his real love, he continued to smoke marijuana, drink liquor, and trip occasionally on acid. His mother was becoming more and more desperate and kept his room under constant surveillance. But he managed to elude most of her checks. His father sometimes, after much insistence by Charlotte, chastised him. His arrest at school angered his mother and irritated his father. The court ordered Garry, as part of his probation, to go to a mental health clinic and a drug rehabilitation program. His rehab lasted about a week. A therapist angered Carl by suggesting that Garry's problems stemmed from a lack of attention from his father. That ended the therapy sessions. Garry just casually stopped attending sessions of the drug program and resumed sniffing the glue. The fights escalated at home.

"I hated being interrupted. I held it against them. Glue was a solitary thing. Getting interrupted and the confiscation of my glue brought me down. And then I had to start all over again. I hated to be interrupted."

During the spring of his senior year Garry's parents decided they had to rent out a room, which meant that Garry had to move into a smaller bedroom. Once he moved he noticed that the "little people" no longer visited him. There were no more magical mystery tours, and the mystical experience that he craved diminished. In a letter he wrote:

Family Disrupts My Glue. As I said before, most of my glue people were related to the old big bedroom where I did most of my sniffing/hallucinating. The move was not an apparent trauma, but it did presage a new course in my glue trip. There came fewer hallucinations and very different. I was only there for a few weeks before Dad died [date]. The hallucinations didn't get as intense in the new room, nor was I able to get to the alternate worlds. . . . Around this time my car, Austin Healey Sprite, passed away. The car was very much connected to glue trips away from home, and I grieved its death (It blew a gasket). At this time I was gluing during the day more often because the change in hallucinations suit it better. Day of Doom: School was over, I sold the car and was taking final exams. It was a Tuesday, English final was over, and I came home. Mom was gone shopping with Larry—neither were expected home until 3 o'clock. At noon I cracked a bottle of whiskey, drank half of it, smoked some pot as a primer to take the glue trip I intended to make on my last half quart of glue. (It took more glue and priming to trip by this time.)

He was primed and ready to go just as his mother arrived unexpectedly and confiscated his glue. She had been worrying about him for months and did not want him alone, so she had dropped Larry off and driven home to check up on her older son. He had set the bed on fire the previous night and he was acting strange. They argued and she chastised him for sniffing glue, setting the bed afire, and being a drain on the family at a time when they needed to rally. His father had been dead for six weeks and they stood a good chance of losing their house. She needed help. Garry was sick of being chastised, especially by his mother.

When she finished scolding him she asked him to help her carry some stuff to their barn. As they walked he was carrying a two-by-four, and suddenly he thought of hitting her in the head but resisted the impulse. On the way back to the house he again thought of killing her but shook loose of the thought. When they walked into the room she was planning to rent to boarders, he spotted a heavy metal chinning bar, picked it up, and played with it in his hands as if to get the feel of it. When Charlotte turned her back on him, he hit her. He thought one blow would do it but she turned suddenly and looked into his eyes. He grabbed her arm and beat her on the head. The blows cracked her skull but did not kill her, so he ran and got a utility knife and cut her throat.

After he had sex, Garry rushed to clean up the blood and conceal his mother's body because his brother would be home soon. He needed time to think of some way of explaining everything to his brother so that he would understand why Garry had had to kill their mother. And Larry was going to have to get used to taking orders from him because he was now running the show, and things were going to be a little different around home. He hopped into his mother's car and drove to a party, where he met some friends and tried, he told the arresting police later, to think about all that had happened. He was willing to tell them everything.

"What I think about it now and what I felt at the time and what I told the police are three different things. Trying to make it all jibe is not easy. I told them what they wanted to hear as to physical police-oriented facts. I thought they would understand and relate to what I was going to tell them. I thought they would understand about the little people. . . . I look at it this way. The whole thing was so bizarre. I don't think a conscious person could have done everything that I did. I was aware of what I did. The right or wrong of it, there's no question. Something had gone wrong. It wasn't something that should have happened. I didn't contemplate jail. Didn't contemplate it. I thought they would question me and let me go. I was honest and because of that honesty I thought they would understand. . . That's the part I can't really grasp. Why? I was honest and because they would understand. When I was busted for the burglaries—we had done about a thousand—they [the police] had asked me to return the goods and let them know where the rest was. It was very understanding. There were no handcuffs. I signed a long statement and that was it. With that kind of cooperation and favorable treatment of me [then] I expected them to let me go [again]. They were the same detectives. I told them it [killing his mother] was the easiest way. It really doesn't describe it."

He told them where to find the chinning bar and the utility knife, but when they showed him a utility knife he refused to identify it as the murder weapon. It was the wrong knife but they kept insisting that it was the right one.

"I wasn't going to argue about it. They were looking for the chinning bar and I told them where to find it. . . I was just trying to save them trouble but I couldn't help them. They wouldn't let me. They got huffy about it. I felt distance between them rather than the closeness I got from talking to them the first time."

They gave him his first glimpse of the disgust people would express for a boy who casually describes killing his mother like an animal and having sex with the body.

"They asked me all sorts of questions. Did I enjoy it? Did it feel good? When they asked those questions they opened up the most private parts of me."

He did not have to talk to them.

"I probably wouldn't now. It's instinctive now. But I was trying to be honest. I wanted them to know the truth. It paid off before."

Rachel visited Garry in jail. He was not the same kid. The last time she had talked with Garry was at his father's funeral. He had been talking about studying art and maybe going into the Coast Guard for a brief stint to get away from home. He was also feeling guilty about skipping the hospital visit the night his father died. But in jail he was "spaced out" and brazen.

"You could have a conversation with him but he was so spacey. He talked to me about castles and kings and stuff. I've done reality orientation in a nursing home. It was interesting. There I was doing it with Garry. When his friends visited him he talked to them in a flip, arrogant tone."

He was Mr. Cool. He had found a way to shock people in a manner that he and Jeff had never even imagined together. This was not a time to be remorseful and weak. Garry wanted them to know that he had panache. When his court-appointed attorney recommended that they use an insanity defense, Garry snapped it up. He thought it would be the fastest and least painful way. He was certain he was not going to be found guilty, and he was not even considering the possibility of going to a mental institution. He was more worried about his take from the estate left behind by his mother and father.

"I also went along with it because it wasn't too hard for me to play the role. He told me to keep the long hair and instructed me not to cooperate with the DA's psychiatrist."

But when Garry asked if he should play the "bugout role," his lawyer said no. The lawyer did not want Garry examined by a psychiatrist or doctor because he believed no one could testify that Garry was insane. The attorney planned to argue that only an insane person or

someone acting under "extreme emotional disturbance" could have
done what Garry had done. Drugs and alcohol had to be a factor.
Because of that approach, he did not try to have Garry's statement to
the police thrown out of court. He needed it in his plan to show just
how crazy Garry really was. He planned to bring in an expert to testify
about how drugs, alcohol, and LSD can warp a personality.

At the start of the trial, the judge instructed the jury that the
burden was on the district attorney. He had to prove beyond a reasonable doubt that Garry had not been insane or acting under extreme emotional disturbance when he killed his mother. The trial
spanned a little more than three weeks. Garry testified about his
little people and how much he needed them, and explained that he
had been close to his father but not his mother. "I could do things
with my father . . . with my mother it was more or less doing things
for her. We talked about painting." He also explained how difficult it
was for him to get along with his brother. The drugs and the alcohol
and the pressures at home had caused him to kill his mother. "I
could not leave the house so I had to kill my mother. It was the only
way to get out of a situation of being prosecuted for doing the glue."
He claimed he had not been angry when he hit her and that he had
not wanted to cause her great pain but only to kill her.

The prosecutor suggested early in his opening remarks that Garry
at one point had considered getting rid of the whole family so that he
could have the house to himself. The prosecutor called to the stand a
psychiatrist who testified that he had found no evidence of psychosis
or severe mental or emotional disorders. He had been unable to examine Garry fully because the boy had been refusing to cooperate,
but he was convinced that Garry was not insane. The psychiatrist
also testified about incest in an almost birds-and-bees analogy: "He,
any boy, learns about life from his father and learns about warmth
and sex and emotions and closeness from his mother." The doctor
also said that necrophilia was an aberration and that Garry was still
cold and insensitive about his mother's murder. Garry's explanation
about his little people, the doctor testified, was a fabrication. He had
made it all up because he had killed his mother and wanted people to
think he was crazy. When Garry's brother testified for the prosecution, he said he could recall his brother speaking with a slurred
speech at times and acting like he was drunk, but he had never
noticed any bizarre change in Garry's behavior. Teachers and counselors and friends testified that he had never acted strange around

them. He had always been funny and good in school and not a problem. At the end of the trial the jury deliberated a day and a half before finding him guilty.

"There was never any question about insanity," said Harold (a pseudonym), a juror, later. "We discarded that fairly early on. The real issue was, was he so emotionally disturbed that it screwed up his judgment at the time?"

Many of the jurors wanted to convict him of murder but others were looking for a "compromise verdict." The first vote for a manslaughter conviction was 7 to 5.

However, "he was so clear. He was articulate in the confession and on the stand. We saw him sitting and acting normally and all the testimony from the past, from his teachers and counselors, all indicated that he seemed totally aware of everything going around him. Everything pointed to that he knew what he was doing."

The jurors did not believe the accounts of the little people because no one ever offered corroborating information that the little people had ever appeared in Garry's life. They also were unimpressed by the "thugs paraded in" by the defense attorney to testify as witnesses for Garry. They were his friends.

"Everything indicated clear rational thinking. We didn't see him out of touch with reality."

What about the sex?

"We did not discuss sex," he said, "but it was there" in the jurors' room.

On the second day, they voted for murder. And the judge, who could have sentenced him to fifteen years, gave him the maximum of twenty-five. Harold was so moved by the whole affair that he began to correspond and visit with Garry.

"It wasn't until the impact of the hard sentence that it hit him," Rachel said. "He had worried about all the wrong things. He was so spaced out. He wasn't tuned into the severity of what he had done. He began to see a little of the reality when they started auctioning off his family's property. When the home was sold, that shook him."

Garry did not start feeling any remorse until he had been in prison for four or five years. Years of deprivation and no freedom made him feel what he had lost. Eventually, whenever he met an older man or woman, he would try to make that person into a surrogate mother or father. He also tried to stay in touch with his brother. For penance, he worked in the prison mental health ward with the jail's "bugouts," when he was not painting or running the facility's newspaper. He also found Jesus.

"The Bible is very real to me. Divine forgiveness is one thing that I needed. Love and patience and understanding is what I was looking for. These are truths."

Did he understand now why he had had sex with his mother's body, besides the drugs?

Though he always insisted that he felt superior to everyone whom he had encountered, it only served to cover up his extreme feelings of inadequacy. "I'm unsure of myself, especially with people. I'm inhibited and didn't have the nerve to talk with a girl about sex. With my girlfriend, we were very close friends and shared a lot of interests. We were companions. It was not enough. I have longings like every other person. I would go around with those guys from bar to bar looking for girls. I felt very much out of place. All I was into was drinking. They were into women. I couldn't even share the same language with them. I wanted . . . to be into the same thing they were. The terrible conclusion? I had mother's dead body there. There was nothing left to do but to make use of it. I felt ashamed of being eighteen years old and being a virgin. That bothered me a lot. It was all in my own thinking. No one else made a point of it; no one taunted me. I had missed that part of life everyone had gone through and learned how to deal with."

Was he sure he hadn't been just making love with his mother in some strange way?

"It was what it was. I [at one point] came up with the rationale, for my own psyche, that it was after beating her I wanted to love her. But it was just a rationale. It doesn't justify anything. But it made me feel better."

Did he believe he should have gone to jail for what he had done? No.

Garry looked like a gangly teenager the first time I met him. Over a green T-shirt he wore a faded green button-down shirt with sleeves that stopped well short of his wrists. The green socks in his generic gym shoes almost matched the color of his shirt. I thought he talked with a vestigial German accent, but it was possible that I thought it was German because I knew his parents came from Germany. He was a careful and attentive listener who monitored my reactions and weighed the intent of my questions. He also still liked to put people on. He acted just a bit goofy and funny so that he would appear more disarming. After thirty minutes or so he got serious. Of the many things we discussed, he spoke with particular pride about how he was no longer trying to play the role of nonconformist or pariah. "I've come a complete hundred and eighty degrees now," he said at one point. "I can wear a suit and tie and get a positive response from people. When I cut my hair I get a bit more respect, and I like the way people look at me." He earned that respect, he explained, "by being what they want instead of what I want." His life went strictly by the rules, he said, and he encouraged new inmates to follow his example.

Garry believed he would not have been imprisoned if his parents had enforced more discipline on him and deprived him of his rock music, drugs and glue, and creepy friends, all of the things that he said got him into trouble. "They didn't demand anything of me," he said. "If I mowed the lawn and took care of the storm windows and screens, as well as take care of my bedroom and my toys or whatever, [that] was enough." His father should have cracked down on him when he was arrested for the burglaries. Carl instead expressed disgust and ignored him. His mother, however, tried to rein him in somewhat, and he resented her for it.

Garry believed his problems had started when the family moved into the farmhouse, and he cited the glue addiction and the burglaries as examples. But I believed that there had been problems well before the family moved, and I believed his parents had either misread the signs or ignored them when he was in grade school. When I asked Garry about his grade school years and inquired if there had been any tension in the family or anything unusual occurring, he said no. He gave a prosaic picture of upper-middle-class living: He went to school, he came home from school, and he played with his friends. And his parents provided him with everything he wanted or needed.

But in his early school years, he casually mentioned during the first interview, he had been an inveterate shoplifter. There had been occasions when his parents took him and his brother shopping with them, and Garry got caught shoplifting. I imagined that his parents had been embarrassed and angry but Garry said they never punished him. It was not clear exactly how many times it had happened or how long he had been a shoplifter. Garry made light of the incidents and only referred to them in passing. He could not recall details or specifics. About the same time he had been fighting regularly with other kids. I suspected that his behavior had been giving off a number of warning signals, and the fights and the shoplifting were just two. Garry had been drifting into serious trouble and no one was paying attention. By the time he was in high school, Garry believed he could not be held accountable for his actions. After a while he believed he did not need his family or friends because he had his glue.

When he talked about his psychedelic experiences, I did not believe he was lying, though I wondered how really vivid his experiences had been. He hinted a few times in the interview, and later in letters, that he was not sure how much of the little people he had actually seen or experienced, and how much had been just in his head. But I did not doubt him when he said his glue had been more important to him than his family. I believed him unhesitatingly when he said that after sniffing his stash, he had conjured up a kingdom of people who were loyal to him. It was probably when he was reveling in the discovery of his new family that he was nearing a crisis with his real family.

I do not know when the alienation between him and his family set in, but he made it obvious that he had never been really close to anyone, not his burglarizing buddies, or even his good friend Jeff, or JoBeth, his girlfriend. When he was imprisoned he missed his freedom, but there was no one in his life he really missed until four or five years later, when he learned to grieve and mourn.

All of this—the fights and shoplifting, the burglaries and bizarre sexual behavior, the glue addiction and drug and alcohol abuse, the brutal murder and necrophilia, expressions of no self-esteem, and the lack of emotion or sympathy for anyone other than himself—was suggestive of a serious disorder. But I was unable to pinpoint the malady. It was not a psychosis, because he was always aware of everything he did. He just lacked inhibitions. So for several months I was stymied.

A few years after he was imprisoned, Rachel, a born-again Christian, gave Garry a Bible. And Garry found salvation. But the first time we met he talked only a little about Christ. In a letter he wrote, "Rachel mentioned in her letter that you were a bit worried that maybe you hadn't let me feel free to talk of my faith in Jesus—I don't think so. I am not the Lord's most vocal advocate. But where my oral testimony lacks I make it up in my daily devotion to lead as an example. And if people desire from me the motive for my actions, then I expound on the subject of God's grace in my life and share his love. I have never appreciated the bold approach of some Christians—I have seen too many people turned off by that. So, I usually only tell someone of my experience with Jesus when they ask me where do I get my patience from or where did I learn to paint like that! or in a number of other ways." One of the reasons he had agreed to an interview, he said, was because he believed it was God's will and another way for him to atone for his crime.

It was during the second interview, when I revealed how I was planning to write the chapter on him, that Garry suddenly believed that he was headed for a crisis. Despite God's will, Garry sensed that there was a good chance he would not like what I wrote. But he would not tell me in the interview. He could not tell me that it was going to be painful or that he might be subjected to more scorn and contempt. In person he wanted to appear amicable and friendly. But a few days after I left the prison, he wrote me the first of two long letters:

> I have come to a tentative grip on the crisis, which has made the past month build into a problem, culminating in distress over the things added, over the reflections come from our recent visit. No less than a ramble-on sentence could begin to describe what I've been through recently! I am told by friends to watch out for a nervous breakdown. I'm counting on God's ever present help—daily!
>
> Yet I slip here a little, there a bit more and am very hard pressed with absorbing the data input, without losing track of loose ends. This is like sailing across the Atlantic, single-handed on a tiny boat—through stormy weather.
>
> I have no doubt that I will make it. The shock of this together is making my eyes open; new angles of insight reveal better what was dark before—or forgotten.
>
> What got me rather flustered after our visit is the doubts it fostered. I doubted your sincerity, my insanity, and my faith in God. I was really shaken to confront my past, in detail. And also I was kind of upset about your being rather loud when talking

about me and my crime. I don't know still how you feel on a person to person level about me. But you must realize that my whole life (now) is dedicated to God, and by this, my only desire is to give back more than I took. If your casual talk brings people to look only on my past state, then I may not live to give— and by having to defend my own existence I am deprived of the little freedom needed to help those around me.

I wish I could get this across to you in a clear, concise way. You see, I probably hate myself more than any other person who hears about my very disgusting crime. And it is just as well this way, for having low self-esteem, I abase myself enough to give my all to the "next guy," who may have a chance to learn, grow and avoid my erroneous life mistakes if I am here to encourage help, and pray for "him."

In prison, he explained, he had acted as a counselor to a small following of inmates who depended upon him to survive in prison and, in some cases, to prepare for their eventual release. It was part of his way of atoning for his crime.

In the second letter, a week later, he wrote, "I'm not quite sure I've made it clear enough to you—so excuse apparent redundancy—I trust you in what you are doing, because I believe God has his hands in this, and will use it to bring a lot of healing into the world. . . I trust that you are sincere, and are truly intending to promote the early detection and correction of misfortunate lives like mine. I trust also that you will include in my chapter a just indication of the *faith* that sustains me in Christ."

A few days after I received the second letter from Garry, I learned, with the help of a friend, some reasons for Garry's actions before he found Christ. After Garry had been arrested, his lawyer consulted with an eminent psychiatrist about his client. The brutal murder, Garry's bizarre behavior, and his obvious lack of remorse and guilt had startled the attorney. What the psychiatrist told him was also unsettling. Garry was a psychopath. He had probably been sick for years and exhibited signs of the personality disorder, but no one had noticed or taken the signs seriously. According to the book *Major Psychiatric Disorders*, psychopathy may be caused by a genetic component, emotional deprivation at an early age, and the lack of caring relationships. "Because an important factor in predicting antisocial behavior is parental pathology, it is not yet clear how genetic and environmental factors interact etiologically," the editors wrote. The glue addiction, plus the drug and alcohol abuse, apparently stripped away the few inhibitions that had kept Garry from being violent.

There were several reasons why Garry's psychopathy, which is also known as sociopathy or antisocial behavior, could have escaped detection by his parents, teachers, and few friends. The disorder can only be reliably diagnosed in adult life because many of its signs— such as lying, stealing, fighting, resisting authority, drug and alcohol abuse, and bizarre or aggressive behavior—can easily be seen in a great many teenagers. For most teenagers, it's a passing phase. For a psychopath it becomes a way of life. Garry's ingratiating charm and upper-middle-class background allowed his excesses to be viewed as either teenage angst or the eccentric behavior of the son of two prominent artists. When he got into trouble—either shoplifting or burglary—his parents bailed him out, but the cause of the crimes was never addressed. Garry's behavior never improved later. He still retained, however, enough inhibitions so that Garry was never considered dangerous. But the glue, drugs, and alcohol changed that. His father's illness and untimely death, plus some other problems in the family, distracted attention from Garry's crisis. Without inhibitions, Garry was capable of anything.

Because the disorder was not a psychosis, Garry's attorney could not allow his client to be examined by a psychiatrist. He had to try to argue that Garry was crazy or that he had acted under extreme emotional distress.

Flagrant criminal behavior in most cases of psychopathy diminishes by the early thirties, though people with the disorder continue to be wracked by a pervasive angst and lack of self-esteem, and cannot form close ties with anyone. Some, however, still can lead "normal lives."

The oppressive regimen of prison life forced Garry to deal with the disorder without benefit of any psychiatric help. Though he did not believe he should have been imprisoned, he eventually accepted that it was his actions that had sent him there. He could even grieve, in a fashion, for everything that he missed. "I miss Mom," he said in the first interview. "I don't think . . . I don't think about it. For the longest time I have had a group photo but I couldn't look at it. I could look at my brother and Dad. But Mother, I remembered her as a different person. I remember her as all smashed up. I look at a picture of her with them and I get them all mixed up with the last memory where she was all shattered and a corpse and [he shuddered] that's no way for me to deal with that."

In prison, he was editor of the newspaper, counselor-at-large to younger inmates, instructor, and artist. His paintings were bringing him modest commissions, and he was still trying to maintain some contact with his brother. He also was spreading the word of God among those willing to listen and hoping that his chapter in this book would not savage him too much.

# Conclusion

Child abuse and mental illness, based on the best information available, account for most of the parricides committed in the country. It was beyond the means of this book to provide an accurate numerical breakdown for each category, but abuse has to be regarded as the number one cause of sons' and daughters' killing their parents. Research for this book showed that abused children killed because they believed, after repeated beatings and threats, that they were in mortal danger. In other cases, physical and psychological abuse coupled with severe emotional disturbances triggered a rage that caused kids to kill, sometimes indiscriminately. When young girls have been involved in parricide, sexual abuse and incest-rape were often contributing factors. The strong normative imperative against killing parents explains why there are at most only four hundred parricides a year. Many kids would rather suffer in silence, run away, or kill themselves than kill abusive parents.

While the popular notion is that all children think about killing their parents at some moment in their lives, it is equally fair to say that all parents at some point think how much easier life would be if the kids disappeared. But it is a statistical fact that more parents act on their wishes and kill their offspring than vice versa. Many experts who study family violence do not question the claim that thousands of toddlers are murdered each year and that their deaths are falsely attributed to accidental causes.

In too many cases of parricide the kids blame themselves for what happened, and so does society. Because of the various state laws that allow children to be prosecuted as adults, and the prevailing myths and pervasive ignorance about the root causes of parricide, youngsters have received less than fair treatment under the law. The paradigm of the battered-child defense (such as that researched by lawyer Paul Mones) suggests how kids could be better treated under the law, and it also gives attorneys, judges, and other professionals a better means for considering the motives of children who kill parents. Through Stephen Levine's efforts, the public defender's office in Miami, Florida, for example, has devised its own strategy for defending kids. The bottom line should be to keep them out of jail and rehabilitate them. The Miami examples and the battered-child paradigm are only stop-gap measures until society decides if and how it plans to reduce violence in the family.

The connection between parricide and mental illness, especially schizophrenia, reveals a tragic irony. Most mentally ill people are not violent, but the small number who *are* attack and harm the people who are trying to help them. Almost all of the parricides in the section on mental illness happened just about when families had exhausted their options for helping their children. It is extremely difficult for a family to tackle the panoply of emotional, physical, and financial problems that arise when a son or daughter becomes sick with schizophrenia. At a time when families need the most their communities can offer, they discover that they are isolated and vulnerable. The National Alliance for the Mentally Ill and other grass-roots self-help organizations are working to provide the kind of support that families need when a son or daughter—or a mother or father—becomes mentally unbalanced. It will take the kind of fervor, commitment, and support that a NAMI can provide to marshal forces to change the way mentally ill people and their families are treated in this society because of ignorance and prejudice.

Parricide has only recently begun to receive attention, and I hope this book will spark more interest and scientific research. I believe that a real understanding of the connection between abuse and parricide can also open up channels for understanding the connection between abuse and delinquency. There are others who also see a connection between violence in the home and violence in society. "The American public needs to understand the consequences of children growing up in violent homes," wrote the authors of *Behind Closed Doors*. "We must explain that street violence is directly traceable to violence in the home, just as violence in the home is traceable to violence in the streets."

# Afterword

The following is a capsulized summary of the events happening in the lives of some of the kids mentioned in this book as it was going to press.

Chapter 2, MARY JANE: A change in prison procedures stopped Mary Jane from taking weekend furloughs. And because of three prison infractions she incurred, she was dropped from the honor cottage and deprived of her special privileges. Two infractions were "subtracting errors" involving money: "I overspent 24¢ and $1.40." The third infraction sounded like an institutional catch 22. She said a teacher allowed her to go to the prison canteen and then decided it was wrong: "He had the authority to write me up but didn't have the authority to give me permission [to go]." She cannot appear before the parole board until September. Some people who knew of her plight were writing letters and making phone calls "to try and get me out of here."

Chapter 5, DAWN: A state appeals court ruled that a trial judge erred by not treating Dawn as a youthful offender. The court ruled that there was sufficient evidence that she had been sexually abused by her father, but there was not enough evidence to show that she was about to be attacked in the garage. She did not act in self-defense or cold-blooded murder but "under emotional trauma brought through no fault of her own." The appeals court decided that she should receive "a reasonable definite term of incarceration along with a probation period which includes the necessary counseling." Youthful offender status means that her criminal records would be sealed and that she might not be incarcerated more than six months. The prosecutor was unhappy with the decision and said he was considering appealing it.

Chapter 8, BUDDY: The facility where Buddy junior was incarcerated started proceedings again to try to commit him to a psychiatric hospital. His appeal was pending, and I could not learn why the previous decision not to try to commit him had been reversed. The American Civil Liberties Union said it was taking an interest in the case.

Chapter 9, THE BATTERED-CHILD DEFENSE: Paul Mones and Lee Adler had been hoping that their medical experts would persuade the court to give Jerry Bald a sentence that would allow him to continue the treatment he needed to be rehabilitated. In his sentencing decision, the trial judge wrote, ". . . I cannot help but be moved by the evidence before me which indicates that he was himself subjected to child abuse." But he also wrote that the medical evidence presented by the Harvard doctors for the defense and the local doctors for the defense "was conflicting" and that therefore he was unable to "conclude that these four murders resulted from the abuse of the defendant as a child." He also wrote that Jerry's rehabilitation could be costly. "To treat the defendant in the manner sought, that is by placing him in one (1) or more therapeutic and/or rehabilitative out-of-state hospital settings, would establish a precedent with far-reaching fiscal repercussions, and one which would hereafter be available to any number of defendants charged with violent crimes," he wrote. He also wrote, "The rehabilitation of the defendant through medical treatment is at best a possibility." He sentenced Jerry to life, with a recommendation for mercy, to be spent in a maximum security prison. Adler appealed and the West Virginia Supreme Court unanimously voted to hear the appeal. Paul Mones, who was working as legal director of the Public Justice Foundation (a citizens' advocacy organization) in Santa Monica, California, said the foundation would be filing a brief in Jerry's behalf.

Chapter 12, BARRY: His brain disease was exacting a toll and he was sent back to the hospital. It was his fourth time, and his mother said the prognosis was very bad.

Chapter 14, VIC: A social worker was finally able to find a place for emotionally disturbed youths that was willing to help him.

# Index

## A

abuse, *see* battered child; child abuse; psychological abuse; sexual abuse, by father
Adler, Lee, 147–48, 150
alcohol abuse
  by father, 26–31, 46, 151, 247, 248, 251
  by juvenile, 30–31, 84, 275, 278, 280, 281
Alliance for the Mentally Ill, 218
Anderson, Paul, 248–51
anger
  child's, 62, 109, 126, 139, 141, 151, 157, 164, 175
  father's, 26–27, 61, 64, 86, 90, 136, 172
appeals, legal, 51–52, 76, 79, 141, 142, 174, 218
arrest and arresting authorities, 32, 81, 128, 173, 245, 272; *see also* custody, child in; police, treatment of juveniles by
Association for Retarded Citizens, 216
attorney(s)
  attitude of, toward abuse, 153–54, 165

juvenile client and, 26, 51, 73, 112, 129, 136–37, 141, 239–40
negligence of, 51, 141
plea bargaining counseled by, 32, 50, 92, 98, 136–37, 153, 159, 165
*see also* Adler, Lee; Gaits, Stephen; McMahon, John; Mones, Paul; Peterson, Stephen B.; prosecutor(s); Vallario, Joseph H.
Attorney General's Task Force on Family Violence, 188

## B

Ball, Jerry, 147–48, 150–51
Barton, Russell, 200–202
battered child, 111, 118, 121, 133, 138, 149, 150, 159–60, 161–62, 167–68
battered-child defense, 153, 159–65, 294
battered-woman syndrome, 150, 154, 168

*Behind Closed Doors: Violence in the American Family* (Stevens, Gelles, and Steinmetz), 21, 188, 294
blaming victim, 40, 146, 293
Bleuler, Eugen, 196, 249
Bloom, Robert M., Jr., 22–23, 162–63
Bonnie, Richard J., 189
borderline personality disorder, 49
brain damage, of battered children, 160
brothers, *see* siblings

# C

chaplain, role of, 73, 75, 81, 83, 93, 101
child abuse, 21–23
    attorneys' attitudes toward, 153–54, 165
    courts and, 25
    delinquency and, 146–47, 153, 294
    parricide and, 148–69, 293–94
    physical, 111, 118, 121, 133, 138, 149, 150, 159–60, 161–62, 167–68
    psychological, 61–62, 77, 105, 159, 160, 161–62, 175, 179–82, 247, 248–49
children's rights, 146, 159, 163
child's death
    feared by child, as imminent, 26, 161, 164
    at parent's hands, 21–22, 165–66
community
    attitudes toward parricide, 16, 69, 124, 151, 152, 283, 294
    ignorance about troubled families, 26, 161, 266
conspiracy to murder, 70–71, 85, 95, 99, 102, 254–58
correctional facilities
    jail

experiences in, 52–56, 79, 81–82, 83, 85, 90, 271
    as perilous, 59, 63
    for juveniles, 36, 51, 79
    experiences in, 137, 245, 246
    *see also* psychiatric hospitals, incarceration in
courts, *see* appeals, legal; attorney(s); child abuse: courts and; judge(s); jury selection; plea bargains; prosecution of juvenile offenders; prosecutor(s); sentences and sentencing; trial(s), court
criticism and humiliation of child, by parent, 28–29, 37, 61, 172, 177
custody, child in, 32, 35–36, 58–59, 81, 94, 129, 131, 173, 240, 271, 283; *see also* arrest and arresting officers; jail, for juvenile offenders

# D

daughter(s)
    relationship to father, 36–38, 45–48, 71, 75–76, 77, 86–87, 89, 90–91, 100, 172–73, 175; *see also* sexual abuse, by father
    relationship to mother, 43–45, 72, 83, 91, 97, 98, 155–56, 171–74
death of child
    feared by child, as imminent, 26, 161, 164
    at parent's hands, 21–22, 165–66
death of parent, *see* matricide; parricide; patricide
death sentence, sought for parricide, 25, 26, 32–33
defenses, legal
    battered-child, 153, 159–65, 294

insanity, 59, 60, 153, 163, 188, 189–90, 197, 210, 283–84

self-defense, 36, 114, 115, 124, 148, 155–56, 158–59

delinquency, abuse and, 146–47, 153, 294

denial (psychological state), 93, 151, 168

depression (psychological state), 49, 52, 60, 61, 85, 109, 142, 172, 233, 240, 271

drinking, *see* alcohol abuse

drugs, violence and, 46, 138, 140, 151, 271, 275, 278, 280, 281

# E

Ebert, Ronald, 150

# F

family (families)
  distress signals from, 251
  dominated by father, 26–29, 61–62, 64, 103, 111, 118, 121–23, 161
  isolated by father, 62, 121, 123, 161, 182
  unknown to outsiders, 26, 161, 266

family violence, 17, 21, 153, 251, 294
  mental illness and, 188
  *see also* battered child; child abuse; psychological abuse; sexual abuse, by father

father(s)
  domination and tyrany over family, 26–29, 61–62, 64, 103, 111, 118, 121–23, 161
  drinking and violence of, 26–31, 46, 151, 247, 248, 251
  fear of, 24–25, 37, 47, 122, 247
  murder of, *see* patricide

rage of, 26–27, 61, 64, 86, 90, 136, 172

relationship to daughter, 36–38, 45–48, 71, 75–76, 77, 86–87, 89, 90–91, 100, 172–73, 175

relationship to son, 28–31, 61–62, 118, 130–31, 133–36, 137, 140–41, 246–47

relationship to wife, 28, 30, 61, 121–23

seductive, 104

*see also* sexual abuse, by father

fear
  of death, child's, 26, 161, 164
  of father, 24–25, 37, 47, 122, 247
  of violent family, neighbor's, 133, 134

Federal Bureau of Investigation, 66–67

Femia, Vincent J., 63–69, 70, 71, 72, 76, 77, 80, 158–59

Frazier, Shervert, 150–51

# G

Gaits, Stephen, 110, 112, 115–16

Gardner, Hugh, 123

Gelles, Richard: *Behind Closed Doors,* 21, 188, 294

glue sniffing, 271, 275, 278–79, 280, 281, 288

Griffin, William Bradley, 220–26

Guggenheim, Frederick G.: *Major Psychiatric Disorders,* 249–50, 290–91

guilt (psychological state), 52, 176, 181, 290

guns
  child taught to use, 37, 109, 229
  in house, 31–32, 48, 109, 117, 118, 129, 251
  *see also* shooting deaths

# H

hallucinations
  auditory, 180, 193
  hypnagogic, 279
  olfactory, 160
Hayden, Steven, 102
HELP (Help Exists for Loved Ones in Prison), 216
Herman, Judith Lewis: *Father-Daughter Incest*, 42, 104
Hinckley, John, Jr., 163, 188–89, 216
homicide, *see* husband, murdered by wife; matricide; parricide; patricide; siblings: murdered
hospitals (psychiatric), incarceration in, 36, 38–41, 141–42, 157, 163, 175–76, 181, 200, 202–3, 244–45; *see also* Patuxent Institute (Maryland); Perkins Hospital (Maryland)
humiliation and criticism by parent, 28–29, 37, 61, 172, 177
husband, murdered by wife, 25–26, 69, 150, 164–65; *see also* father(s)

# I

incarceration, *see* custody, child in; jail, for juvenile offenders; juvenile correctional facilities; psychiatric hospitals, incarceration in
incest, 100–101
  of father and daughter
    fondling, 100–101, 103–4, 111, 118, 145, 172–73, 175
    rape, 39, 41, 47, 48, 103, 112–13, 115, 166
  legal defense and, 115–16, 158

overt *vs.* covert, 103–4
psychiatrists and, 39–40, 42
of son and mother, 273, 284, 286
insanity defense, 59, 60, 153, 163, 188, 189–90, 197, 210, 283–84
isolation
  of child, 27, 28, 62, 123, 139
  of family, 62, 121, 123, 161, 182

# J

Jahnke, Richard, Jr., 117–19, 148, 152, 153, 159, 164
jail, for juvenile offenders
  experiences in, 52–56, 79, 81–82, 83, 85, 90, 271
  *vs.* juvenile facilities, 36, 51, 79
  as perilous, 59, 63
journalists, *see* publicity and press coverage
judge(s)
  attitudes of
    toward accused, 33, 50–51, 63–67 *passim*, 71, 72, 76, 77, 124, 157, 175, 176
    toward sexual abuse, 55
  conflict of interest, 110
  role of, 67–69
  sentencing by, *see* sentences and sentencing
jury selection, 165
juvenile correctional facilities
  experiences in, 137, 245, 246
  *vs.* jail, 36, 51, 79

# K

knife murders, 49, 57–58, 70, 92, 157, 170, 173, 192, 200, 209, 231–32, 237, 260–61, 262, 263, 272, 282
Kosinski, Stanley, 128–31

## L

lawyer(s), *see* attorney(s)
Levine, Steven J., 170–83
Lewis, Dorothy, 160

## M

McCarty, Edward, 155
McMahon, John, 110, 112
*Major Psychiatric Disorders*
    (Guggenheim and Nadelson),
    249–50, 290–91
matricide, 102, 103, 127–28, 147,
    156, 157, 178, 188, 195,
    224, 231–32, 237, 259–60,
    265, 272, 281–82
  by daughter, 155
  *see also* parricide
mental hospitals, *see* Patuxent
    Institute (Maryland); Perkins
    Hospital (Maryland);
    psychiatric hospitals,
    incarceration in
mental illness, 187–225, 294
  schizophrenia, 181, 196, 198,
    204–14, 294
    hebephrenic, 201–2
    latent, 249–50
    paranoid, 193, 200, 201–2, 210
molesting, *see* sexual abuse, by
    father
Mones, Paul, 146–48, 150–54,
    160–69 *passim*
money, as motive for murder, 102,
    255–58
mother(s)
  murder of, *see* matricide
  psychologically impaired, and
    child's violence, 161
  relationship to daughter, 43–45,
    72, 83, 91, 97, 98, 155–56,
    171–74
  relationship to husband, 28, 30,
    61, 121–23
  relationship to son, 126–27,
    138–40, 149, 151, 232, 236,
    251, 254, 284, 291–92
  role in family dissension, 28, 62,
    101, 136, 138, 149, 151,
    171–73, 180, 182
motivation and precipitating factors
    (in parricide), 37, 41, 49–50,
    66, 70, 72, 97, 99, 100,
    101–5, 114, 131, 137,
    140–41, 147, 170
murder, *see* husband, murdered by
    wife; matricide; parricide;
    patricide; siblings: murdered
*Myths and Realities* (National
    Commission on the Insanity
    Defense), 189

## N

Nadelson, Carol: *Major Psychiatric
    Disorders*, 249–50, 290–91
National Alliance for the Mentally
    Ill (NAMI), 215–19, 294
National Association for the
    Prevention of Child Abuse,
    165–66
National Commission on the
    Insanity Defense, 189
necrophilia, 273, 284, 286
neglect, benign, 151
neighbors
  ignorance of trouble in families,
    26, 161, 266
  recollections and opinions about
    juvenile murderers, 131–36,
    232
  troubled families and, 118, 133
neurological damage, to battered
    child, 160, 168

# O

orthomolecular psychiatry, 206, 217

# P

parents
    murdered, see matricide;
        parricide; patricide
    murdering children, 21–22,
        165–66
    see also father(s); mother(s)
parricide
    explanations for, 148–54
    incidence and extent of, 152–53,
        293
    motivation for, 37, 41, 49–50, 66,
        70, 72, 97, 99, 100, 101–5,
        114, 131, 137, 140–41, 147,
        170
    popular beliefs and perceptions
        about, 16, 69, 124, 151, 152,
        283, 294
    see also matricide; patricide
pathological psychiatric condition,
    178, 180
patricide
    by daughter, 34, 48–49, 70, 92,
        102, 107, 166, 171, 173
    by son, 25, 31–32, 57–58, 102,
        117–18, 122, 147, 149, 156,
        157, 192, 200, 209, 229,
        249, 265
    see also parricide
Patuxent Institute (Maryland), 72
Perkins Hospital (Maryland), 191,
    193, 195
Peterson, Stephen B., 123
Petrila, John, 189, 190
physical abuse, see battered child
plea bargains, 70, 123, 211, 218–19,
    240
    counseled by attorneys, 32, 50,

92, 98, 136–37, 153, 159,
    165
police, treatment of juveniles by,
    58–59, 81, 94, 107–8, 173,
    245, 282–83; see also arrest
    and arresting authorities;
    custody, child in; Kosinski,
    Stanley
press coverage, see publicity and
    press coverage
prison, for juvenile offenders
    experiences in, 52–56, 79,
        81–82, 83, 85, 90, 271
    vs. juvenile facility, 36, 51, 79
    as perilous, 59, 63
prosecution of juvenile offenders
    as adults or as juveniles, 36, 43,
        72, 79, 136, 148, 157, 158,
        159, 170, 249, 263–65, 294
    death sentence sought, 25, 26,
        32–33
    murder or manslaughter charged,
        32, 35, 36, 43, 59, 71, 109,
        119, 136, 156, 167, 170,
        174, 238–39, 249, 265
    see also appeals, legal; plea
        bargains; sentences and
        sentencing; trial(s), court
prosecutor(s)
    dilemmas of, 59, 63
    portrayal of accused by, 32–33,
        70–71, 74, 76–77, 80, 95,
        114, 284
psychiatric examination of accused,
    36–42, 60, 72, 101, 110,
    111, 112, 123, 141, 158,
    167, 178, 249, 291
psychiatric hospitals, incarceration
    in, 36, 38–41, 141–42, 157,
    163, 175–76, 181, 200,
    202–3, 244–45; see also
    Patuxent Institute
    (Maryland); Perkins Hospital
    (Maryland)

psychiatrists and psychologists
  incest and, 42
  juvenile murderers and, 36, 38,
    39–40, 42, 48, 52
psychoanalysis, schizophrenia and,
  207
psychological abuse, 61–62, 77, 105,
  159, 160, 161–62, 175,
  179–82, 247, 248–49
psychopathy, 290–91
psychotherapy, for rehabilitation,
  142, 151, 176; see also
  psychiatric hospitals,
  incarceration in
public attitudes toward parricide,
  16, 69, 124, 151, 152, 283,
  294
publicity and press coverage, 113,
  231–33, 234, 236, 237, 244,
  252, 262, 265, 266
  of the mentally ill, 209–10, 212


R

rage
  child's, 62, 109, 126, 139, 141,
    151, 157, 164, 175
  father's, 26–27, 61, 64, 86, 90,
    136, 172
rape
  of daughter, 39, 41, 47, 48, 103,
    112–13, 115, 166
  in mental hospital, 40
rehabilitation
  as correctional goal, 72, 158
  vs. punishment, 141, 148
  difficulty of, 132–33
Reinstein, Jerome L., 234–36, 240
religious convictions, 29, 149,
  171–72, 286, 288–89
remorse, lack of, 60, 76, 87, 95,
  129, 181, 250, 285–86, 290
rights, children's, 146, 159, 163

running away from home, 35, 37,
  43–44, 126, 135, 154, 162,
  251, 293

S

Salk, Lee: "Blood Ties or Bad
  Blood," 151–52
Sargent, Douglas, 148–49, 251
Sauerwein, Joseph C., 70–71, 77,
  94–99, 105
schizophrenia, 181, 196, 198,
  204–14, 294
  hebephrenic, 201–2
  latent, 249–50
  paranoid, 193, 200, 201–2, 210
Schreuder, Frances Bernice, 102
seductiveness, of father, 104
self-defense, as legal defense, 36,
  114, 115, 124, 148, 155–56,
  158–59, 163–64, 174; see
  also battered-child defense
sentences and sentencing (legal),
  32–33, 51, 68, 71–72, 115,
  119, 124, 136, 159, 174,
  211, 219, 258, 285
  commuting sentence, 119
  reduction of sentence, 142, 213
sexual abuse, by father, 293
  fondling, 100–101, 103–4, 111,
    118, 145, 172–73, 175
  judges and, 55
  psychiatrists and, 42
  rape, 39, 41, 47, 48, 103,
    112–13, 115, 166
shame, of child, 27, 272
shooting deaths, 22, 25, 34, 48–49,
  107, 117–18, 122, 127–28,
  147, 156, 157, 166, 177–78,
  224, 229, 249, 259, 260,
  262, 265
shoplifting, 30, 43, 287–88
siblings
  abused, 162

siblings (*cont.*)
   murdered, 22, 147, 151, 157,
      177, 260–61, 263, 265
sisters, *see* siblings
son(s)
   relationship to father, 28–31,
      61–62, 118, 130–31,
      133–36, 137, 140–41,
      246–47
   relationship to mother, 126–27,
      138–40, 149, 151, 232, 236,
      251, 254, 284, 291–92
   stabbing deaths, 49, 57–58, 70, 92,
      157, 170, 173, 192, 200,
      209, 231–32, 237, 260–61,
      262, 263, 272, 282
status offenses, 154; *see also* running
   away from home
Steinmetz, Suzanne: *Behind Closed
   Doors,* 21, 188, 294
stepparents, 31–32, 37, 45, 46–47,
   166, 171
Stevens, Murray: *Behind Closed
   Doors,* 21, 188, 294
suicidal intentions, 34, 61, 109,
   142, 151, 162, 177, 209,
   210, 211, 221, 225, 251, 271

## T

therapy, for rehabilitation, 142, 151,
   176; *see also* psychiatric
   hospitals, incarceration in
Torrey, E. Fuller, 196
trial(s), court, 26, 114–15, 256–58,
   284–85
   avoiding, 32–33, 50, 98, 240
   *see also* appeals, legal; attorney(s);
      child abuse: courts and;
      judge(s); jury selection; plea
      bargains; prosecution of

juvenile offenders;
   prosecutor(s); sentences and
   sentencing

## V

Vallario, Joseph H., 71, 72–77, 98,
   101, 105
victim, blame of, 40, 146, 293
violence, *see* battered child; child
   abuse; family violence; sexual
   abuse, by father
violent children, *vs.* parricides, 152,
   160–61

## W

weapons, *see* guns; knife murders;
   shooting deaths
Whatley, Donna, 121–23
Whatley, Vincent, 120–24, 161,
   164
"When Kids Kill Their Parents"
   (*Newsweek,* 1983), 152
wife (wives)
   battered, 150, 154, 168
   murdering husband, 25–26, 69,
      150, 164–65
   relationship to husband, 28, 30,
      61, 121–23; *see also*
      mother(s): role in family
      dissension
Winkler, Richard, 102
work ethic, 110, 121

## Z

Zimmer, Perry, 262–64